AF266848

How to Stop Ruining Your Relationships 10-in-1

The Complete Guide to Overcome Toxic, Negative, Rude, and Hurtful Behaviors, Master Anger Control, Build Empathy, and Strengthen Trust

Claim Your Free Bonus

As a thank you for reading, I've put together a powerful digital bonus pack to help you apply what you've learned — even if you only have a few minutes a day.

 **Inside you'll find:**

✔ Quick-access emotional reset tools

✔ A printable clarity map for focus and purpose

✔ 30 powerful journaling prompts

✔ Daily progress & reflection trackers

✔ A mini affirmation deck for calm and confidence

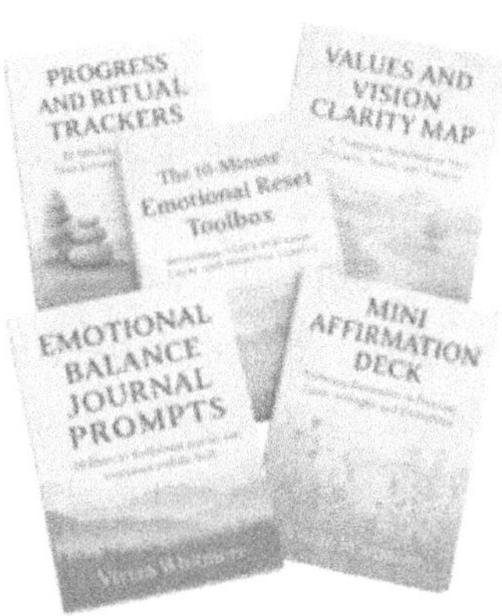

Access below to download your full bonus pack:

https://livetolearn.lpages.co/vivian-withmore-how-to-stop-ruining-your-relationships-10-in-1-paperback/

Or, scan the QR code

TABLE OF CONTENTS

PART 2: HOW TO STOP BEING NEGATIVE, RUDE, AND HURTFUL 5-IN-1

PART 1: HOW TO STOP BEING TOXIC 5-IN-1

The Complete Guide to Control Anger, Build Empathy, Talk with Respect, Set Boundaries, and Fix Broken Trust

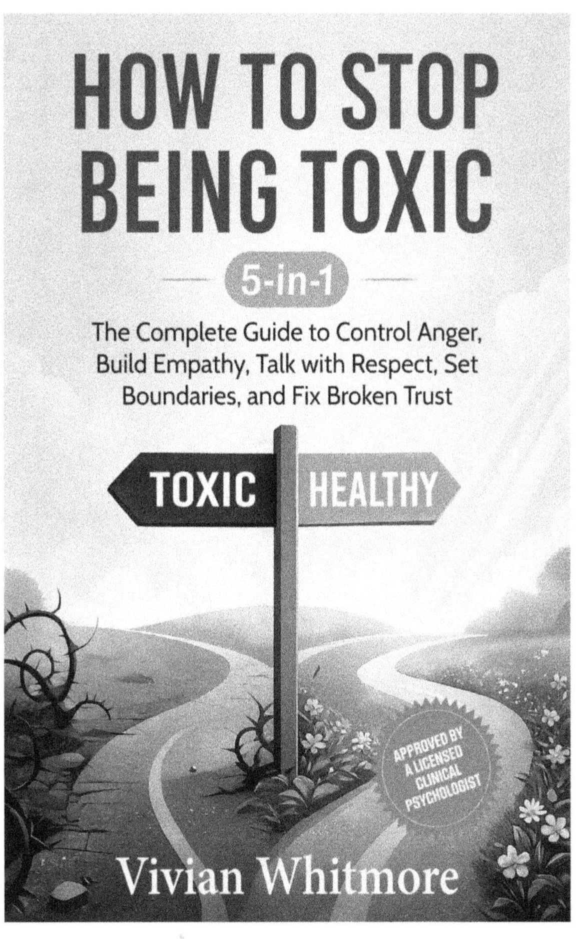

How to Stop Being Toxic 5-in-1: The Complete Guide to Control Anger, Build Empathy, Talk with Respect, Set Boundaries, and Fix Broken Trust

By Carolina Estevez, Psy.D., Licensed Psychologist

"How to Stop Being Toxic 5-in-1: The Complete Guide to Control Anger, Build Empathy, Talk with Respect, Set Boundaries, and Fix Broken Trust" offers a practical, skills-based roadmap for individuals seeking meaningful behavioral change. As a psychologist, I found the book's structure—five focused mini-books bundled into one—to be especially helpful for readers who need clear guidance, actionable steps, and reassurance that change is possible through consistent practice.

The first section, Control Anger, stands out for its grounding in cognitive-behavioral principles. The chapters on identifying triggers, recognizing physiological warning signs, and changing hostile thinking patterns align closely with empirically supported anger-management frameworks. The book places emphasis on immediate cooling strategies such as grounding, paced breathing, and time-outs—techniques that reduce sympathetic arousal and help prevent impulsive reactions. Particularly strong is the chapter on expressing needs assertively, which reframes anger not as something to suppress but as a signal that unmet needs require healthy communication. The included checklist reinforces habit development and self-monitoring.

In the section Build Empathy, the author introduces core therapeutic communication skills. The focus on attending behaviors, paraphrasing, reflecting emotions, and offering non-judgmental presence mirrors foundational components of client-centered therapy. These chapters are valuable for readers who struggle with emotional attunement and interpersonal sensitivity. The encouragement to deepen connection through open inquiry promotes curiosity rather than defensiveness, a shift essential for reducing toxic communication patterns.

Book 3, Talk with Respect, provides a concise but impactful exploration of assertive communication. The chapters on "I" statements, avoiding blame, and staying anchored to the current issue will resonate with individuals who tend to ruminate on past conflicts or escalate discussions. The reminders to align non-verbal cues with verbal intent highlight a psychologically important principle: authenticity strengthens trust, while incongruence breeds uncertainty.

The fourth section, Set Boundaries, offers some of the most therapeutically relevant material in the entire collection. The book skillfully addresses internal barriers—such as guilt, fear of conflict, or people-pleasing—that often sabotage boundary-setting efforts. Readers receive step-by-step guidance on how to state limits, follow through with consequences, and tolerate discomfort during interpersonal pushback. This section is particularly useful for individuals emerging from enmeshed family systems or codependent dynamics.

The final book, Fix Broken Trust, emphasizes accountability, transparency, and behavioral consistency—three components strongly supported by research on relational repair. Chapters on non-defensive apology and long-term loyalty to the healing process highlight that trust is not restored through words alone but through sustained, predictable action.

Overall, "How to Stop Being Toxic 5-in-1: The Complete Guide to Control Anger, Build Empathy, Talk with Respect, Set Boundaries, and Fix Broken Trust" is a practical, psychologically informed resource for anyone committed to self-improvement and healthier relationships.

INTRODUCTION:
COMMIT TO CHANGE NOW

You pick up this book because you are ready to stop causing pain. You recognize the crushing cost of toxic behavior. You see the deep damage in your relationships. You feel the constant internal conflict in your own life. This self-awareness is the essential first step. You must face the problem directly. Change begins with this moment of commitment.

Toxic is not a fixed identity. It is a set of learned, highly destructive behaviors. These actions are habits. They are automatic responses built over time. You do not need to be defined by them. You can replace these habits with effective, respectful skills. You can change your behavior.

This guide is an operational manual for that change. It views destructive behavior as a skill deficit. You will replace harmful, automatic reactions with deliberate, constructive responses. Change is action. It is built through small, consistent, measurable steps. You are not simply wishing for different emotions. You are choosing different actions.

The Neurological Core of Toxicity

The human brain's architecture ensures quick reaction. When you perceive a threat, whether it is physical danger or a simple verbal slight, the amygdala fires instantly. This small, ancient cluster of neurons triggers a massive physiological stress response. Your heart races. Your muscles tense. Rational thought, located in the prefrontal cortex, is effectively hijacked. This is the core problem of behavioral toxicity. You react quickly, often violently, before you can think clearly. You are reacting from an ancient, survival-driven part of your mind.

Your behavior becomes destructive when your emotional response is disproportionate to the event. A forgotten key or a differing opinion does not require survival panic. The immediate goal is to interrupt this rapid cycle. You must insert a thoughtful pause between the trigger and the reaction. Cognitive Behavioral Therapy, or CBT, provides the principles necessary to achieve this intervention. You learn to control the cycle of negative thoughts and overwhelming feelings. You regain capacity for rational choice.

Chronic, unchecked anger consumes massive mental energy. It clouds your thinking. This constant emotional turmoil makes it harder to concentrate or enjoy your life. Toxic behavior is simply poor emotional management. You must learn to translate the emotional message without causing damage.

Skill Set 1: Establishing Internal Control

How do you interrupt a reaction built over decades? You start by identifying the warning signs. Your body gives the earliest and most reliable signal before your mind shuts down. This includes a racing heart, tightened jaw, or rapid breathing. Early awareness of these signals creates the necessary window for intervention.

You must take a deliberate pause. You step away from the immediate situation physically. This timeout is not avoidance. It is operational necessity. It restores your brain's ability to think rationally. Emotional skill is built on physical control.

You need immediate cooling strategies. Deep breathing or progressive muscle relaxation helps reduce the physical stress response. Consciously slowing your physiology prevents the cognitive part of the brain from becoming overwhelmed. You must reset your internal state before attempting to communicate.

Toxicity often involves hostile thinking patterns. These are negative, irrational thoughts based on assumptions, not facts. You must address these thoughts directly. This is **cognitive restructuring**. You challenge the belief that triggered the anger or aggression. For instance, if you think, "They did this on purpose to hurt me," you must ask yourself what objective evidence proves that hostile intent.

You find alternative, objective interpretations of the event. You replace an automatic negative response with a balanced perspective. You separate the emotion from the thought, restoring rational decision-making. This consistent practice effectively reduces overall hostility. Research, including a comprehensive meta-analysis of CBT interventions, consistently shows that changing hostile cognitions significantly reduces hostility. This practice is based on evidence.

This deliberate effort is difficult. Change requires accountability. You must take full responsibility for your actions. This means stopping the habit of blaming others for your emotional state. Your feelings are yours. Taking responsibility for them bypasses the defense mechanism in others. You report an undeniable internal state.

Skill Set 2: Mastering Assertive Dialogue

The heart of respectful living is structured communication. Respectful talk replaces reactive, toxic habits with structured, assertive dialogue. Assertiveness is the skill of expressing your thoughts, feelings, and needs clearly, without infringing on the rights of others. This reduces conflict stress and strengthens relationships.

How do you stop blaming people? You reframe the complaint. You shift observations about the person into specific, observable behaviors. You focus on what they did, not what you assume about their character. Behavior is changeable. Character attack feels like a fixed, unmanageable assault.

You must construct powerful "I" statements. This ensures clarity and emotional responsibility. The structured XYZ formula helps here. You state your specific emotion clearly. You name a feeling like "frustrated" or "concerned," not a judgment like "ignored." Then you state the specific, observable behavior that caused the emotion. This systematic formula prevents arguments and misunderstandings.

Assertive communication requires you to state your needs without guilt. Do not assume others know what you want. You must articulate the resolution you seek. You end your assertive statement with a clear request for a change in behavior or action. Your needs are equal to the needs of others. Asking for what you need prevents you from feeling underappreciated. The **Locus of Control** concept shows this shift toward self-responsibility is psychologically healthy. You claim ownership of your emotional state.

Crucially, your non-verbal signals must align with your words. Your tone and posture carry immense weight. Albert Mehrabian's influential research concluded that nonverbal and vocal cues overwhelmingly convey emotional information. If your tone is aggressive, your calm words are ignored. You must maintain congruence.

Skill Set 3: Building Active Empathy

The next major skill you must master is connection. Respectful communication requires empathy. Empathy is a learnable skill. It allows you to move conversations out of conflict by showing the speaker they have been heard, understood, and supported. The foundation of empathy is structured, reflective listening.

You start with physical and psychological attention. These are called **Attending Skills**. They communicate non-verbally that you are fully engaged. You maintain appropriate eye contact. You use open body language, avoiding crossed arms or defensive postures. If your posture signals distraction, the speaker distrusts your sincerity, making any later verbal effort useless.

Reflective listening confirms you correctly process information. You practice **rephrasing the factual content** the speaker shared, using your own words. This step confirms your understanding. It gives the speaker feedback on what was heard. This avoids the illusion of understanding.

High-level empathy reflects the emotion underpinning the words. This changes the conversation from a fight about facts to an acknowledgment of human experience. You reflect the feelings you perceive. You say, "You sound disappointed," or "I hear how frustrated you are." This **validation** acknowledges their emotional reality. You simply accept their feelings as a reasonable response to their situation.

Empathy requires non-judgment. You must set aside your own opinions. You consciously suppress reactive thoughts. Embrace **silences**. Do not rush to fill quiet moments. Silence helps the speaker focus, vent, and articulate clearly. Toxic communication often dismisses or invalidates feelings. Empathy provides necessary emotional safety.

The next core skill is setting limits. Boundaries are interpersonal limits. They define appropriate behavior in your relationships. Setting and enforcing healthy limits is crucial for self-care and mutual respect.

A boundary is an edge that defines you as separate from others. Healthy limits give you empowerment and self-respect. They separate your wants, needs, thoughts, and feelings from those of others. You must know what you want. Clarify your comfort levels regarding physical space, emotional effort, and time commitment.

Boundaries must be clearly stated. Unstated limits are just preferences. You must deliver the message calmly and confidently. State your request directly in terms of what you want. This frames the boundary positively.

Setting a boundary can cause internal discomfort. You may feel guilt, shame, or fear of conflict. You must accept this feeling to maintain the limit. Tolerate the feeling of guilt instead of retreating. You are disrupting an old, unhealthy pattern. You must build **Distress Tolerance**, the capacity to endure negative emotional states without engaging in destructive behaviors to make the feeling stop. Research shows that low distress tolerance is correlated with higher overall psychological distress. This is why the boundary work is hard but essential.

When someone challenges your new limits, you must respond firmly. If you allow challenges to succeed, the boundary erodes instantly. You reiterate the boundary simply. You use short, firm sentences. Do not justify or over-explain why you need the limit.

An unenforced boundary is merely a suggestion. When a person violates a clearly expressed limit repeatedly, you must implement consequences. Consequences protect you. They are not intended to control the other person. Consequences often involve removing your effort, time, or presence from the interaction. You define these consequences in advance. You must follow through consistently. This is difficult, but necessary.

Skill Set 5: Restoring Relational Security

The final skill area addresses relational security. Trust is the foundation of intimate relationships. Once trust is broken, words alone are not enough. Trust must be rebuilt through visible behavioral change and sustained consistency. You are creating a new relationship after the damage.

Trust repair demands immediate, comprehensive ownership of the damage. You take full responsibility for your actions. Do not attempt to sidestep the issue or shift blame. Acknowledge the mistake openly. You recognize the gravity of the betrayal without rationalizing. Trust begins with honesty and integrity. **Attribution Theory** in trust repair shows that the injured party seeks to understand the cause of the betrayal. You must prove the cause was a behavioral choice, not a permanent lack of integrity.

A sincere apology is only the beginning. The apology must acknowledge the depth of the pain caused. Be prepared to apologize repeatedly, accepting the other person's ongoing hurt. You must listen to their anger and hurt feelings without defense or excuse. Use the empathy skills you learned.

Trust cannot be rebuilt in secrecy. Openness counters the fear and uncertainty betrayal creates. Engage in complete honesty and open communication. This involves answering questions openly and avoiding any secrecy. This **radical transparency** is the antidote to manipulation tactics like **gaslighting**, which makes the victim question their own reality.

Trust is fixed by consistent, observable action, not by promises. You must consistently show up with reliability. Be true to your word. Follow through with every commitment, large or small. Consistent follow-through demonstrates reliability. You must understand **Loss Aversion**. The pain of a loss is psychologically twice as powerful as an equivalent gain. This means your integrity must be aggressively consistent.

This process requires unwavering loyalty. You must commit to the healing process. You show commitment through sustained positive actions. You hold space for the partner's timeline. You must accept that the old relationship cannot exist anymore. You are rebuilding the foundation together. Focus on small positive moments and consistent efforts over time.

You have five distinct, measurable skill sets to master. Controlling reactive internal states. Building active connection. Communicating needs clearly. Setting essential limits. Rebuilding relational security. These skills are measured by your consistent choices, not by your innate feelings.

Self-correction is necessary. Continuous effort is required. You will replace toxic patterns with competence and respect. Maintaining a non-toxic life means choosing skill over reaction every single time. Your deliberate, consistent commitment to these actions defines your new, respectful path. This guide provides the operational roadmap.

This deliberate effort is difficult. Change requires profound accountability. You must take full responsibility for your actions. This means stopping the habit of blaming others for your emotional state. Your feelings are yours. Taking responsibility for them bypasses the defense mechanism in others. You report an undeniable internal state. This shift from external to internal locus of control is necessary for self-esteem.

The heart of respectful living is structured communication. Respectful talk replaces reactive, toxic habits with structured, assertive dialogue. Assertiveness is the skill of expressing your thoughts, feelings, and needs clearly, without infringing on the rights of others. This reduces conflict stress and strengthens relationships.

How do you stop blaming people? You reframe the complaint. You shift observations about the person into specific, observable behaviors. You focus on what they did, not what you assume about their character. Behavior is changeable. Character attack feels like a fixed, unmanageable assault.

You must construct powerful "I" statements. This ensures clarity and emotional responsibility. The structured XYZ formula helps here. You state your specific emotion clearly. You name a feeling like "frustrated" or "concerned," not a judgment like "ignored." Then you state the specific, observable behavior that caused the emotion. This systematic formula prevents arguments and misunderstandings.

Assertive communication requires you to state your needs without guilt. Do not assume others know what you want. You must articulate the resolution you seek. You end your assertive statement with a clear request for a change in behavior or action. Your needs are equal to the needs of others. Asking for what you need prevents you from feeling underappreciated.

The second major skill you must master is connection. Respectful communication requires empathy. Empathy is a learnable skill. It allows you to move conversations out of conflict by showing the speaker they have been heard, understood, and supported. The foundation of empathy is structured, reflective listening.

You start with physical and psychological attention. These are called attending skills. They communicate non-verbally that you are fully engaged. You maintain appropriate eye contact. You use open body language, avoiding crossed arms or defensive postures. If your posture signals distraction, the speaker distrusts your sincerity, making any later verbal effort useless.

Reflective listening confirms you correctly process information. You practice rephrasing the factual content the speaker shared, using your own words. This step confirms your understanding. It gives the speaker feedback on what was heard.

High-level empathy reflects the emotion underpinning the words. This changes the conversation from a fight about facts to an acknowledgment of human experience. You reflect the feelings you perceive. You say, "You sound disappointed," or "I hear how frustrated you are." This validation acknowledges their emotional reality. You simply accept their feelings as a reasonable response to their situation.

Empathy requires non-judgment. You must set aside your own opinions. You consciously suppress reactive thoughts. Embrace silences. Do not rush to fill quiet moments. Silence helps the speaker focus, vent, and articulate clearly. Toxic communication often dismisses or invalidates feelings. Empathy provides necessary emotional safety.

The third core skill is setting limits. Boundaries are interpersonal limits. They define appropriate behavior in your relationships. Setting and enforcing healthy limits is crucial for self-care and mutual respect.

A boundary is an edge that defines you as separate from others. Healthy limits give you empowerment and self-respect. They separate your wants, needs, thoughts, and feelings from those of others. You must know what you want. Clarify your comfort levels regarding physical space, emotional effort, and time commitment.

Boundaries must be clearly stated. Unstated limits are just preferences. You must deliver the message calmly and confidently. State your request directly in terms of what you want. This frames the boundary positively. For example, you ask for a specific time alone instead of demanding silence.

Setting a boundary can cause internal discomfort. You may feel guilt, shame, or fear of conflict. You must accept this feeling to maintain the limit. Tolerate the feeling of guilt instead of retreating. You are disrupting an old, unhealthy pattern. Recognize that setting limits will not disrupt a healthy relationship.

When someone challenges your new limits, you must respond firmly. If you allow challenges to succeed, the boundary erodes instantly. You reiterate the boundary simply. You use short, firm sentences. Do not justify or over-explain why you need the limit.

An unenforced boundary is merely a suggestion. When a person violates a clearly expressed limit repeatedly, you must implement consequences. Consequences protect you. They are not intended to control the other person. Consequences often involve removing your effort, time, or presence from the interaction. You define these consequences in advance. You must follow through consistently. This is difficult, but necessary.

The final skill area addresses relational security. Trust is the foundation of intimate relationships. Once trust is broken, words alone are not enough. Trust must be rebuilt through visible behavioral change and sustained consistency. You are creating a new relationship after the damage.

Trust repair demands immediate, comprehensive ownership of the damage. You take full responsibility for your actions. Do not attempt to sidestep the issue or shift blame. Acknowledge the mistake openly. You recognize the gravity of the betrayal without rationalizing. Trust begins with honesty.

A sincere apology is only the beginning. The apology must acknowledge the depth of the pain caused. Be prepared to apologize repeatedly, accepting the other person's ongoing hurt. You must listen to their anger and hurt feelings without defense or excuse. Use the empathy skills you learned.

Trust cannot be rebuilt in secrecy. Openness counters the fear and uncertainty betrayal creates. Engage in complete honesty and open communication. This involves answering questions openly and avoiding any secrecy. Be prepared to endure discomfort as you reveal the truth.

Trust is fixed by consistent, observable action, not by promises. You must consistently show up with reliability. Be true to your word. Follow through with every commitment, large or small. Consistent follow-through demonstrates reliability.

This process requires unwavering loyalty. You must commit to the healing process. You show commitment through sustained positive actions. You hold space for the partner's timeline. You must accept that the old relationship cannot exist anymore. You are rebuilding the foundation together. Focus on small positive moments and consistent efforts over time.

You have five distinct, measurable skill sets to master. Controlling reactive internal states. Building active connection. Communicating needs clearly. Setting essential limits. Rebuilding relational security.

These skills are measured by your consistent choices, not by your innate feelings.

Self-correction is necessary. Continuous effort is required. You will replace toxic patterns with competence and respect. Maintaining a non-toxic life means choosing skill over reaction every single time. Your deliberate, consistent commitment to these actions defines your new, respectful path. This guide provides the operational roadmap.

This deliberate effort is difficult. Change requires profound accountability. You must take full responsibility for your actions. This means stopping the habit of blaming others for your emotional state. Your feelings are yours. Taking responsibility for them bypasses the defense mechanism in others. You report an undeniable internal state.

The heart of respectful living is structured communication. Respectful talk replaces reactive, toxic habits with structured, assertive dialogue. Assertiveness is the skill of expressing your thoughts, feelings, and needs clearly, without infringing on the rights of others. This reduces conflict stress and strengthens relationships.

How do you stop blaming people? You reframe the complaint. You shift observations about the person into specific, observable behaviors. You focus on what they did, not what you assume about their character. Behavior is changeable. Character attack feels like a fixed, unmanageable assault.

You must construct powerful "I" statements. This ensures clarity and emotional responsibility. A formula helps here. You state your specific emotion clearly. You name a feeling like "frustrated" or "concerned," not a judgment like "ignored." Then you state the specific, observable behavior that caused the emotion. This formula prevents arguments and misunderstandings.

Assertive communication requires you to state your needs without guilt. Do not assume others know what you want. You must articulate the resolution you seek. You end your assertive statement with a clear request for a change in behavior or action. Your needs are equal to the needs of others. Asking for what you need prevents you from feeling underappreciated.

The second major skill you must master is connection. Respectful communication requires empathy. Empathy is a learnable skill. It allows you to move conversations out of conflict by showing the speaker they have been heard, understood, and supported. The foundation of empathy is structured, reflective listening.

You start with physical and psychological attention. These are called attending skills. They communicate non-verbally that you are fully engaged. You maintain appropriate eye contact. You use open body language, avoiding crossed arms or defensive postures. If your posture signals distraction, the speaker distrusts your sincerity, making any later verbal effort useless.

Reflective listening confirms you correctly process information. You practice rephrasing the factual content the speaker shared, using your own words. This step confirms your understanding. It gives the speaker feedback on what was heard.

High-level empathy reflects the emotion underpinning the words. This changes the conversation from a fight about facts to an acknowledgment of human experience. You reflect the feelings you perceive. You say, "You sound disappointed," or "I hear how frustrated you are." This validation acknowledges their emotional reality. You simply accept their feelings as a reasonable response to their situation.

Empathy requires non-judgment. You must set aside your own opinions. You consciously suppress reactive thoughts. Embrace silences. Do not rush to fill quiet moments. Silence helps the speaker focus, vent, and articulate clearly. Toxic communication often dismisses or invalidates feelings. Empathy provides necessary emotional safety.

The third core skill is setting limits. Boundaries are interpersonal limits. They define appropriate behavior in your relationships. Setting and enforcing healthy limits is crucial for self-care and mutual respect.

A boundary is an edge that defines you as separate from others. Healthy limits give you empowerment and self-respect. They separate your wants, needs, thoughts, and feelings from those of others. You must know what you want. Clarify your comfort levels regarding physical space, emotional effort, and time commitment.

Boundaries must be clearly stated. Unstated limits are just preferences. You must deliver the message calmly and confidently. State your request directly in terms of what you want. This frames the boundary positively. For example, you ask for a specific time alone instead of demanding silence.

Setting a boundary can cause internal discomfort. You may feel guilt, shame, or fear of conflict. You must accept this feeling to maintain the limit. Tolerate the feeling of guilt instead of retreating. You are disrupting an old, unhealthy pattern. Recognize that setting limits will not disrupt a healthy relationship.

When someone challenges your new limits, you must respond firmly. If you allow challenges to succeed, the boundary erupts instantly. You reiterate the boundary simply. You use short, firm sentences. Do not justify or over-explain why you need the limit.

An unenforced boundary is merely a suggestion. When a person violates a clearly expressed limit repeatedly, you must implement consequences. Consequences protect you. They are not intended to control the other person. Consequences often involve removing your effort, time, or presence from the interaction. You define these consequences in advance. You must follow through consistently. This is difficult, but necessary.

The final skill area addresses relational security. Trust is the foundation of intimate relationships. Once trust is broken, words alone are not enough. Trust must be rebuilt through visible behavioral change and sustained consistency. You are creating a new relationship after the damage.

Trust repair demands immediate, comprehensive ownership of the damage. You take full responsibility for your actions. Do not attempt to sidestep the issue or shift blame. Acknowledge the mistake openly. You recognize the gravity of the betrayal without rationalizing. Trust begins with honesty.

A sincere apology is only the beginning. The apology must acknowledge the depth of the pain caused. Be prepared to apologize repeatedly, accepting the other person's ongoing hurt. You must listen to their anger and hurt feelings without defense or excuse. Use the empathy skills you learned.

Trust cannot be rebuilt in secrecy. Openness counters the fear and uncertainty betrayal creates. Engage in complete honesty and open communication. This involves answering questions openly and avoiding any secrecy. Be prepared to endure discomfort as you reveal the truth.

Trust is fixed by consistent, observable action, not by promises. You must consistently show up with reliability. Be true to your word. Follow through with every commitment, large or small. Consistent follow-through demonstrates reliability.

This process requires unwavering loyalty. You must commit to the healing process. You show commitment through sustained positive actions. You hold space for the partner's timeline. You must accept that the old relationship cannot exist anymore. You are rebuilding the foundation together. Focus on small positive moments and consistent efforts over time.

You have five distinct, measurable skill sets to master. Controlling reactive internal states. Building active connection. Communicating needs clearly. Setting essential limits. Rebuilding relational security. These skills are measured by your consistent choices, not by your innate feelings.

Self-correction is necessary. Continuous effort is required. You will replace toxic patterns with competence and respect. Maintaining a non-toxic life means choosing skill over reaction every single time. Your deliberate, consistent commitment to these actions defines your new, respectful path. This guide provides the operational roadmap.

BOOK ONE

CONTROL ANGER:
ACTION STEPS TO MASTER YOUR REACTIONS

INTRODUCTION

You chose this book for one precise reason. You want to regain control over your explosive temper. You are ready to stop the internal chaos. You are tired of the damage that small triggers cause in your life. This weariness is not failure. It is commitment. It is the necessary starting point for change. You are acknowledging the cost of your fury.

Anger is a basic, natural human emotion. It is not an error in your personality. Like fear or sadness, anger provides information. It signals a message. It tells you that a boundary has been crossed. It warns you that a situation is threatening, unfair, or unjust. The emotion itself is a messenger.

The problem is the **reaction** to the feeling. When your automatic response is immediate, violent expression, the message is lost. It is replaced by destruction. Uncontrolled anger is simply toxic behavior. It is a sign of poor emotional management.

You might believe that venting your fury is healthy release. You might feel justified in your rage. You might think only an angry outburst gets attention. The evidence proves otherwise. Uncontrolled anger damages relationships permanently. It clouds your decision-making. It works against your success and personal peace.

The consequences of allowing anger to spiral out of control are severe. These consequences are observable. They affect your body, your mind, and your personal connections.

Your physical health suffers measurably. When you operate at high levels of stress and anger constantly, your body becomes highly vulnerable. Your system is flooded with stress hormones frequently. This chronic arousal leads to serious, documented health problems. Studies consistently link persistent hostility to an increased risk of heart disease, diabetes, and high blood pressure. Your immune system weakens over time. Unchecked anger disrupts your sleep quality. It makes achieving deep, restorative relaxation nearly impossible. You live in a constant state of internal conflict. This sustained vigilance drains your physical resources completely.

Your mental health pays an equally high price. Chronic anger consumes enormous mental energy. This constant internal fight clouds your thinking. It makes concentration difficult. You struggle to focus on tasks that require sustained attention. This persistent agitation contributes significantly to stress and depression. Uncontrolled anger is a major, debilitating mental obstacle. It stops you from enjoying simple, peaceful moments. Anger management is a required step toward mental well-being.

The core issue is physical, not moral. Your brain is structured to prioritize immediate survival. It chooses speed over careful thought when it senses any threat. A triggering event bypasses your conscious mind instantly. It activates the amygdala. This primitive part of your brain manages the fight-or-flight response. It initiates a rapid, powerful physiological stress response.

This response is instantaneous. Your body reacts before your conscious, logical mind can fully process the situation. This is why you say and do things you immediately regret. Your heart pounds heavily. Your muscles tighten painfully. Your breath shortens rapidly. The part of your brain responsible for rational thought, the prefrontal cortex, is temporarily disabled. You become impulsive. You act before you think clearly. This is the automatic, destructive anger cycle.

Your behavior is destructive when your emotional response is wildly disproportionate to the event. A canceled appointment does not require a crisis level of rage. A minor critique does not justify yelling. You must learn how to insert a thoughtful pause. You must stop the cycle between the trigger and the destructive reaction. This book provides the skills to achieve that specific interruption.

You will learn the structured, tested techniques of Cognitive Behavioral Therapy. CBT is highly effective for anger control because it directly targets the connections between your thoughts, your feelings, and your actions. You learn how to systematically manage the cycle of negative thinking and overwhelming physical feelings. You restore your capacity for rational choice and appropriate response.

The effectiveness of these cognitive-behavioral techniques is supported by extensive scientific evidence. Studies consistently show that CBT interventions work for anger management. These are not abstract theories. They are precise skills refined over decades of clinical application. They offer an action-based path toward measurable change.

For evidence, look to the clinical standard. The Center for Substance Abuse Treatment at the Substance Abuse and Mental Health Services Administration (SAMHSA) produced a detailed, structured resource. The *Anger Management for Substance Use Disorder and Mental Health Clients: A Cognitive–Behavioral Therapy Manual* outlines the exact structured treatment design used successfully with thousands of clients over the past three decades. This system is an evidence-based roadmap for anger control.

Your first required skill is self-interception. You must become a meticulous observer of yourself. You must translate the message of your anger before it escalates into an uncontrollable expression. This demands profound self-awareness.

You need to know your precise warning signs. Your body provides the earliest, most reliable clues. These physical changes always precede the failure of rational thought. When you ignore these physical signals, you lose the crucial opportunity to intervene effectively.

Your physical warning signs are concrete. They include a noticeable acceleration of your pulse. You feel muscle tension in your jaw or shoulders. Your breathing becomes fast and shallow. You might feel a sudden, intense rush of heat.

Mental warning signs appear simultaneously. You start cycling hostile, repetitive thoughts. You automatically assume the worst possible intentions from others. You begin to rehearse arguments internally. You tell yourself the situation is intolerable and that you have been deeply wronged. Ignoring these symptoms means the thoughtful part of your brain is already losing the battle. Early, immediate awareness of these physical and mental signals is the critical first step in anger management.

Once you recognize these signs, you must use immediate physical interventions. The presence of stress hormones like adrenaline prevents clear thinking. You need a fast, effective reset button.

You must take a deliberate timeout. You must step away from the triggering situation physically. You need distance. You need space to breathe. Stay away until your thinking is clear and your body calms down. Timeouts are not retreats. They are acts of responsible emotional regulation. They restore your brain's ability to think rationally.

You employ relaxation techniques intentionally. Conscious relaxation is a powerful, studied countermeasure against rising anger. You must slow your physical system. Deep, controlled breathing helps. Progressive muscle relaxation helps release the tension in your braced muscles. You consciously operate to reduce the physiological stress response. You must lower your heart rate before you attempt to engage the thinking part of your brain. This sequence is mandatory.

Physical activity serves as another necessary reset tool. It reduces the overall stress levels that feed your anger. A quick, brisk walk or a short, intense exercise session can safely discharge built-up tension. This moves the energy out of your body. It ensures the energy does not discharge as fury toward another person.

The second foundational pillar of change is cognitive. You must change the way you think about triggers. Anger frequently stems from patterns of irrational, negative thoughts. These hostile thoughts are based on assumptions, not on objective facts. You must confront them directly.

This process is called cognitive restructuring. You challenge your automatic, irrational beliefs head-on. This technique specifically targets the hostile cognitions that trigger aggression. You question the evidence supporting your angry thought. If you automatically think, "They did this just to make me look foolish," you must immediately ask yourself what objective evidence proves that hostile intent. You gather facts only. You look for proof.

You train yourself to find alternative interpretations of the situation. These interpretations must be balanced. They must be non-hostile. You stop the automatic negative response. You replace it with a calm, proportional perspective. You focus on the objective facts of the event. You disregard the perceived insult.

The effectiveness of this specific method is well-documented. A major meta-analysis was conducted by DiGiuseppe and Tafrate. This analysis reviewed 23 studies focused on cognitive restructuring interventions. The findings, cited in subsequent research, showed that cognitive restructuring is effective in reducing overall hostility with moderate to large effect sizes (d = 0.51 to 1.87). This confirms the profound impact of simply changing your inner dialogue. You learn to separate the emotion from the thought. This restores your capacity for rational decision-making.

Hostile thinking often relies on faulty logic. You might turn a small annoyance into a total disaster. You might use black-or-white thinking. Things are either perfect or ruined. You must recognize these faulty patterns instantly. When you see a faulty thought pattern, you stop it. You replace it with a factual, proportional statement. This systematic replacement of hostile thinking builds emotional stability over time.

Anger often points to an underlying, unresolved problem in your life. Managing anger long term means solving that recurring issue. You must stop simply reacting to the constant fallout. You must start solving the root cause of the frustration.

You must view challenges as problems to be solved. They are not threats to be avoided or fought against. Properly channeled anger can motivate necessary resolution. You identify the specific, recurring problem your anger points toward.

You generate multiple solutions to that problem. You do not limit yourself to the first idea. You objectively weigh the pros and cons of each option. You select the best solution. You implement it. This constructive, systematic process replaces the destructive cycle of chronic, unresolved anger.

The third area of skill acquisition involves clear expression. Once you are calm and thinking clearly, you must express your frustration assertively. This is assertive communication. Assertiveness is the skill of expressing your feelings and needs clearly and directly. You do this respectfully. You do not violate the rights of others in the process.

You must use "I" statements. This technique focuses on your internal state. It avoids blaming the other person for your feelings. Your message must be direct and clear. Practicing assertiveness reduces conflict stress. It builds stronger relationships.

You must use neutral, positive language. Assertive communication is honest. It is direct. It avoids belittling or dismissing others' opinions. Assertiveness training, a component of CBT, includes practicing skills like role-playing and active listening. This improves communication effectiveness. It ensures your needs are heard without escalating the situation.

Controlling anger is a project of disciplined, consistent action. It requires recognizing your physical limits. You must interrupt the escalation cycle before you lose control. The specific techniques you learn in this book, physical cooling, cognitive restructuring, problem-solving, and assertive expression, build consistent self-control.

You are training your brain to choose skill over raw reaction. You are developing new neural pathways deliberately. You replace old, toxic, automatic reactions with effective, deliberate responses. This is the goal of Book 1. The work is challenging. It requires unwavering commitment. You must choose disciplined action over uncontrolled fury every single time. Your sustained commitment to these steps defines your new path toward calm control.

The chapters ahead provide the specific, actionable steps for this operational change. You will learn how to identify your precise physical and mental warning signs. You will learn the four-step process for challenging hostile thought patterns. You will learn immediate physical cooling methods. You will learn structured problem-solving techniques. You will learn exactly how to use assertive language to express needs without aggression. Mastery of these actions provides the consistent calm control you need to succeed.

CHAPTER 1
IDENTIFY YOUR TRIGGERS AND WARNING SIGNS

The first step in achieving calm control is precision. You must become a scientist of your own anger. You must systematically identify what initiates the destructive cycle. This means identifying two separate things: your external triggers and your internal warning signs. Without this knowledge, you are simply waiting for the next explosion.

Locate Your External Triggers

An external trigger is the event, person, or situation that reliably sparks your fury. This trigger sends the immediate alarm to your brain. It starts the physiological process that leads to loss of control. Identifying these situations is crucial. It separates the root cause of your anger from the subsequent reaction.

You need to move past generalizations. Do not say, "Everything makes me angry." You must pinpoint the specifics.

Start logging your anger events immediately. Use a small notebook or a phone note. Note the exact time, place, and who was involved. Describe the situation in objective, factual terms. For example, do not write, "My partner was being lazy." Write, "My partner left dishes in the sink after I asked them to clean up."

Look for patterns in your log. Ask yourself these precise questions about each event:

• **Situational:** Was the anger always sparked by waiting in traffic? Was it always related to poor customer service? Was it caused by feeling trapped or helpless?

• **Relational:** Did the anger only occur with a specific person? Was it only when you felt disrespected by an authority figure? Was it tied to interactions where you felt unheard?

• **Environmental:** Did it happen when you were hungry or tired? Did it happen when you were already stressed or rushed? Research confirms that environmental factors like hunger or poor sleep can heighten your emotional reactivity, making you more susceptible to anger triggers.Clear identification of these specific triggers does two things. First, it allows you to anticipate when you are most vulnerable. Second, it gives you measurable targets for intervention. You cannot solve a diffuse problem. You can manage a specific situation.

Recognize Your Internal Warning Signs

The most vital moment for intervention occurs inside your body. You need to recognize your personal warning signs. Your body provides the earliest and most reliable signal that rational thought is about to fail. This physical signal gives you the necessary window to intervene before the anger fully takes over.

Ignore these physical symptoms and your brain's cognitive centers will become overwhelmed. You must learn to notice the symptoms before you lose control.

Physical signs are often consistent and reliable. Look for these internal cues:

Symptom Type	Specific Physical Signs to Watch For
Cardiovascular	A sudden, noticeable increase in your heart rate. Your chest feels tight or pressured.
Muscular	Your jaw clenches tightly. Your fists ball up without conscious thought. Your neck or shoulders

	tense immediately.
Respiratory	Your breathing becomes fast and shallow. You feel a sudden rush of heat or a flush in your face.
Gastrointestinal	A knot forms suddenly in your stomach. You feel immediate nausea or digestive upset.

Your psychological warning signs appear at the same time. These are the thoughts that accompany the physical surge. These mental signs involve immediate, hostile thinking patterns:

- **Catastrophizing:** You immediately believe the worst possible outcome is certain. ("This small mistake will ruin everything.")
- **Blaming:** You automatically assign hostile intent to others. ("They did that on purpose to disrespect me.")
- **Rehearsing:** You begin cycling hostile internal monologues. You rehearse exactly what you will say to inflict maximum damage.

The Science of Interruption

Your goal is to disrupt the physiological cascade. The moment a trigger is identified, your amygdala fires instantly. The amygdala is the ancient part of the brain that governs immediate survival reactions. This rapid firing disables the prefrontal cortex, which is the region responsible for logic, planning, and rational decision-making. Your survival response overrides your capacity to think clearly.

The physical warning signs you identified are the direct evidence of this neurological hijacking. They signal that adrenaline is flooding your system. You must intervene at this moment.

Early awareness of these signals is the critical first step in Cognitive Behavioral Therapy for anger management. Clinical approaches emphasize this awareness. For example, the comprehensive program outlined in the *Anger Management for Substance Use Disorder and Mental Health Clients* manual requires participants to track and identify these exact warning signs to create a map of their personal anger cycle. This is systematic work.

When you notice a clenched jaw or a sudden rush of heat, you are not angry yet. You are at the moment of choice. This moment is brief. You must recognize it and act. This physical awareness is the foundation upon which all other control strategies are built. You cannot apply cognitive restructuring or assertive communication if you are already operating without a rational mind. You must respect the signal. You must interrupt the cycle immediately.

You have the tools to create your personal anger map. You must commit to recording every instance of intense anger. Note the trigger. Note the specific physical and mental warnings that preceded the explosion. This commitment to observation provides the precise data you need to take back control.

CHAPTER 2
CHANGE YOUR HOSTILE THINKING PATTERNS

Anger is fueled by thought. The intense physical sensation you feel, the pounding heart, the clenched jaw, is triggered by what you tell yourself about a situation. These thoughts are often hostile. They are irrational. They are based on assumptions, not facts. If you want true control, you must address these thoughts directly.

The goal is cognitive restructuring. This is a scientific technique used in therapy to replace automatic, destructive thought patterns with objective, balanced interpretations. Hostile thinking keeps you trapped in the anger cycle. Changing your mind changes your response.

Identify Faulty Thought Patterns

Your automatic angry thoughts often fall into specific categories of faulty logic. You must learn to spot these patterns instantly.

1. Catastrophizing: This pattern turns a small problem into a massive disaster. A minor setback becomes "the end of everything." If a coworker submits a report late, you think, "This is going to ruin my entire project, and I will be fired." This thought is disproportionate.

2. All-or-Nothing Thinking: You see situations in extremes. Things are either perfect or ruined. You use words like "always" or "never." If your partner forgets one chore, you think, "You never listen to me. This relationship is hopeless." This generalization ignores all positive history.

3. Mind Reading and Blaming: This is the most toxic pattern. You instantly assume you know the hostile intent of others. If someone cuts you off in traffic, you think, "They did that just to annoy me." You assign malicious intent without evidence. This thought triggers immediate aggression.

The Four Steps of Cognitive Restructuring

You must actively challenge these hostile cognitions. You use logic and objective fact to dismantle the angry thought before it disables your prefrontal cortex. This systematic process restores your rational capacity.

Step 1: Identify the Hostile Thought. Pinpoint the exact thought that occurred right before your anger surged. Do not focus on the event. Focus on your internal interpretation of the event. Example: "They intentionally ignored my request to undermine my authority."

Step 2: Question the Evidence Supporting the Thought. This is the moment of truth. You challenge your assumption. Ask yourself, "What objective proof do I have that they intended to undermine me?" Ask, "Is there any other reason their request was ignored?" Most angry thoughts cannot withstand this factual examination.

Step 3: Find Alternative, Objective Interpretations. Replace the hostile thought with a balanced, non-hostile perspective. Focus only on the facts of the event. Find three other non-angry reasons for the situation. Example: "They might have been genuinely overwhelmed and forgot." Example: "The email may have gone to their spam folder."

Step 4: Test and Internalize the New Thought. You practice repeating the alternative thought. This replaces the automatic hostile response with a calm one. You must focus on the facts of the event, not the perceived insult. This consistent practice effectively reduces overall hostility.

Proven Results of Cognitive Change

The principle behind cognitive restructuring is supported by extensive research in psychology. Studies show that focusing on changing these hostile cognitions is directly effective at reducing aggression.

A major meta-analysis, or study of studies, reviewed 23 different research trials focused on cognitive restructuring interventions for anger control. The findings showed that cognitive restructuring is effective in reducing overall hostility. Researchers DiGiuseppe and Tafrate conducted this analysis. They found that these cognitive interventions produced moderate to large effect sizes, meaning the change was significant and measurable. These results confirm the profound power of simply changing your inner dialogue about a trigger.

You are training your brain to choose logic over reaction. When you identify and challenge a hostile cognition by gathering evidence for **and** against it, you are actively exercising your prefrontal cortex. This exercise rebuilds your capacity for self-control.

You must internalize this truth: Your thoughts are not facts. They are interpretations. You can change your interpretation. This practice restores your ability to make rational decisions, even when faced with frustrating situations. You separate the thought from the feeling, thereby regaining control.

CHAPTER 3
PRACTICE IMMEDIATE COOLING STRATEGIES

When warning signs appear, you must act instantly. You need immediate physical interventions to regain cognitive control. High levels of stress hormones like adrenaline prevent rational thought from working effectively. Immediate cooling strategies are essential reset buttons. They are non-negotiable actions that stop the neurological cascade before it results in a toxic outburst.

You cannot think clearly when your heart is racing. You cannot communicate assertively when your jaw is clenched. The physical state dictates the mental state. You must respect this biological hierarchy. You must manage the body first. Only then can you manage the mind. The goal of this chapter is to teach you how to physically override the emergency signal.

The Tactical Timeout: Create Necessary Distance

The moment you feel the physical warning signs, the heat, the tension, the racing heart, you must create space. You need a deliberate timeout. This is the most important physical intervention you can perform. It is a mandatory separation from the trigger.

A timeout is a specific action. You step away from the triggering situation physically. You remove yourself from the source of the conflict. This physical distance gives your system the time it needs to clear the adrenaline and cortisol that are fueling your rage. It restores your brain's capacity for rational thinking.

You must understand this is not avoidance. This is operational necessity. Your brain's prefrontal cortex, the part responsible for logic and problem-solving, is offline during peak anger. You are not capable of resolution. You are only capable of reaction. Stepping away forces a physical pause. This pause is the moment you wait for your rational mind to reconnect.

How to Announce a Tactical Timeout

You must communicate this need assertively and respectfully. You cannot storm out. That simply escalates the conflict further. You use direct, clear language. You take responsibility for your own emotional state.

Use a simple, committed statement:

- "I feel too frustrated to talk clearly right now. I need five minutes to calm down, and then I will come back."

- "I am starting to lose control. I am taking a quick break now. We will finish this conversation when I return."

- "I need distance. I am stepping away now. I will check in with you in ten minutes."

The key is to state your need for distance and clearly announce your intention to return. This shows responsibility. It shows commitment to the resolution, not just avoidance of the conflict. You are not running from the issue. You are running toward self-control.

Execute the Timeout Effectively

Where do you go? You go to a place where you are genuinely alone. You must remove yourself from sight and sound of the trigger. This might be another room, a quiet corner, or even just stepping outside.

What do you do when you get there? You do not replay the argument. You do not rehearse hostile responses. Replaying the event only fuels the fire and extends the physical response. You use the timeout to apply the physical cooling strategies below.

You give yourself a time minimum. Five to ten minutes is often necessary to reduce the adrenaline surge effectively. You only re-engage when you are genuinely thinking clearly again.

Relaxation: Reset Your Nervous System

Once you are in your safe space, you must focus on regulating your physiology. You are using conscious action to talk your body down from emergency mode. Relaxation techniques are a powerful tool against anger. They directly reduce the physical symptoms of the stress response.

The Power of Measured Breathing

Deep, controlled breathing is the fastest way to signal safety to your brain. This technique works because it mechanically stimulates the vagus nerve. The vagus nerve runs from your brain stem down to your abdomen. Stimulating this nerve signals your body to switch from the sympathetic nervous system, the fight or flight state, to the parasympathetic nervous system, the rest and digest state. You are telling your body to stand down.

- **The Technique:** You must breathe deeply, using your diaphragm, not just your chest. Place one hand on your chest and one on your abdomen. When you breathe in, the hand on your abdomen should rise more than the hand on your chest.

- **The Counted Rhythm:** You must breathe rhythmically. Inhale slowly through your nose to a count of four. Hold the breath for a count of two. Exhale slowly through your mouth to a count of six. The exhale must be longer than the inhale. This ratio is crucial for activating the calming response. Repeat this process ten times. This focused, intentional, counted breathing forces your entire system to slow down.

- **Consistency:** Research confirms that intentional use of relaxation skills, like deep breathing, helps reduce the physical symptoms of anger. You must practice this technique when you are calm. Practice builds memory. When chaos strikes, your body will automatically recall the rhythm.

Anger causes immediate, painful muscle tension. Your jaw clenches. Your shoulders rise. Your fists tighten. Progressive Muscle Relaxation, or PMR, systematically releases this physical tension. This technique is often included in comprehensive anger management programs.

The method is simple. You systematically tense and then completely relax different muscle groups in your body.

- **Process:** Start with your hands. Clench your fists as tightly as you can for five seconds. Notice the tension. Then, release the tension completely and let your hands go limp. Notice the feeling of release.

- **Sequence:** You move through the body systematically. Move to your arms, tensing your biceps and forearms. Release. Move to your shoulders and neck, tensing them toward your ears. Release. Continue down to your facial muscles, stomach, legs, and feet.

- **Result:** This process heightens your awareness of physical tension. It teaches your body how to intentionally release that tension. This physical release directly combats the adrenaline surge.

You are using your body to change your mind. You are consciously operating to reduce the physiological stress response. This deliberate action is the core of effective cooling.

Physical Interruption: Move the Energy

Anger generates massive amounts of physical energy. This is the adrenaline and cortisol flooding your system. This energy is prepared for fight. If it is not discharged safely, it will discharge as fury. You must use immediate physical activity to channel this energy safely.

Physical activity reduces the overall stress levels that feed anger. A quick burst of movement acts as a shock absorber for your system.

- **Brisk Movement:** Take a quick, brisk walk. Do it alone. Walk fast enough to raise your heart rate slightly. This physical action uses the adrenaline productively.

- **Stretching:** Engage in simple stretches. Stretch your arms wide. Stretch your neck and shoulders. The physical release in your muscles helps relieve tension.

- **Simple Exercise:** Perform thirty seconds of jumping jacks or ten pushups. These activities discharge the fight energy safely. They allow you to process the event without lashing out.

You must move the energy out of your body. You cannot sit and wait for the feeling to pass. You must participate in the calming process actively. The goal is to move the stress hormones through your system quickly.

Operationalizing Your Calm-Down Kit

You need to prepare for these moments in advance. You cannot invent a cooling strategy while you are raging. You need a personalized "Calm-Down Kit" of physical actions ready to deploy instantly.

This kit is a small list of actions you know will work. This list should be stored on your phone or written on a small card in your wallet. It is your emergency plan.

Your personal kit should include three things:

1. **Your Timeout Script:** The exact sentence you will use to leave the situation. "I need five minutes."

2. **Your Breathing Technique:** The exact count you will use. "In 4, hold 2, out 6. Ten times."

3. **Your Movement Discharge:** The exact physical action you will perform. "Fifteen minutes of fast walking."

You must commit to using this kit the moment you recognize the physical warning signs. When the jaw clenches, the clock starts. You have a narrow window of opportunity. Using these strategies is not optional. It is the immediate, operational requirement for maintaining calm control.

The process is sequential. First, recognize the physical signs. Second, announce and take the timeout. Third, use deep breathing to regulate your nervous system. Fourth, use physical movement or muscle relaxation to discharge the residual adrenaline. Only after completing these steps are you prepared to re-engage the problem with a rational mind. This disciplined approach builds consistent self-control.

CHAPTER 4

SOLVE PROBLEMS THAT FUEL YOUR ANGER

Recurrent anger is frequently a response to specific, ongoing problems. When an issue remains unresolved, it becomes a chronic trigger. You cycle through the same frustration again and again. You stop managing the issue and simply start managing your reaction to it. This approach is unsustainable. Long-term anger control requires solving the underlying problem, not just suppressing the resulting rage.

You must stop viewing difficulties as threats or personal attacks. You must start viewing them as engineering challenges to be solved. Anger, when channeled productively, can drive you toward necessary resolution. This chapter teaches you a structured problem-solving approach. This method replaces the destructive cycle of chronic anger with a productive cycle of resolution.

Identify the Root Problem

Anger is often a signal pointing to a deeper need that is not being met. You must translate the signal.

Start by reviewing your anger log from Chapter 1. Look for patterns in the triggers. Do your explosions consistently follow a few specific scenarios?

- **Example 1: Perpetual Latency.** If your anger is consistently sparked by your partner being late, the surface trigger is the lateness. The underlying problem is likely a lack of mutual respect for time, or perhaps a breakdown in communication regarding schedules. The problem is not the *lateness*. The problem is the unmet need for respect and reliability.

- **Example 2: Recurring Task Imbalance.** If you frequently become enraged over household chores, the problem is not the dirty dishes. The problem is an unfair division of labor, or a lack of clear expectations and accountability.

You must clearly define the problem in neutral, objective terms. Do not use judgmental language. Define the problem as the gap between what you need and what is currently happening. "I need the living room clean by 7:00 PM every night to feel relaxed, but the children's toys are consistently left out until 9:00 PM." This defined gap is the target for resolution.

The Four Steps of Problem-Solving

This structured approach is a core component of Cognitive Behavioral Therapy for anger management. It ensures that you address the issue logically, using your newly restored rational mind. You must only engage in this process after you have successfully completed a cooling strategy from Chapter 3.

Step 1: Define the Problem Clearly. State the problem factually, without blame or emotion. Focus on specific, observable behaviors or circumstances. Avoid generalizations. Example: "We need a system for handling incoming mail so that important bills are not missed."

Step 2: Generate Multiple Potential Solutions. Do not limit yourself to the first idea. Brainstorm at least five different ways to solve the problem. Include unconventional ideas. Do not evaluate the solutions yet. The goal is quantity.

- *Solution Examples for Mail Problem:* 1. Set aside 15 minutes every Sunday for one partner to handle all mail. 2. Get a separate mail sorter for bills only. 3. Sign up for electronic billing for everything. 4. Hire a personal assistant for one hour a week. 5. Agree that the first person to see the mail processes it immediately.

Step 3: Evaluate and Select the Best Solution. Now you analyze the options objectively. Weigh the pros and cons of each potential solution. Consider effort, cost, and long-term sustainability. Select the solution that is most likely to resolve the problem and that both parties can commit to. If the problem involves another person, their input is necessary here.

Step 4: Implement and Review the Solution. Put the chosen solution into action immediately. Define clear, measurable actions and assign responsibility. "We will try electronic billing for three months, and John will be responsible for setting it up by Friday." Set a review date. After one week or one month, review the solution. Did it resolve the problem? If the anger trigger reappears, the solution was unsuccessful. Return to Step 2 and choose a new solution. This practice replaces the destructive cycle of anger with a productive cycle of resolution.

Research on Problem-Solving Efficacy

Problem-solving training is a robust, evidence-based intervention in managing chronic frustration. Research shows that teaching individuals to systematically identify and solve the sources of their anger leads to significant reductions in overall aggression and hostility.

For instance, problem-solving is identified as a key skill in comprehensive cognitive behavioral interventions. By learning to view challenges as solvable issues, rather than emotional threats, you activate the rational, controlled part of your brain. The *Anger Management for Everyone* program, developed by prominent clinical psychologists Kassinove and Tafrate, includes structured problem-solving as one of the ten proven-effective skills for anger management. This systematic training helps people effectively interrupt the anger escalation process by substituting destructive rumination with constructive thought.

You stop wasting energy on the explosion. You redirect that energy toward constructive resolution. This shift from reaction to action is the definition of mastering your emotional state.

CHAPTER 5
EXPRESS NEEDS ASSERTIVELY, NOT AGGRESSIVELY

Getting your emotions under control is just the first step. Once you've taken a moment to cool off and think things through, it's time to re-engage. Now, you need to express your frustration in a calm, respectful way. This is the most important skill in handling anger—you swap the impulse to lash out for a way to speak up clearly and kindly.

Being assertive means sharing what you need, how you feel, and what you think without beating around the bush. You do so in a way that respects others and keeps things from heating up. Assertive talk actually makes your relationships stronger and cuts down on stress caused by fights.

The key shift here is moving away from blaming others to taking responsibility for yourself.

Turn "You" Blame Into "I" Responsibility

Blaming "You" phrases are toxic—they make people immediately defensive and shut down the conversation. When you say, "You never listen," the other person stops hearing and starts protecting themselves.

1. Don't Blame Others for Your Feelings

   Your feelings belong to you. Saying "I feel angry" is true and undeniable. It stops the blame game and keeps the other person open.

2. Talk About What You See, Not What You Think

   Say what happened, not what you guess about who they are. For example, instead of "You're rude," say, "When you interrupted me, the talk stopped." Actions can be changed. Character labels can't.

3. Keep It Positive and Respectful

   Say what you mean clearly but kindly. Avoid words that shame or attack. Your tone should invite peace and problem-solving, not start a fight.

Use the XYZ Formula for Clear "I" Statements

This handy formula helps make your feelings clear and your point easy to understand. Many trainers teach it because it works so well.

1. Say Your Feeling (X)

   Be specific: "frustrated," "worried," "sad." Don't say things like "ignored" or "attacked" because those sound like judgments, not emotions.

2. Say Exactly What Happened (Y)

   Give a fact: "when you speak loudly" or "when dishes pile up."

3. Say Where or When It Happened (Z)

   Add context: "at the family dinner" or "during our meeting."

4. Ask for What You Want (Resolution)

   Finish with a clear request: "Please text me if you'll be late."

Putting it all together might sound like:

"I feel frustrated when you arrive twenty minutes late for the third time this week, and I would like you to text me before if you expect to be late."

To keep healthy boundaries, you need to say what you want.

1. Say What You Need

A complaint without a request is just venting. Tell people what would make things better so they know how to help.

2. Say "No" Politely but Firmly

Don't just avoid or agree to things to keep peace. Try, "Thank you for asking, but I can't right now."

3. Remember Your Needs Are Equal to Anyone Else's

Asking for what you want is self-respect and stops resentment from building up.

Stay Focused on the Present

Old issues have no place in today's talk.

1. Avoid "Always" and "Never"

Words like "You never…" spark more arguing and distract from the real problem.

2. Deal With One Problem at a Time

Keep your attention on what's happening now. Don't bring up past fights. Focus keeps it manageable and calmer.

Words alone aren't enough. Your body needs to say the same thing.

- Stand or sit confidently and relaxed.
- Keep steady eye contact—not staring, but interested.
- Choose the right time for big talks—don't start when someone's rushing or stressed.

Research shows assertive talk lowers anger and conflict. Using "I" statements helps listeners stay open instead of feeling attacked. It prevents fights and helps everyone feel understood.

Training in assertiveness is a core part of anger management therapies like Cognitive Behavioral Therapy. These programs teach that speaking your needs respectfully keeps anger from building up and bursting out. When you master assertive talking, you create fair and steady relationships with clear ways to handle frustration.

CHAPTER 6
BOOK 1 CONCLUSION:
MAINTAIN YOUR CALM CONTROL

You have learned five fundamental skills for anger control. This mastery is not based on feeling different. It is based on acting differently. Control is measured by your consistent choices. You have replaced reactive fury with deliberate, respectful responses. This is an operational change. You are not waiting for anger to disappear. You are choosing skill over reaction every single time.

This disciplined approach is how you build true, consistent self-control. You must maintain this operational focus. The techniques you learned are effective only when applied immediately. The moment of decision is brief. You must act the instant you recognize your warning signs.

Your new system of control is built on five necessary actions. Each action serves a specific purpose in disrupting the toxic anger cycle.

Pillar One: Intercepting the Surge. You must know your physical and mental warning signs. This is the first step in control. You are training yourself to notice the body's earliest signals. The racing heart is a signal. The clenched jaw is a signal. Hostile thoughts cycling in your head are signals. These signs tell you the amygdala has fired instantly. This neurological event means your rational mind is temporarily disabled. You are not capable of complex thought or civilized discussion at this point. Early awareness creates the vital window for intervention. You must respect the signal. You must interrupt the cycle immediately. You use your personal anger map to monitor yourself.

Pillar Two: Physical De-escalation. You must physically restore calm before attempting rational thought. This is non-negotiable. You take a deliberate timeout. You announce your need to step away clearly and respectfully. This is not escape. This is self-regulation. You must remove yourself from the trigger physically. Distance allows the adrenaline to clear. Then you activate your relaxation response. Deep, measured breathing is the fastest way to signal safety to your brain. You breathe in slowly. You exhale slowly. The long exhale stimulates the vagus nerve.

This action mechanically signals your nervous system to switch from emergency mode to calm mode. You use progressive muscle relaxation. You systematically tense and release muscle groups. This releases the painful tension stored in your body. This discharge uses the energy prepared for fight. You use physical movement to channel residual stress safely. This step manages the body first. It restores the capacity for rational thought.

Pillar Three: Cognitive Restructuring. You must challenge the thoughts that fuel the fury. Anger is sustained by irrational, hostile interpretations of events. You stop assuming the worst intent. You stop catastrophizing small mistakes. You stop using all-or-nothing thinking. You use the four-step process. You identify the hostile thought. You question the objective evidence for that thought. You find three alternative, non-hostile explanations. You practice repeating the balanced thought. This conscious process actively engages your rational brain. Research confirms that focusing on changing these hostile cognitions is effective in reducing aggression and hostility. You are training your mind to prioritize facts over assumptions. You restore your ability to make rational decisions.

Pillar Four: Structured Problem-Solving. You must solve the underlying issues that generate chronic frustration. Recurrent anger is often a response to specific, ongoing problems. You stop wasting energy managing the reaction. You start solving the root cause. You define the problem neutrally. You generate multiple potential solutions. You select the best, most sustainable solution. You implement it. You set a review date. This systematic action replaces the destructive cycle of chronic anger with a productive cycle of resolution. This problem-solving approach is a key skill in comprehensive cognitive behavioral interventions. It stops anger from recycling.

Pillar Five: Assertive Expression. You must communicate your frustration respectfully once you are calm. This skill replaces reactive blame with proactive responsibility. You stop using "You" statements. You stop attacking the person. You start reporting on your internal state. You use powerful "I" statements. The XYZ formula ensures clarity. You state your specific emotion (X). You state the specific behavior (Y). You state the situation (Z). You request a clear resolution. This structured communication reduces conflict stress and ensures your needs are heard without belittling the other person. Assertive dialogue establishes equal footing in your relationships.

Sustaining Control: The Path Forward

Maintaining your calm control requires continuous effort. You are replacing decades of automatic reaction with disciplined skill. This takes time. This takes consistency.

The Role of Consistency. The old toxic patterns are deeply ingrained neural pathways. They fire instantly. Your new skills must become the new default response. This only happens through consistent practice. You must commit to using the tactical timeout every single time you feel the warning signs. You must commit to challenging hostile thoughts even when you are alone. Every time you choose skill over fury, you reinforce the new, healthier pathway. Small, repeated wins build the habit. Inconsistency ensures the old patterns remain dominant. Consistency is the measurement of your commitment.

Self-Correction is Mandatory. You will make mistakes. You will occasionally lose control. This is part of the process. A mistake is not an invitation to quit. It is data. When you have an anger episode, you do not punish yourself. You return to your anger log. You analyze the failure. Where did the process break down? Did you miss the physical warning sign? Did you refuse to take the timeout? Did you use all-or-nothing language? You correct the failure point immediately. You adjust your strategy. You plan for the next encounter. Self-correction is learning. It keeps the process focused on growth, not guilt.

Separating Feelings from Actions. You will still feel angry sometimes. Anger is a necessary human emotion. The goal is never to eliminate the feeling. The goal is to separate the feeling from the destructive action. You respect the feeling. You acknowledge the message. Then you choose a skillful, respectful action. You use the emotional energy for problem-solving or assertive communication. You stop using it for attack. You control your behavior. You do not try to control the feeling. This separation is the true definition of emotional maturity.

Preparing for High-Stress Triggers. You know your triggers are most powerful when you are hungry, tired, or already stressed. Research confirms that environmental factors like poor sleep can heighten emotional reactivity. You must build buffers against this vulnerability. You manage your sleep consistently. You eat regularly. You do not engage in crucial conversations when you are depleted. You respect your physical limits. You avoid putting yourself in situations where you know your self-control will be lowest. You preemptively deploy cooling strategies when you anticipate a difficult trigger.

Building the New Foundation. Your commitment to these five pillars creates structural integrity in your life. You are building a new foundation for all your relationships. When you consistently control your anger, you provide predictability. You provide safety. You provide respect. These are the necessary conditions for building trust, which is the subject of later books. You cannot build deep connection on an unpredictable foundation. Calm control is the prerequisite for all healthy interaction.

You have the tools. You have the map. You have the scientific basis for success. Your work now is maintenance. You choose control. You choose respect. You choose consistent action.

Reflection Questions

1. Detail three specific situations from the past week where you successfully used a cooling strategy. What technique did you use and how effective was it?

2. What specific hostile thought pattern (e.g., blaming, catastrophizing) caused your last moment of intense frustration? Rewrite that thought using a balanced, objective interpretation.

3. Describe a recent instance where you used an "I" statement. Identify the X (emotion), Y (behavior), and Z (situation) you used.

4. What recurring problem does your most frequent anger pattern point toward? What is one new, measurable solution you will implement to address the root cause this week?

5. Where did your control process break down the last time you lost your temper? What adjustment to your current plan will you make to prevent that failure point from recurring?

CHECKLIST
MAINTAIN YOUR CALM CONTROL

This checklist is your operational guide for **Book 1: Control Anger**. It breaks down the five chapters into daily, actionable tasks. Use this list immediately when you encounter frustration. These are the measurable choices that define your transformation.

I. Intercepting the Surge: Identifying Warning Signs

Before you can intervene, you must become a scientist of your own anger. You are training yourself to notice the body's earliest signals. If you miss this moment, the rest of the skills fail. This section focuses on observation and immediate awareness.

Have you committed to the following actions this week?

- **Identified Three Specific External Triggers:** Did you move past generalizations like "traffic" or "money"? Did you pinpoint specific, external situations that reliably start the anger cycle? You need precision. Think about the specific person, time, or circumstance that reliably sparks your fury. You are separating the root cause of anger from the subsequent, destructive reaction. You must know what sets the stage for your explosion. This clear identification allows you to anticipate when you are most vulnerable.

- **Logged Your Anger Events with Factual Detail:** Did you log every instance of intense anger? Did you note the exact time, place, and involved people? You must describe the situation in objective, factual terms. For example, do not write, "My partner was being rude." Write, "My partner left the lights on when leaving the room." This focus on observable behavior, not assumed intent, is necessary for clean data collection. Accurate logging is the first step in CBT for anger control.

- **Recognized Your Personal Physical Warning Signs:** Did you feel the surge? You know your body gives the earliest and most reliable signal before your mind shuts down. You must identify the physical cues that precede rational thought failure. Did you notice your heart rate suddenly increase? Did your jaw clench tightly? Was there a sudden rush of heat in your neck or chest?

You must respect this signal. The physical sensation is the direct evidence of a neurological takeover.

- **Identified Your Hostile Mental Signs:** Did you recognize the toxic thoughts that accompanied the physical surge? You must pinpoint the immediate, hostile interpretation you made. Did you start **Catastrophizing** ("This small mistake will ruin everything")? Did you automatically engage in **Blaming** ("They did that on purpose to insult me")? Did you start **Rehearsing** the argument internally? Recognizing these mental signs is crucial because they fuel the escalation of anger. You must catch the thought before it accelerates the physical response.

- **Practiced Self-Monitoring Proactively:** Did you perform periodic body checks throughout the day? Set an alarm on your phone for noon and 4:00 PM. Check your body for physical tension or shallow breathing at those specific times. This deliberate monitoring prevents the anger from building up unnoticed. This practice builds consistent self-awareness, which is the foundational skill for all emotional management.

II. Challenging Hostile Thoughts: Cognitive Restructuring

The anger cycle is sustained by irrational assumptions. You must use logic to dismantle these thoughts before they disable your prefrontal cortex. This section focuses on applying the four-step cognitive restructuring process every time a hostile thought arises.

When a hostile thought occurred, did you perform the following steps?

- **Successfully Identified the Core Hostile Thought (Step 1):** Did you pinpoint the precise thought that triggered the emotional surge? You must separate the external event from your internal interpretation. Example: You must identify, "This person is actively trying to make my life harder," not just, "I feel frustrated." This precision is essential. You are identifying the target for intervention.

- **Questioned the Evidence Supporting the Hostile Thought (Step 2):** Did you challenge your assumption? You must immediately ask yourself what objective evidence proves that hostile intent. Ask, "What factual proof do I have that they intended to undermine me?" Ask, "Is there any other, less hostile reason for this situation?" Most hostile thoughts cannot withstand this rigorous factual examination. You are gathering evidence for and against your automatic emotional conclusion. This is the moment you choose logic over reaction.

- **Generated Alternative, Objective Interpretations (Step 3):** Did you replace the hostile thought with a balanced perspective? You must find at least three alternative, non-hostile reasons for the situation. Example: Instead of deliberate disrespect, choose "They might have been overwhelmed and forgot," or "They might be facing an external pressure I do not know about." This practice ensures you focus only on the facts of the event. You neutralize the assumed insult.

- **Practiced Internalizing the New, Balanced Thought (Step 4):** Did you actively repeat the alternative thought to replace the automatic, hostile response? You must internalize the non-hostile perspective. This repetition reinforces the new, rational neural pathway. This consistent practice effectively reduces overall hostility. You are choosing to rewire your brain for calm.

- **Eliminated Toxic Thought Patterns:** Did you catch yourself using specific toxic thought patterns? Did you stop **Catastrophizing** a small inconvenience into a disaster? Did you avoid **All-or-Nothing Thinking** (using "always" or "never")? You must recognize these faulty logical traps. Eliminating these patterns of thinking is crucial for proportional emotional responses. You train your mind to think proportionally.

III. Practicing Immediate Cooling: Physical De-escalation

Once the warning signs appear, intervention must be physical and immediate. You must manage the body first to clear the adrenaline surge. This section focuses on disciplined action to restore physiological calm.

The moment warning signs appeared, did you execute these actions?

- **Took a Deliberate Tactical Timeout:** Did you physically step away from the triggering situation? You must create distance instantly. This timeout is not avoidance; it is operational necessity to restore rational thought capacity. Did you remove yourself from the sight and sound of the trigger? You must give your system time to clear the adrenaline that fuels your rage.

- **Used an Assertive Timeout Script:** Did you communicate your need to step away respectfully, without storming out? You must use direct language. You state your intention to return. Example: "I feel too frustrated to talk clearly. I need five minutes to calm down, and I will be back." This clear communication shows responsibility for the resolution, not just avoidance of the conflict.

- **Activated Measured Breathing (The 4-2-6 Count):** Did you immediately use deep, controlled breathing to signal safety to your brain? You must stimulate the vagus nerve to switch from fight-or-flight to rest-and-digest mode. Did you inhale slowly to a count of four? Did you hold for two? Did you exhale slowly and deliberately to a count of six? You must repeat this rhythm ten times. This focused, intentional breathing forces your system to slow down.

- **Discharged Physical Tension with Relaxation Skills:** Did you use Progressive Muscle Relaxation? You must systematically tense and then completely relax different muscle groups (jaw, fists, shoulders). This releases the physical tension stored in your body, which directly combats the adrenaline surge. This active release teaches your body how to consciously let go of stress.

- **Used Movement to Channel Adrenaline Safely:** Did you engage in immediate physical activity? You must move the fight energy out of your body. Did you take a brisk walk? Did you perform thirty seconds of jumping jacks? This physical action uses the adrenaline productively. You do not wait for the feeling to pass. You actively participate in the calming process.

IV. Solving the Root Problems: Structured Resolution

Recurrent anger is a predictable response to unresolved issues. You must stop simply managing the reaction. You must start solving the problem. This section focuses on structuring your rational capacity toward constructive resolution.

When a recurring issue sparked frustration, did you follow these four problem-solving steps?

- **Defined the Root Problem Neutrally (Step 1):** Did you clearly state the problem factually, without blame or emotion? You must define the problem as the gap between what you need and what is currently happening. Example: "We need a system for clear task assignment," not "You are always messy." You identify the underlying problem your anger points to.

- **Generated Multiple Potential Solutions (Step 2):** Did you brainstorm at least five different ways to solve the problem? You must not limit yourself to the first, obvious idea. You encourage creativity and quantity. Did you include unconventional ideas? This generates options for negotiation.

- **Evaluated and Selected the Best Solution (Step 3):** Did you weigh the pros and cons of each option objectively? You must select the solution that is most likely to resolve the problem and that all parties can commit to. If it involves another person, did you ensure their input and commitment? You choose feasibility over perfection.

- **Implemented and Reviewed the Solution (Step 4):** Did you put the solution into action immediately? Did you define clear, measurable actions and assign responsibility? Did you set a review date? If the anger trigger reappeared, did you return to Step 2 and choose a new solution? This practice replaces the destructive cycle of chronic anger with a productive cycle of resolution.

V. Expressing Needs Assertively: The Language of Respect

Once you are calm and thinking clearly, you must express your frustration using structured, respectful language. This section focuses on applying the assertive communication skills you mastered.

In your recent communications, did you ensure the following?

- **Shifted Language from Blame to Responsibility:** Did you stop using accusatory "You" statements? Did you acknowledge that your feelings are yours? You must focus on your internal state. Example: "I feel frustrated when..." not "You make me frustrated." This honesty bypasses the listener's defense mechanism.

- **Constructed Powerful "I" Statements (XYZ):** Did you use the complete, structured formula when expressing a key need? Did you state your specific emotion (X)? Did you identify the specific, observable behavior (Y)? Did you state the situation (Z)? This structure ensures your message is clear and complete.

- **Articulated a Clear Resolution:** Did you end your assertive statement with a clear request for a change in behavior or action? A complaint without a request is venting. You must define the desired outcome in clear, measurable terms. Example: You must request, "I need you to commit to loading the dishwasher," not "I need you to be more helpful."

- **Eliminated Absolute Language and Maintained Present Focus:** Did you avoid bringing up the past? Did you stop using generalizations like "you always" or "you never"? You must address only the current, single issue. This present focus gives the listener a manageable problem to solve.

- **Ensured Non-Verbal Congruence:** Did your non-verbal signals align with your assertive words? You must maintain a calm, even, low tone of voice. Did you use confident, open posture? You must maintain direct, non-glaring eye contact. Your calm body language provides the credibility necessary for your assertive words to be heard as a request, not a threat.

BOOK TWO

BUILD EMPATHY:
TOOLS TO TRULY UNDERSTAND OTHERS

INTRODUCTION

You have established internal calm. You have mastered your aggressive impulses. You can intercept the anger cycle and communicate your own needs assertively. This control is the necessary foundation for deep connection. You cannot build a relationship if you are a walking time bomb. Now you must shift your focus externally. You must learn to truly hear and understand the people around you.

Empathy is the critical next skill. Empathy is not sympathy. Sympathy feels pity. Empathy allows you to connect with another person's feeling. It allows you to sense the emotion they are experiencing. This connection transforms dialogue. Empathy is a learnable skill.

Toxic behavior dismisses feelings. It rushes to judgment. It assumes hostile intent. Empathy dismantles these toxic habits. When you show the speaker they have been genuinely heard and understood, you move conversations out of pain and conflict.

The foundation of empathy is structured, reflective listening. This is not passive hearing. It is active engagement. Reflective listening ensures you have correctly processed both the factual content and the emotional underpinning of what the speaker shared. This process avoids the illusion of understanding. It builds immediate safety.

You must accept this basic truth: giving understanding is the best way to ensure you receive understanding later. When you offer validation and true listening, you create an environment where the other person feels safe enough to be vulnerable. This ability to hear and affirm pain is essential for repairing any relational damage you caused in the past.

This book will teach you the four stages of empathic listening. You will move from simple physical attention to deep emotional reflection.

First, you will learn the **Attending Skills**. These are the physical and non-verbal cues that signal you are fully present. You must prove you are listening before a single word is exchanged.

Second, you will practice **Rephrasing Content**. You confirm that you have processed the factual information shared. You check your accuracy.

Third, you will practice **Reflecting Feelings**. This moves the conversation from argument to acknowledgment. You identify and name the emotion underpinning the words.

Finally, you will combine these skills into **Deep Inquiry**. This is the highest level of connection. You integrate both the facts and the emotions. You determine what the speaker needs from you right now.

Empathy is work. It requires consistent effort to shift your focus from self-preoccupation to genuine focus on the other person. You must suppress your own reactive thoughts and judgments during the dialogue. You are giving the speaker your full mental and physical attention. This skill provides the depth and connection that toxic behavior inherently lacks. You are committing to understanding over attack.

Research on Empathy and Connection

Structured listening and empathy are recognized as necessary tools for constructive communication and conflict resolution. Marshall B. Rosenberg, the creator of Nonviolent Communication, emphasized that the ability to offer empathy allows people to stay vulnerable and defuses potential conflict. He noted that the best way to get understanding from another person is to give that person understanding first.

Empathy is consistently shown to de-escalate conflicts. It combats loneliness. It builds human connection even in challenging circumstances. By focusing on reflective listening, you learn how to translate anger and blame into productive dialogue. This systematic approach transforms relationships, providing the necessary emotional safety for both parties to speak freely.

This structured approach is a powerful tool for self-transformation. You are training yourself to be present. You are building connection deliberately. You are making empathy your new default response. This work establishes the necessary conditions for healing and relational growth.

CHAPTER 1
ADOPT ATTENDING SKILLS FOR FOCUS

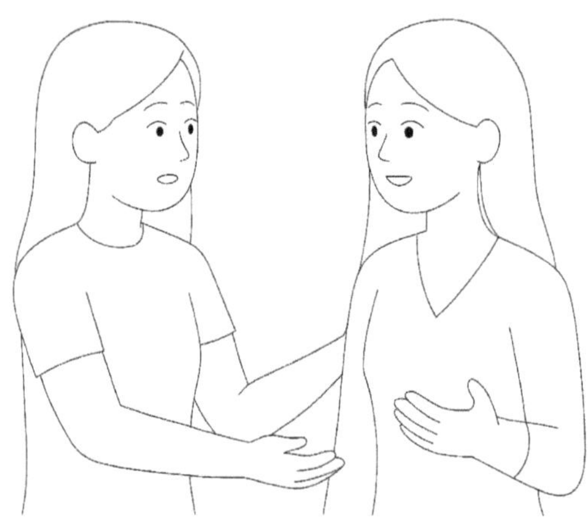

Empathy begins with attention. You cannot understand someone if you are distracted, defensive, or rehearsing your next comment. Attending skills are the physical and psychological actions you take to communicate non-verbally that you are fully present and engaged. This physical commitment is the gatekeeper of effective listening.

If your non-verbal signals convey distraction or disinterest, the speaker will immediately feel unsafe. They will doubt your sincerity. This renders any later verbal reflection useless. You must prove you are listening before a single word is exchanged.

Master Your Non-Verbal Signals

Attending involves all elements of your physiology: your eyes, your posture, and your movement. These signals establish immediate rapport.

1. Maintain Appropriate Eye Contact. Looking at the speaker demonstrates that they have your full attention. This non-verbal cue signals engagement. However, you must avoid staring intently. Staring can make a person feel uncomfortable, signaling aggression or intensity instead of connection. You must be natural. Adjust your eye contact based on cultural norms. The goal is to show interest and focus, not dominance.

2. Use Open Body Language. Your posture must invite the other person to talk freely. Avoid defensive postures at all cost. Do not cross your arms tightly across your chest. Do not turn your body away from the speaker. Crossed arms and tight postures signal disagreement or emotional withdrawal. They shut down communication before it starts.

You should lean slightly forward in your chair. This small movement demonstrates active engagement. It shows you are actively listening to what the speaker is saying. Your posture must convey relaxation and openness.

- **3. Employ Non-Verbal Feedback and Mirroring.** Use small, physical actions to show you are tracking the conversation. This establishes immediate rapport.

- **Nodding:** Simple, small nods indicate that you are following the thread of their thought.

- **Mirroring Tone:** Adjust your facial expressions to reflect the speaker's tone. If they are talking about something sad, your expression should show gentle concern. If they express surprise, reflect that surprise momentarily. This subtle mirroring demonstrates you are connecting with their emotional state.

- **Minimal Encouragers:** Use quiet, brief vocal sounds like "Hmm," "I see," or "Go on." These small vocalizations show continued engagement without interrupting the speaker's flow.

Create Psychological Space

Attending is not just physical. It is also psychological. You must prepare your mind to receive information without immediate judgment. You must temporarily set aside your own agenda.

1. Practice Mindfulness During Dialogue. You must be aware of your own internal desire to argue, refute, or jump ahead to a solution. You must consciously suppress these reactive thoughts. Stay focused entirely on the present moment and the speaker's narrative. You are not listening to prepare your reply. You are listening to understand their experience.

2. Embrace Silences. Do not rush to fill quiet moments. Silence can feel awkward, but it is a powerful tool in communication. Silence helps the other person focus on themselves. It allows them space to vent, sort out complex issues, and articulate their thoughts and feelings clearly. Respecting silence shows patience. It demonstrates you are willing to wait for them to process their own experience at their own pace.

3. Focus Completely on the Speaker. If your posture or eye signals communicate distraction, the speaker immediately distrusts your sincerity. They will believe you are merely waiting for your turn to talk. Attending means giving your complete physical and psychological attention to the other person. This commitment is the necessary first stage of empathic listening.

The Scientific Basis of Attending

The practice of attending skills is the foundation of the reflective listening process, a clinically recognized approach to improving communication. Reflective listening research consistently shows that non-verbal communication is vital for building trust and ensuring the speaker feels supported.

These physical actions communicate empathy non-verbally. They demonstrate caring and support, which are necessary for psychological safety. When a speaker feels safe, they are more likely to express their feelings and address issues at a deeper level. This physical commitment to listening is the first active step away from your toxic past. You are showing respect for the speaker's presence and experience.

CHAPTER 2
LISTEN BEYOND WORDS: REPHRASE CONTENT

You've already shown you're fully present, both physically and mentally. The speaker feels comfortable because you're open and keeping steady eye contact. Now, it's time to move into the next important step of verbal empathy: making sure you really got the facts right.

This step is called rephrasing content. It's a key part of reflective listening and comes in handy anytime conversations get tough. The goal is to double-check that you understood the speaker's objective info correctly. This helps avoid misunderstandings and stops arguments that spiral out of control over mere facts.

Why Thinking You Understand Isn't Enough

It's easy to assume you know what someone said—you think you're listening but your mind's already rushing ahead to what you'll say next. This gives you a false sense of understanding. If you jump in too soon, you risk shutting down the real message. That's when frustration and conflict creep in fast.

Lots of toxic talks skip this crucial step, rushing straight to debate or solutions. But if you want to truly connect, you need to verify you heard facts correctly before moving forward.

How to Rephrase Content: Basic Steps

Rephrasing content is taught in active listening classes and is the second stage of empathic listening. It's simply about repeating back what the speaker said, but using your own neutral words. Focus is purely on facts, not emotions.

Here's how you do it:

- Wait for a Pause: Let the speaker finish their point without cutting in.

- Start Your Response Clearly: Begin with something like, "So, what I'm hearing is..." or "If I got that right, you're saying..." or "Let me check I've got the details straight."

- Summarize the Facts: Use plain language to restate the key info—who, what, where, when. Leave out feelings or judgments.

- Check for Accuracy: End with a question like, "Did I get that right?" or "Is that accurate?" so they can clarify or fix any mistakes.

Example in Action

Speaker: "I asked Sarah to finish the budget spreadsheet by Tuesday morning, so I could review it before the meeting. But when I checked at noon, it wasn't there. Now I don't have time to check her work before presenting."

Listening You: "Okay, if I understand, you needed the finished spreadsheet from Sarah by Tuesday morning so you could review it. Then, when you looked for it at noon, it wasn't in the file folder. Did I get that right?"

Why Rephrasing Matters

This simple back-and-forth actually does a lot:

- Checks Your Understanding: You make sure you heard the facts right, so you won't later say, "You never said that."

- Builds Speaker Trust: They know you're really paying attention and their words matter.

- Keeps You Focused: It stops your mind from drifting off and keeps you tuned in to their story.

- Clarifies the Issue: You organize their info in your head, making the problem clearer to both of you.

Reflective listening, especially rephrasing content, is a proven way to make tough talks productive. It's about using the logical side of your brain which you practiced way back in Book 1. Applying that self-control out loud helps you take in what's being said before you react.

Make this your go-to move in every tricky conversation. Hold back the urge to fix the problem or share your judgment right away. Your first job is just to understand the facts. The next part will be about connecting with the feelings behind those facts.

CHAPTER 3
REFLECT FEELINGS TO VALIDATE EXPERIENCE

Okay, so you've got the facts right, and you've been there in person. You've put the basic info in your own words. But now, here's the tricky part: tuning into what the speaker *feels*. This is where things really start to click. It's called Stage 3 of empathic listening: reflecting feelings. Basically, you're showing that you get what's going on inside their head, emotionally speaking.

You know how toxic behavior pretty much shuts down feelings? Like, it tells people, "Hey, you're not supposed to feel that way," and then rushes to downplay whatever hurt they're experiencing? Empathy? It's the total opposite. It says, "Yeah, I see what you're going through. That feeling? It's valid." This changes the whole thing from some dry, fact-based argument to a real human exchange.

Finding the Real Feeling Behind the Words

Good empathy means picking up on the actual emotion behind what they say. Most folks don't state their feelings straightforwardly. They might complain about stress from work deadlines, but their voice, body language, and face might be saying, "I'm tired," or "I'm disappointed," or maybe even, "I'm scared." So your job is to listen for these deeper feelings.

- Listen for tone. Is their voice a bit tight or quick? Are they sounding frustrated or maybe even relieved?
- Watch their body language. If they're grinning but telling you about a loss, that probably means there's more beneath the surface.
- Use exact emotion words. Don't just say "bad" or "upset." Try "disappointed," "anxious," "relieved," or "overwhelmed." It shows you're actually paying attention.

How to Reflect Feelings

The trick here is to say back what you hear, linking the feeling to what they said. It's like putting a label on their inner experience.

Start with something like, "Sounds like you're frustrated," or "You seem anxious about..." Then say the feeling you noticed and connect it to their story. Maybe, "Sounds like you're overwhelmed because of the sudden change in your project deadline."

Why It Matters to Validate

Validation is huge, it means accepting their feelings as reasonable, even if you don't necessarily agree with the situation. You're not judging or fixing, just acknowledging.

Why bother? Because it helps calm things down. When people feel heard, their emotional intensity drops. It creates a safe space for them to open up.

Research backs this up. John Gottman's work shows that couples who validate each other's feelings tend to have stronger, longer-lasting relationships. And Marshall Rosenberg's Nonviolent Communication teaches us that empathy helps avoid conflict and keeps us open.

Wrapping It Up

When you reflect and validate, you hand the speaker the chance to clarify. Maybe they'll say, "Actually, I'm not overwhelmed, just disappointed because I felt disrespected." That's your cue to follow their lead.

In the end, toxic communication brushes off feelings. Empathy is about welcoming them, reflecting them, and saying, "I get you." It takes real effort and focus but helps build trust and make a true connection.

CHAPTER 4
AVOID JUDGMENT AND OFFER NON-VERBAL SUPPORT

You have mastered the mechanics of listening. You attend to body language. You confirm facts. You validate feelings. Now you must address the single greatest obstacle to connection: your own internal judgment.

Empathy requires you to set aside your own judgments. You focus entirely on the speaker's worldview. You must consciously suppress your desire to argue, fix, or offer unsolicited advice. Toxic behavior assumes the listener knows best. Empathy acknowledges the speaker is the expert on their own experience.

Consciously Suppress Your Internal Reaction

When someone shares a difficulty, your mind races. You want to offer a solution. You want to point out where they went wrong. You want to compare their problem to one of your own. These internal reactions are instant. They are self-focused. They block true empathy.

You must view your reactive thoughts as distractions. Practice mindfulness during the exchange. Be aware of your own desire to argue or refute, but choose not to voice those internal judgments. Stay focused entirely on the present moment and the speaker's experience. Your primary job is to provide a non-judgmental container for their feelings.

This restraint is difficult. It requires constant self-monitoring. You are choosing to sacrifice your own immediate need to be right or to fix the problem. You are prioritizing the speaker's need to be heard.

Embrace and Utilize Silence

Silence can feel intensely awkward. Your instinct is to fill the quiet moment immediately. You feel pressure to offer a comment or a solution. Resist this urge completely.

Embrace silences fully. Do not rush to fill quiet moments. Silence is a powerful communication tool. It benefits the speaker immensely.

- **Processing Time:** Silence helps the other person focus on themselves. It gives them necessary time to process their emotions.
- **Venting and Sorting:** It allows them space to vent a feeling. It gives them time to sort out complex issues internally.
- **Clearer Articulation:** Silence encourages them to articulate their thoughts and feelings more clearly.

Respecting silence shows patience. It demonstrates you are willing to wait for them to process their own experience at their own pace. When you respect silence, you are validating their right to control the speed of the conversation.

Use Open-Ended Inquiry

When you do speak, your questions must encourage deeper sharing. You use open-ended questions that invite elaboration. Avoid closed-ended questions that can be answered with a simple yes or no.

Closed questions focus on facts. They keep the conversation shallow. Open-ended questions require descriptive answers. They encourage the speaker to explore their feelings and motivations.

- **Closed Question:** "Did that make you angry?" (Answer: Yes/No)
- **Open-Ended Question:** "What were the feelings that came up for you when that happened?"
- **Closed Question:** "Do you know what you should do next?" (Answer: Yes/No)

- **Open-Ended Question:** "What outcomes would satisfy you here?"

This technique allows the speaker to guide the conversation in the direction they choose. It shows you trust them to know their own path. You are not imposing your agenda. You are facilitating their self-discovery.

Offer Non-Verbal Support

Attending skills continue to play a vital role in this stage. Even when you are silent, your body language must convey patience and acceptance.

- **Open Posture:** Maintain relaxed, open body language. Do not shift restlessly. Avoid crossing your arms.

- **Non-Verbal Feedback:** Use small, quiet gestures. Use gentle nodding. This indicates you are following the emotional thread. Mirroring the speaker's tone or facial expression subtly shows you are connecting with their experience.

This non-verbal commitment provides a constant signal of psychological safety. If your body language signals judgment, the speaker will immediately withdraw. You must stay focused on the present moment. You must stay focused on the speaker's worldview.

The Scientific Necessity of Non-Judgment

The therapeutic process relies heavily on the counselor's ability to maintain unconditional positive regard. This means accepting the client without judgment. This principle applies directly to empathic communication in your relationships.

Research shows that non-judgmental acceptance is critical for allowing individuals to process difficult emotions. When a speaker feels judged, the brain's defense mechanisms activate instantly. They become guarded. They stop sharing honestly. Their vulnerability disappears.

By avoiding judgment, you provide a safe space. This safety allows the speaker to truly vent, sort out complex issues, and deal more effectively with their emotions. You are enabling their process of self-healing. You are not fixing them. You are simply creating the conditions under which they can fix themselves. This willingness to hold a space of non-judgment is a deliberate choice. It is a fundamental action that builds trust and repairs relational damage.

CHAPTER 5
DEEPEN CONNECTION THROUGH OPEN INQUIRY

You have moved through the initial stages of empathy. You have attended. You confirmed the facts. You validated the emotions. You held a space free of judgment. The speaker now feels heard and safe. The final, highest stage of empathic listening requires integration. You must combine content rephrasing with feeling reflection to capture the full, complete meaning of the communication. This is the step that guides the conversation toward a constructive end.

Toxic communication leaves the speaker feeling abandoned after they have opened up. It says, "Thanks for sharing," and then moves on. Empathy requires you to process their entire narrative. You must determine what action, if any, is required from you. You move from listening to purposeful inquiry.

Summarize the Entire Narrative

Do not rely on small reflections here. You must summarize larger segments of what has been said. This integration demonstrates that you have tracked the entire narrative. It gives the speaker confidence in your sustained attention and capacity to understand complexity.

A comprehensive summary integrates the main facts, the key emotions, and the overall context. This technique shows the speaker you have organized their experience internally. It allows them to confirm or correct your overall understanding before moving forward.

The process is deliberate:

1. **Use an Integration Phrase:** Begin with a phrase like: "Let me pull this all together and make sure I understand the full picture..." or "So, summarizing the whole situation, what I hear is..."

2. **State the Facts:** Briefly list the critical factual points the speaker shared.

3. **State the Emotions:** Acknowledge the core feelings you validated throughout the discussion.

4. **Confirm the Need:** Ask if your summary accurately reflects their full experience.

Example of Integration:

- **You Summarizing:** "So, summarizing, you had a hard conversation with your boss [Fact] where you were assigned extra work [Fact] which makes you feel **overwhelmed** and **frustrated** [Emotions]. And this is happening because you feel the responsibility is unbalanced [Content]. Is that a fair summary of the problem?"

This integrated summary is the final check of your accuracy. It shows you respected the entirety of their sharing.

Ask Clarifying Questions for Action

The speaker has now defined their problem and vented their emotional experience. The next step is to clarify what happens next. You must determine what role, if any, you are expected to play. You move the conversation from feeling to function.

Avoid assuming you know the solution. Avoid jumping in with unsolicited advice. Toxic behavior immediately tries to fix the problem, often minimizing the feeling in the process. Empathy transfers control back to the speaker.

You must ask clarifying questions to determine their needs or required action. This inquiry focuses on their desired outcome.

- **Ask for Needs:** Ask, "What do you need from me right now?" This is the most important question. Do they need listening, advice, or active support?

- **Ask for Outcome:** Ask, "What outcome would satisfy you right now?" or "What do you plan to do next?" This helps the speaker clarify their own next steps.
- **Ask for Support:** If they ask for help, ask, "How can I support you best with that?"

This deliberate inquiry clarifies expectations. It helps the speaker articulate exactly what you are expected to do. If they simply needed to vent, the conversation ends respectfully. If they need active support, you now have clear, assertive directions.

The Science of Reciprocity and Vulnerability

The ability to offer this deep level of structured empathy is not just good communication. It has measurable psychological benefits for both parties.

Marshall B. Rosenberg, a pioneer in nonviolent communication, stated that the ability to offer empathy allows us to stay vulnerable and helps us hear negative messages without taking them as personal rejection. He noted that giving understanding is the best way to ensure you receive understanding later. This establishes a powerful, positive cycle of relational reciprocity.

Furthermore, research emphasizes that the security provided by empathic communication allows for deeper vulnerability. When a speaker is confident that their entire narrative, facts and feelings, will be received without judgment, they are more willing to share honestly. This openness is essential for resolving long-standing issues.

The systematic use of reflective listening creates emotional safety. This safety is a necessary condition for rebuilding any damaged relationship foundation. You are proving that your new, calm control (from Book 1) is now dedicated to the security of your partner.

Concluding the Exchange Respectfully

Once the need is clarified, the exchange should conclude with respect. You confirm the agreed-upon action.

- If they needed only to vent, you say, "Thank you for sharing that with me. I appreciate you letting me know how you feel."
- If you agreed to a specific action, you state, "I understand. I will handle the scheduling change by the end of the day, as we discussed."

Recognize that giving understanding is the best way to ensure you receive understanding later. By consistently providing a non-judgmental space and clarifying needs, you establish empathy as your new, reliable mode of interaction. This consistency builds the trust necessary to move forward constructively.

CHAPTER 6

BOOK 2 CONCLUSION: MAKE EMPATHY YOUR DEFAULT

You have completed the essential work of empathy. You moved from internal self-preoccupation to external, focused attention. You mastered the four stages of structured listening. This shift requires immense, consistent effort. Empathy is not a natural state for someone accustomed to toxic, reactive patterns. It is a disciplined skill you must choose every time you engage with another person.

By developing reflective listening and non-verbal attending skills, you create an environment where the other person feels safe enough to be vulnerable. This ability to hear and validate pain is critical for repairing relational damage. You are proving that your newfound self-control (from Book 1) is dedicated to the security of your partner.

Your new system for connection is built on a structured, deliberate process. You must execute these steps sequentially.

Stage 1: Adopt Attending Skills for Focus. You communicate your presence non-verbally. This is the physical gateway to connection. You maintain appropriate eye contact. You use open body language, avoiding defensive postures like crossed arms. You lean slightly forward to demonstrate active engagement. Your non-verbal signals must establish immediate rapport. If your body language signals disinterest, the speaker distrusts your sincerity. You must prove you are listening before a word is exchanged. You suppress your own reactive thoughts. You practice mindfulness during the exchange.

Stage 2: Listen Beyond Words: Rephrase Content. You confirm factual understanding. This step prevents later conflict over details. You restate the factual content the speaker shared, using your own neutral words. You summarize the who, what, where, and when. You end with a question: "Did I get that right?" This preemptive check avoids the illusion of understanding. It builds confidence in the speaker that their message is being processed seriously. This skill forces you to focus completely on the narrative. You are organizing the information into manageable units.

Stage 3: Reflect Feelings to Validate Experience. This is the core act of connection. You recognize and reflect the emotion underpinning the words. You listen beyond the facts to the tone and body language. You use precise emotion words, such as "frustrated" or "disappointed." You state the perceived feeling and link it to the content. The most important action here is validation. Validation is acknowledging that the speaker's feelings are a reasonable, human response to their situation. You accept their emotional reality without having to agree with their conclusions. Research confirms this is a necessary clinical skill. Emotional validation helps regulate intense feelings and is key to successful conflict management.

Stage 4: Deepen Connection Through Open Inquiry. You combine content rephrasing with feeling reflection to capture the full meaning. You summarize larger segments of the narrative, integrating both the facts and the emotions. This demonstrates sustained attention. Then, you move the conversation toward function. You ask clarifying questions to determine their needs. You ask, "What do you need from me right now?" or "What outcome would satisfy you?" This inquiry transfers control back to the speaker. It helps them clarify exactly what action is required from you. You avoid unsolicited advice.

The Science of Reciprocity and Safety

Empathy is effective because it establishes a cycle of relational reciprocity and safety.

Marshall B. Rosenberg, a creator of Nonviolent Communication, emphasized that the ability to offer empathy allows people to stay vulnerable. It helps us hear negative messages without taking them as personal rejection. He noted that giving understanding is the best way to ensure you receive understanding later. This establishes a powerful, positive cycle.

Furthermore, research confirms that the security provided by empathic communication allows for deeper vulnerability. When a speaker is confident that their entire narrative—facts and feelings—will be received without judgment, they are more willing to share honestly. This openness is essential for resolving long-standing issues and repairing relational damage. The systematic use of reflective listening creates this emotional safety. This safety is a mandatory condition for rebuilding any trust foundation. You are proving that your internal calm is now dedicated to the security of your relationship.

Maintaining Empathy as the Default

Empathy requires you to suppress your own immediate response. You must fight the impulse to fix, argue, or deflect. This work builds your capacity for self-transcendence.

Practice Non-Judgment. You must consciously suppress your desire to argue or offer advice. Practice viewing your reactive thoughts as distractions. You are providing a non-judgmental container for their feelings. This restraint requires constant self-monitoring. Research shows that non-judgmental acceptance is critical for allowing individuals to process difficult emotions. When a speaker feels judged, their brain's defense mechanisms activate instantly, blocking vulnerability. You are creating the conditions under which they can solve their own problems.

Embrace Silence as a Tool. Do not rush to fill quiet moments. Silence is a powerful communication tool. It helps the other person focus on themselves. It allows them necessary time to process their emotions. Respecting silence shows patience. It demonstrates you are willing to wait for them to process their own experience at their own pace.

Choose Skill Over Reaction. Empathy, like anger control, is a choice. You must choose to listen actively over reacting defensively. You must choose reflection over rebuttal. By consistently making empathy your default, you provide the structural integrity needed to make your relationships stronger than the old, toxic versions. This consistency defines your transformation.

Reflection Questions

1. Identify an emotion someone recently expressed that you initially missed or ignored. How could you have reflected that feeling using a more precise emotion word?

2. Describe three specific non-verbal skills (eye contact, posture, nodding) you successfully used this week during a difficult conversation. How did the speaker respond to your physical attention?

3. How did rephrasing content help you avoid a specific misunderstanding or factual argument this week?

4. Identify a moment you rushed to fill a silence. What might the speaker have used that time for if you had waited?

5. Who is the one person you will commit to using Stage 4 integrated listening with consistently this month? What specific action will you ask them about after summarizing their narrative?

CHECKLIST
MAKING EMPATHY YOUR DEFAULT MODE

You're using structured listening to build a safe emotional space. Empathy isn't automatic, it's a choice you have to make. And to get it right, you need to follow four important steps, one after the other. Doing this helps you really grasp both the facts and feelings the person is sharing.

I. Stage One: Mastering Your Attending Skills to Stay Focused

Empathy starts with how you show up—physically and mentally. Your body language has to say, "I'm here and I'm safe" before a word is even spoken. This is all about non-verbal signals and getting your head in the right place.

Before you start talking, did you do some of these things?

- Keep your posture open and relaxed? No crossed arms or looking away—that kind of stuff says "I'm not interested." A slight lean forward shows you're engaged and available.

- Make eye contact, but not too intense. You want to be natural—like you really want to listen, not stare someone down.

- Use small gestures and sounds like nodding or saying "I see" or "Go on." These little things build an instant connection. If they sound upset, gently mirror their expression to show you understand.

- Clear your mind of judgment and don't start planning your reply. This means no quick fixes or pointing out problems. Just listen.

- When there's silence, don't rush to fill it. Silence gives them space to think and keeps the flow honest.

- And if you notice they're pulling back, check yourself—are you distracted or looking too serious? That might shut down trust.

II. Stage Two: Rephrasing Content to Confirm You Got It Right

Now that you've made them feel safe, check you understood the facts. This avoids pointless debates over details because you're making sure you're on the same page.

After they finish a thought, did you:

- Wait until they completely stopped talking before jumping in? Interrupting says you think your point is more important.

- Start with phrases like, "So, if I'm hearing you right…" or "What you're saying is…" This makes it clear you're just trying to understand.

- Put their facts in your own words, stick to the who, what, where, and when, without any personal opinions.

- Ask, "Did I get that right?" This allows them to clear up any misunderstandings right away.

- Resist the urge to jump in with advice at this point. Your job here is simply to absorb information.

- If they correct you, take it in and rephrase until they confirm you're accurate.

III. Stage Three: Reflecting Feelings to Show You Understand

Facts are one thing, but now comes the real heart of empathy—recognizing their feelings behind those facts.

Ask yourself:

- Did you pick up on emotions behind their words? Maybe their tone or body language said more than the facts alone.

- Are you using real, specific words for their feelings? Words like "frustrated," "overwhelmed," or "disappointed" show you're really listening.

- Have you connected the feeling to their story? Saying something like, "It sounds like you're anxious because of the sudden changes at work," ties it all together.

- Did you validate their feelings? Validation means letting them know their emotions make sense and are okay, without judging or trying to "fix" things.

- Avoid pushing phrases like, "It's not that bad," or "You're overreacting"—those only shut down empathy.

- If you see them closing off, maybe you missed something. Go back and say, "I'm sorry, I didn't catch how much this hurt you. Can you tell me more?"

IV. Stage Four: Deepening the Connection and Clarifying Next Steps

You've listened carefully to facts and feelings. Now it's time to bring it all together and figure out where to go from here.

Consider these:

- Can you keep judgment at bay and resist the urge to solve everything immediately? Your goal is to keep the space safe so they feel free to share fully.

- Summarize their full story, blending facts and feelings: "So, to sum up, you're saying [facts], and that makes you feel [emotions]. Am I right?"

- Ask open questions to dig deeper, like "What are you feeling most right now?" or "What options have you thought about?"

- Hand the control back by asking, "What do you need from me?" or "What outcome would feel right for you?"

- End with clear confirmation: if you're just listening, say thanks for sharing; if you agreed on a next step, repeat the plan so you're both clear.

BOOK THREE

TALK WITH RESPECT:
COMMUNICATE CLEARLY AND DIRECTLY

INTRODUCTION

You have mastered internal control. You can stop the anger cycle. You have mastered external attention. You can listen with genuine empathy. Now you must bring these two skills together. You must learn to speak honestly and clearly without aggression.

Toxic habits are rooted in poor expression. When you cannot state your needs clearly, frustration builds. This suppressed emotion often explodes as rage or retreats into silent resentment. Neither option works. You must replace reactive habits with structured, assertive communication.

Assertive communication is the third necessary skill set for a non-toxic life. Assertiveness involves stating your feelings and needs clearly and directly. You do this respectfully, while fully acknowledging the position of others. It ensures your message is conveyed accurately.

This skill is crucial because it strengthens your relationships. Assertive talk reduces stress that comes from constant conflict. It prevents misunderstanding. When you are assertive, you express your opinion without belittling or dismissing other people's thoughts. You claim your own rights while respecting theirs.

This book is about action. It teaches you how to structure your language to prevent arguments before they start. You will move from attacking the person to describing the behavior.

First, you learn to **Shift Language from Blame to Responsibility**. You stop using "You" statements that trigger defensiveness. You own your feelings.

Second, you practice the **XYZ Formula**. This is a precise structure for constructing powerful "I" statements. You learn to articulate your need without resorting to accusations.

Third, you learn to **State Your Needs Without Guilt**. You recognize your needs are equal to the needs of others. You ask for what you want directly.

Fourth, you practice **Present Focus**. You stop using history as a weapon. You address only the current, solvable issue.

Finally, you ensure **Non-Verbal Signals Align with Your Words**. Your body must communicate confidence and calm, not aggression.

Mastery of assertive dialogue creates equal footing in the relationship. This ability to appropriately ask for and obtain what you need, while preserving important relationships, has benefits for your physical and emotional well-being. This is the language of mutual respect.

The Scientific Basis of Assertive Dialogue

The principles of assertive communication are foundational to behavioral therapy. The classic way to define Assertiveness is by contrasting it with its two extremes: aggression and submissiveness. Aggression denies the rights of others. Submissiveness denies your own rights. Assertiveness is the middle ground. It acknowledges both your rights and the rights of others simultaneously.

This skill is directly linked to self-esteem and relational success. Assertiveness is one of the daily habits that produces self-esteem. When you know you have a right to express what you want, you are behaving assertively and confidently.

Researchers, including A. J. Lange and P. Jakubowski, in their work on *Responsible Assertive Behaviour*, define Assertiveness as this crucial "third way of behaving." It is a deliberate choice to operate in the middle lane of confidence, avoiding the extremes of weakness and dominance.

Furthermore, the focused language used in assertiveness, particularly the use of "I" statements, is clinically supported. Research shows that using "I" statements helps prevent arguments and misunderstandings because you are taking responsibility for your feelings and thoughts, not placing blame on the listener.

This book provides the practical structure for this behavioral change. You are learning a new, respectful language. You are replacing the destructive language of attack with the constructive language of clarity.

CHAPTER 1

SHIFT LANGUAGE FROM BLAME TO RESPONSIBILITY

Toxic communication begins with blame. When conflict arises, the immediate reflex is to point outward. You use "You" statements. You make accusations about the other person's character or intent. This approach is highly destructive. It triggers immediate defensiveness. It shuts down all possibility of rational dialogue.

Respectful talk replaces this reactive habit with proactive responsibility. Responsibility is the foundation of respectful dialogue. You must focus the language on your internal state and observable external behavior, not on the assumed failures of the other person.

The Problem with "You" Statements

"You" statements are accusations disguised as communication. When you say, "You make me feel angry," you assign ownership of your feelings to the listener. This is psychologically incorrect. No one can truly *make* you feel anything. Your feelings are your internal response to an event, filtered through your own thoughts and coping mechanisms.

This blame instantly causes the listener to stop listening to the content. They start defending against the attack. They feel cornered.

This leads to escalation and gridlock. You are guaranteed to fail at communicating your need effectively if you start with blame.

Acknowledge Your Feelings are Yours

The first necessary shift is internal. You must stop blaming others for your emotional state. You acknowledge that your feelings are yours alone. You are responsible for your reactions. Taking responsibility for your feelings bypasses the defense mechanism in the listener.

- **Do not say:** "You make me so frustrated when you forget the trash."
- **Say instead:** "I feel frustrated when the trash is left overflowing."

You are reporting an internal state. This is an undeniable fact about your experience. The statement is focused on you, not the listener's character. This is the difference between accusation and assertion. This honesty is essential for effective communication.

Reframe Complaints to Observable Behavior

Toxic communication often attacks a person's identity. It uses generalizations. You say, "You are inconsiderate," or "You are lazy." These attacks feel like a fixed, personal assault. A person cannot change who they "are." They can change what they "do."

You must reframe your complaint. Change the generalization about the person into an observation about their specific, observable behavior.

- **Focus on Behavior:** Focus on what they *did*, not what you assume they *meant*. Instead of calling them inconsiderate, describe the action that led to that feeling. Example: "You left your laundry on the floor for three days."
- **Behavior is Changeable:** Focusing on behavior ensures your complaint is manageable. It gives the other person a clear, practical path to resolution. They can easily clean the laundry. They cannot easily change their entire character in response to an insult.

The Locus of Control Shift

This change in language reflects a fundamental psychological shift in accountability. This concept is called Locus of Control, developed by psychologist Julian B. Rotter.

- **External Locus of Control:** A person with an external locus of control believes events in their life are controlled by outside factors. They blame circumstances, fate, or other people for their outcomes. Toxic behavior is often rooted here: "I lost my temper because *you* provoked me."

- **Internal Locus of Control:** A person with an internal locus of control believes their behavior is guided by their personal decisions and efforts. They praise or blame themselves and their actions for outcomes.

Shifting your language from blame ("You make me angry") to responsibility ("I feel frustrated when...") is an active choice to move toward an internal locus of control. You are claiming ownership of your emotional state. This internal accountability is generally seen as psychologically healthy. It is a prerequisite for self-control and assertion. You must believe you control your response before you can effectively assert your needs.

Using Positive, Non-Threatening Language

Assertive communication requires using neutral, positive language. You must avoid words meant to shame, blame, or belittle the other person.

Your words must invite resolution, not provoke a defense. Assertive talk is honest and direct, but it avoids dismissing or insulting other people's opinions.

You are moving away from the language of dominance and weakness, and toward the language of confidence. Assertion simultaneously acknowledges your rights and the rights of others. This mutual respect is the environment in which difficult conversations succeed. You communicate your needs without making the other person feel attacked.

This change in language is the necessary first step. It transforms an aggressive demand into a manageable request. It creates the psychological space for the listener to hear and process your need without going into immediate defense mode.

CHAPTER 2
CONSTRUCT POWERFUL "I" STATEMENTS

You have accepted responsibility for your own feelings. You have shifted your focus from attacking the person to observing their behavior. The next step is construction. You need a precise tool to express your frustration clearly, ensuring emotional responsibility and clarity.

The power of assertion lies in the "I" statement. It is a communication model developed by psychologist Thomas Gordon in the 1960s and discussed in his book, *P.E.T.: Parent Effectiveness Training*. This technique ensures your thoughts and feelings are expressed from the first-person perspective. It avoids the accusatory tone that makes listeners defensive.

When you use an "I" statement, you are not placing blame. You are simply stating a fact about your internal experience in response to an external action. This honesty is necessary for effective, respectful dialogue.

Effective communication requires structure. The XYZ formula provides a science-backed method for assertive communication. It is taught in communication training programs because it is measurable and repeatable. It ensures all critical elements—your emotion, the specific behavior, the context, and the desired resolution—are included.

The XYZ formula has four components. You must state them in a respectful, calm tone.

1. Identify and State Your Specific Emotion Clearly (X). You must name a genuine feeling. This is the "I feel" component. Use precise emotion words: "frustrated," "sad," "concerned," or "overwhelmed." Avoid using a judgment dressed up as a feeling, such as "ignored" or "attacked." Those are interpretations, not emotions. You are reporting an internal state. This is undeniable.

2. Identify the Specific, Observable Behavior (Y). This is the "when you do" component. You must state exactly what the person *did*. This must be factual, specific, and observable. Do not state your assumption about their intent. Focus on the action. For example: "when you interrupt me" or "when you leave your coat on the floor."

3. State the Situation (Z). This is the "in situation" component. Define the specific context where the behavior occurred. This limits the scope of the conversation. Example: "during our weekly team meeting" or "when we are rushing out the door in the morning." Using this component prevents the conversation from spiraling into generalizations.

4. State What You Want (Resolution). This is the final, most crucial component. A complaint without a request for change is simply venting. You must articulate the resolution you seek. This ends your assertive statement with a clear request for a change in behavior or action. This ensures your needs are met while promoting respectful relationships.

Applying the Formula: From Blame to Clarity

Toxic communication often uses only one or two vague components, instantly leading to conflict.

Formula Component	Toxic Example (Blame)	Assertive Example (XYZ Formula)
I feel (X)	You make me feel angry.	I feel **frustrated**.
When you do (Y)	When you are always late.	When you **arrive twenty minutes late** to our appointments.
In situation (Z)	You disrespect my time.	**For the third time this week.**
I would like (Resolution)	(Implied demand or silence)	I would like you to **text me ten minutes before you expect to be late**.

You combine these parts into a single, respectful statement: "I feel frustrated when you arrive twenty minutes late for the third time this week, and I would like you to text me ten minutes before you expect to be late." This approach is complete. It includes the emotion, the observable facts, and the path to resolution. It makes it easy for the listener to understand and comply. This statement is honest and direct, but it avoids belittling others' opinions.

The Scientific Necessity of "I" Messages

The practice of using "I" statements is supported by extensive research in communication psychology.

1. Reducing Listener Defensiveness: The primary benefit is reduced defensiveness. Research shows that "you-messages" contain heavy loads of blame, judgment, and criticism. These automatically provoke resistance in the listener and lower their self-esteem. "I-messages" avoid accusations. They focus on the speaker's internal experience. This makes the listener feel less cornered. They are more likely to hear the content of your message.

2. Preventing Arguments: When you use "I" statements, you take responsibility for your feelings and thoughts. This helps prevent arguments and misunderstandings. You are offering constructive criticism because you are expressing concerns without increasing tension. This focuses the discussion on a solvable problem, not a personal failure.

3. Enhancing Emotional Honesty: Using this structure forces you to identify your true emotion (X). This prevents you from disguising hurt as anger. Forcing emotional honesty is essential to effective communication.

4. Defining the Solution: Including the final resolution step ensures your needs are met. This practice transforms the conversation from a fight into a negotiation. It ends the interaction with a productive request, not a lingering complaint.

Practice and Application

You must practice this formula until it becomes automatic. Do not wait for a crisis. Practice it in low-stakes situations.

- **During low-stakes annoyance:** If a friend is late, practice saying, "I feel concerned when you are ten minutes late because I worry about your safety, and I would like you to let me know if you are delayed."

- **In daily frustrations:** If a coworker uses your desk, practice saying, "I feel uncomfortable when my papers are moved from my desk because I lose track of important documents, and I would like you to ask me first."

This consistent practice builds memory. When a high-stress trigger occurs, your body will default to the structured, assertive response instead of the toxic, aggressive reaction. Mastering this formula is a daily, disciplined action. It is the core of respectful, clear communication.

CHAPTER 3
STATE YOUR NEEDS WITHOUT GUILT

You have the language of assertion. You know how to construct a non-blaming "I" statement. The hardest part remains. You must overcome the psychological barrier that stops you from using that language. You must state your needs clearly, directly, and without apology.

Toxic habits thrive on silence. When you fail to state your needs, resentment builds. This suppressed frustration eventually fuels an aggressive outburst. You feel underappreciated. You assume others should know what you want. This assumption is incorrect. Assertive communication requires you to articulate the resolution you seek. Do not assume the other person knows what you want.

The Problem of People-Pleasing

The primary barrier to stating needs is the fear of conflict or rejection. This often stems from people-pleasing behaviors. You silence your own needs to gain or maintain approval from others. This creates a cycle where you deny your rights, lead to burnout, and generate internal resentment.

Guilt is the powerful emotion that keeps you trapped in this cycle. Psychologist Zulmaury Saavedra notes that many people struggle with the cycle of guilt and overcommitment. They constantly feel they "should" do something for others. This internal "should" stems from a desire to maintain approval.

When you act on the "should," you follow the script of what you think the other person wants. When you fail to act, you feel guilty for holding back. Both action and inaction lead to the same conclusion: guilt. This means you are not living life in your own best interest. You are allowing someone else to control the script. This denial of your needs directly leads to feeling used and underappreciated.

Recognize the Equality of Your Needs

You must internalize one simple truth: your needs are equal to the needs of others. Assertive communication involves interacting in a way that respects both your rights and the rights of others. You have a right to your time, your space, and your preferences.

Asking for what you need is not selfish. It is necessary self-respect. When you ask for what you need directly, you prevent yourself from internalizing frustration. You strengthen your confidence.

Articulate the Resolution Directly

Once you have constructed your powerful "I" statement, you must deliver the request for action clearly. The request is the resolution. It is the action you want the other person to take to fix the problem you identified.

Do not use vague requests. Do not hope the person guesses what you want. You must define the desired outcome in clear, measurable terms.

- **Vague Request:** "I need you to be more helpful around the house." (Unmeasurable, invites argument)
- **Direct Request:** "I need you to commit to loading the dishwasher immediately after dinner, Monday through Friday." (Measurable, specific action)

This direct articulation ensures your needs are met. It gives the other person a clear pathway to success. This practice promotes respectful relationships because it defines expectations clearly.

One of the most essential ways to state a need is by declining a request. You must learn to say "no" politely but firmly. This helps you avoid getting overwhelmed by overcommitment. This skill strengthens your confidence in your boundaries.

Saying "no" assertively is not aggressive. You do not need to justify or over-explain your decision. Justify means apologize.

- **Aggressive:** "No, I am too busy with my own important things to help you with that."
- **Submissive:** "Oh, I guess I can, but I really have so much to do, I will just stay up late." (Leading to resentment)
- **Assertive:** "Thank you for asking, but I cannot take that on right now."

If the person insists, you simply reiterate your firm "no" without providing further details or apology. You do not owe anyone an explanation for managing your own schedule. This practice is necessary for setting healthy limits.

The Scientific Benefits of Assertion

The ability to appropriately ask for and obtain what you need, while preserving important relationships, has numerous benefits for your well-being.

1. Reduced Stress and Conflict: Assertive communication, by defining needs clearly, strengthens relationships by reducing stress from constant conflict. You eliminate the frustration of constantly feeling unheard. When you ask for what you need directly, you reduce the emotional burden on yourself.

2. Increased Self-Efficacy: When you successfully state a need and the outcome is positive, you reinforce your sense of self-efficacy. You gain confidence that you can control your environment and your relational outcomes. This moves your psychological orientation toward an internal Locus of Control. You see that your behavior—your assertive communication—guides your success.

3. Preventing Resentment: Assertive talk prevents chronic, suppressed anger from building up and eventually exploding. By providing a clear, consistent outlet for frustration, you prevent the accumulation of resentment. This proactive approach is mentally healthier.

This commitment to stating your needs without guilt or apology is a daily action. It is the consistent choice for self-respect. This discipline ensures that your assertive language is backed by genuine internal conviction.

CHAPTER 4

STAY PRESENT:

FOCUS ON THE CURRENT ISSUE

You have the tools to assert your needs. You know how to state your feelings without blame. The greatest threat to this skill is contamination. Conflict often escalates immediately when past grievances contaminate the current conversation. Toxic communication uses history as a weapon.

You must maintain a present focus. You need to address the immediate behavior that caused the concern. If you allow yourself to bring up previous mistakes, you instantly distract the conversation. You prevent resolution of the current problem. This chapter teaches you how to keep dialogue clean, focused, and manageable.

The Danger of Contamination

When a new frustration arises, the toxic reflex is to reach into the past. You use history to justify the intensity of your current emotion. This manifests as phrases like, "This is exactly what you did last year," or "I cannot believe you are making this mistake **again**."

This contamination achieves two destructive ends:

1. **It Triggers Defense:** The listener stops hearing the current, small problem. They feel overwhelmed by the entire catalogue of past failures. They immediately stop engaging the current issue and start defending their history. This guarantees gridlock.

2. **It Undermines Progress:** Bringing up the past invalidates any efforts the person has made to change. If they successfully fixed the issue from last year, reminding them of it shows you are not tracking their positive effort. This poisons the well of motivation.

You must stop using history as a weapon. Maintain present focus. Avoid bringing up the past. When you feel tempted to mention a historical error, pull your focus back immediately to the immediate situation.

Eliminate Absolute Language

Absolute language is the single most common contaminant in dialogue. It destroys credibility and guarantees rebuttal. Stop using generalizations like "you always" or "you never."

These phrases instantly invite the other person to refute the generalization. If you say, "You always leave the cap off the toothpaste," the listener will instantly recall the single time last month they did put the cap on. They focus on refuting your absolute statement. They ignore the current issue. The original problem disappears in a fight over grammar.

Toxic Absolute	Clean, Present Focus
You **always** criticize my effort.	I felt **discouraged** when you edited the memo this morning without discussing it with me.
You **never** help with the planning.	I feel **concerned** that I have been solely responsible for planning the last two trips, and I need help with the next one.

By eliminating absolute language, you demonstrate that you are addressing one specific incident. This is manageable. It shows respect for the other person's capacity for change.

Focus on One Issue at a Time

A clean conversation addresses only one need or one behavior at a time. This prevents feelings of overwhelming frustration that lead to conflict escalation.

Toxic communicators "kitchen sink" the argument. They pile every unresolved issue onto the current problem. You may be frustrated by a late bill, but then you add complaints about chores, their social media habits, and a comment they made three weeks ago. The sheer volume of issues ensures failure.

Assertive communication is surgical. It addresses one thing only.

1. **Identify the Core Issue:** What is the most important problem that needs resolution right now?
2. **Use the XYZ Formula:** Deliver your complete "I" statement about that single issue.
3. **Stay on Target:** If the listener attempts to deflect by bringing up your past, gently pull the focus back. You can say, "I understand that, but I need us to focus on the current problem of the late bill first. We can talk about X later."

This focused approach is necessary for relationship stability. It allows the conversation to conclude with a successful resolution. This practice teaches both parties that problems are solvable.

The Scientific Value of Present Focus

The ability to stay present and non-reactive is a clinically supported skill. It is a core principle in therapies designed to foster psychological flexibility.

1. **Psychological Flexibility (ACT):** Acceptance and Commitment Therapy (ACT) is a mindfulness-based behavioral therapy. ACT emphasizes processes that foster psychological flexibility. This is the ability to accept difficult emotions while committing to meaningful, present-focused actions. ACT promotes psychological flexibility by integrating mindfulness and value-driven behavior. This approach helps individuals manage stress and emotional challenges by embracing life's difficulties with openness. Staying present is fundamental to this model. You accept the reality of the current conflict without letting past failures define or control your response.

2. Mindfulness in Relationships: Research also confirms the benefits of mindfulness—the practice of present awareness—in relational settings. A study published in the *Journal of Consulting and Clinical Psychology* found that greater mindfulness practice on a given day was associated with improved relationship happiness, reduced relationship stress, and enhanced stress coping efficacy on subsequent days. Mindfulness helps you avoid reactivity. It keeps you from contaminating the current conversation with historical arguments.

By maintaining present focus, you are utilizing an evidence-based skill to improve your relationship outcomes. You stop allowing history to control your future. You give yourself and the listener the respect of addressing one single, manageable problem. This deliberate choice for clarity is the foundation of constructive dialogue.

CHAPTER 5:
ENSURE NON-VERBAL SIGNALS ALIGN WITH YOUR WORDS

By now, you've got the basics of respectful communication down—you know the XYZ formula and how to stay present. The last piece of the puzzle is making sure what you say lines up with how you act. Respectful communication isn't just about words; it depends a lot on your non-verbal signals matching your message.

If you say something calm and assertive but your fists are clenched and you're glaring, the person hearing you gets mixed signals. They're going to believe the body language over your words every time. So, your non-verbal cues have to back up what you're saying. They need to show confidence, calmness, and respect—not anger or threat.

Why Non-Verbal Matters: The Science Behind it

Non-verbal communication includes your posture, tone, facial expressions, and movements. Research consistently shows these signals carry huge weight in face-to-face talks.

Albert Mehrabian, an expert in body language, broke this down famously: communication is about 55% body language, 38% tone and pitch, and only 7% actual words. While that's not a perfect formula for every situation, it makes a strong point—most of what people pick up on isn't the words themselves, but how you say them.

So, if your stance or voice come off aggressive, your carefully chosen words don't stand a chance. You've got to be congruent—make sure your body language supports the respectful message, or else it falls flat.

How to Master Non-Verbal Assertiveness

There are three big things to keep an eye on:

1. Posture that Shows Confidence and Openness
2. Your stance is like a billboard for how you feel inside.
    - Don't loom or point fingers—that comes off as aggressive and makes others defensive.
    - Don't slouch or fidget nervously—that makes you seem unsure or weak.
    - Stand or sit straight, with open hands visible. This signals you're calm and not ready to fight.
2. Eye Contact That's Honest and Engaged
3. Good eye contact says you're sincere and listening.
    - Keep your gaze steady while you speak—it shows you believe in your message.
    - But don't stare down the person. A hard glare feels like a challenge or threat. Your goal is to connect, not to intimidate.
3. Use Your Voice to Back Up Your Words
4. Your tone, pitch, and pace can totally change how your message lands.
    - Avoid sharp or loud tones—those scream anger and make you seem unstable.

o   Aim for a lower pitch and steady, calm pace. People hear authority and control in those voices, which helps your words stick.

Pick the Right Moment and Place

How and when you say something matters just as much as what you say.

- Don't catch someone off guard when they're rushing or upset—that usually backfires.
- Instead, ask to set up a time: "I have something important to talk about. When's a good time for you?"
- Choose a quiet, private spot for serious chats—away from coworkers or kids.

Showing this kind of thoughtful timing shows you respect the other person and want a real, positive outcome—not just to get your anger out.

Why Matching Words and Actions Is So Important

When you ask for change, the other person has to believe you really mean it. This match between what you say and how you behave is called congruence, and it's what gives your message power.

If your voice shakes or your stance looks unsure, they'll think you're scared or bluffing—the boundary won't hold. If you come off aggressive, they'll hear a threat, not a request.

Practice is key. Say your full XYZ statement with calm words, open posture, steady eye contact, and a low, steady voice. This shows you've got control over your anger and that you respect the other person. When you get this right, your needs get heard, respected, and taken seriously.

CHAPTER 6
BOOK 3 CONCLUSION:
MASTER ASSERTIVE DIALOGUE

You have completed the third essential step toward a non-toxic life. You moved from internal control and external empathy to clear, respectful expression. Mastering assertive dialogue requires moving from reactive blame to proactive responsibility. You have replaced the destructive language of attack with the constructive language of clarity.

This is not passive communication. It is a highly structured, disciplined way of speaking. By consistently employing the XYZ formula, you ensure that your needs are articulated clearly, respectfully, and without resorting to toxic accusations. This skill creates equal footing in the relationship. It reduces conflict. It demonstrates self-respect.

Your new system for clear communication is built on five deliberate choices. You must maintain consistency across all five pillars.

Pillar One: Shift Language from Blame to Responsibility. You must own your feelings. You stop using accusatory "You" statements. You move from blaming the person to observing their specific, changeable behavior. You acknowledge that your feelings are your internal response. They are not controlled by the listener. This shift activates your Internal Locus of Control. This psychological orientation acknowledges that your behavior is guided by your decisions, not external factors. This internal accountability is necessary for effective assertion.

Pillar Two: Construct Powerful "I" Statements. You use the XYZ formula for assertion. This provides the structure necessary for difficult conversations. You identify and state your specific emotion (X). You state the specific, observable behavior (Y). You define the situation (Z). You request a clear resolution. This structure, pioneered by Thomas Gordon in his work on effective communication, ensures your message is honest and direct. It prevents arguments and misunderstandings by avoiding the accusatory language that provokes defense.

Pillar Three: State Your Needs Without Guilt. Assertive communication requires you to ask for what you want directly. You must overcome the psychological barriers of people-pleasing and fear of conflict. You must recognize that your needs are equal to the needs of others. This prevents resentment from building up. You articulate the resolution you seek in specific, measurable terms. You practice saying "no" politely but firmly. This non-apologetic refusal is necessary for setting healthy limits and strengthening your self-respect.

Pillar Four: Stay Present: Focus on the Current Issue. You must keep your dialogue clean. You stop using history as a weapon. You avoid contaminating the current conversation with past grievances. This means eliminating absolute language like "you always" or "you never." You address one specific need or behavior at a time. This focused approach is a form of mindfulness in dialogue. Research confirms that greater mindfulness practice is associated with improved relationship happiness and reduced stress. By staying present, you give yourself and the listener the respect of addressing a solvable problem.

Pillar Five: Ensure Non-Verbal Signals Align with Your Words. Respectful talk relies on congruence. Your body language and vocal tone must support your assertive words. You use confident, open posture. You maintain direct, non-glaring eye contact. You regulate your vocal tone, using a measured pace and low volume. Research confirms that non-verbal cues carry the majority of emotional and intentional weight in a conversation. If your tone is aggressive, your message is lost. You must achieve congruence between your calm words and your supportive body language.

Assertiveness and Self-Esteem

Mastery of assertion is not just about getting what you want. It is about transforming your internal sense of worth. Assertiveness is one of the daily habits that produces self-esteem. When you consistently honor your rights by expressing what you want clearly, you are thinking and behaving assertively and confidently.

This confidence establishes you in the "Confidence Lane," avoiding the extremes of submissiveness (denying your own rights) and aggression (denying the rights of others). This consistent choice for the middle ground is psychologically healthy. It provides the stability necessary for long-term relational success.

Maintaining the Assertive Default

This skill set, like anger control, requires sustained maintenance. You must commit to using the XYZ formula automatically, even when you are rushed or stressed.

Practice Self-Correction: When you slip into blame or contamination, you do not abandon the effort. You notice the failure immediately. You analyze the conversation. You identify the moment you lost focus. You re-engage the issue later, using the correct assertive language. Self-correction is learning. It is necessary for lasting behavioral change.

Focus on Measurable Outcomes: Use the resolution component of the XYZ formula to measure your success. Were you clear about the needed change? Was the other person able to comply? If the issue persists, the problem is not the person. The problem is likely the clarity or specificity of your request. Return to the formula and refine the needed action.

By making assertive dialogue your default, you eliminate the ambiguity that fuels resentment. You create equal footing in your relationship. This foundational work establishes clarity and accountability, the next essential requirement for setting boundaries.

1. Identify a recent instance where you used the generalization "you always" or "you never." Rewrite that sentence using the complete XYZ assertive communication formula, focusing only on the specific event.

2. What is one need you have recently kept silent about due to fear of guilt or conflict? Draft the assertive statement you will use to articulate this need this week.

3. Describe a moment when your posture or tone contradicted your words during a difficult conversation. What specific non-verbal adjustment will you make next time?

4. Identify a moment in a past conversation when the issue was contaminated by historical grievances. How did this distraction prevent resolution of the current problem?

5. Practice saying "no" politely but firmly to one small, non-essential request this week. How did you feel after you successfully maintained the boundary without apologizing?

CHECKLIST
MASTERING ASSERTIVE CONVERSATION

You're swapping out reactive, harmful habits for clear, respectful communication. Use this guide to steer every tough or annoying talk. You're picking words that show mutual respect, not blame.

I. Change Your Words: Own Your Feelings, Don't Blame

Toxic talks usually start with finger-pointing. Assertive talks start with taking responsibility, for yourself. Make sure your words focus on how you feel and what you saw, not on what the other person supposedly did wrong.

- Did you cut out "You" phrases that put blame on someone else? Saying "You make me mad" puts your feelings in their hands, and that just sparks defensiveness.

- Are you saying your feelings belong to you? Try, "I feel upset when..." rather than "You're upsetting me." It's a simple but powerful switch.

- Are you talking about specific actions, not the person's character? So instead of "You're lazy," say, "You didn't do the dishes for three days." It makes the issue easier to solve.

- Use positive, non-threatening words. Be honest but don't insult. Your words should open the door to fixing things, not slam it shut.

- Are you owning your response? Remember, how you react is your choice, not fate. That mindset shift really helps keep things healthy.

- Clear communication needs structure. The XYZ formula helps you make strong "I" statements that move from venting to asking for what you need.

- Did you name the exact feeling? Use real emotions like "worried," "sad," or "frustrated." Avoid words that sound like judgments, like "ignored" or "betrayed."

- Did you specify the exact behavior? Avoid guessing intentions. Stick to facts like "when you interrupt me" or "when you missed the deadline."

- Did you say when and where it happened? For example, "during the meeting" or "in the morning rush." Giving context helps keep things focused.

- Did you say clearly what you want? A simple, actionable request like "Please text me if you'll be late" turns complaints into solutions.

- Keep it one clear message at a time. Don't mix in excuses, justifications, or unrelated stuff.

II. Speak Up with Confidence, Not Guilt

Now that your words are set, it's time to say what you mean—clearly and confidently. Push through any fear of conflict and stop people-pleasing yourself away.

- Did you treat your needs like they're just as important as anyone else's? Asking for what you want is self-respect.

- Is your request clear and measurable? Avoid vague asks like "be nicer." Say exactly what you want.

- Did you practice saying "No" politely but firmly? It's okay to say, "Thanks for asking, but I can't right now."

- Resist explaining or defending your "No." You don't owe extra reasons; your boundary stands on its own.

- Did you notice any guilt feelings and still hold your ground? That discomfort is part of breaking the habit of putting others first all the time.

III. Keep It Honest: Focus on Now and Match Your Message

Respect means being truthful, in timing and delivery. Keep things about the current issue, and make sure your body backs up your words.

- Did you stop saying "You always" or "You never"? Those phrases make people want to argue and distract from the now.

- Did you stick to one issue at a time? Bringing up old problems just clutters the conversation.

- Does your voice and posture show calm confidence? Non-verbal signals speak louder than words.

- Are your eyes steady but not glaring? Avoid pointing or aggressive stances.

- Did you choose the right time to talk? Avoid launching serious talks when they're stressed, busy, or around others. Scheduling shows respect and helps get better results.

BOOK FOUR

SET BOUNDARIES: DEFINE YOUR LIMITS AND PROTECT YOUR SPACE

INTRODUCTION

You have achieved internal calm. You can communicate your needs clearly. You now possess the three essential tools for managing toxicity: self-control, empathy, and assertion. This control provides predictability. Predictability is the necessary condition for building trust.

However, assertion is useless without limits. Assertiveness is the language you use to state your needs. Boundaries are the **structure** that protects those needs. Boundaries are interpersonal limits. They define what behavior is appropriate in your relationships.

When you lack clear boundaries, you invite toxic behavior. You allow others to invade your emotional, physical, and time limits. This leads to burnout, resentment, and a complete loss of self-respect. Toxic people often seek out individuals with poor boundaries because they are easier to manipulate and control.

Setting and enforcing healthy boundaries is crucial for self-care. It promotes your autonomy. It ensures mutual respect in your interactions. A boundary is simply an edge. It defines you as separate from others.

You must internalize this truth: setting limits will not disrupt a healthy relationship. Healthy relationships respect limits. Only unhealthy relationships collapse when a boundary is established. If a relationship falls apart because you said "no," that relationship was not based on respect. It was based on your compliance.

This book provides the operational steps to define and enforce your limits. You are moving from talking about your needs to defending them.

First, you learn to **Define Your Personal and Emotional Limits**. You clarify your needs for space, time, and emotional energy.

Second, you learn to **Clearly Communicate Expectations and Needs**. Boundaries must be stated assertively. Unstated boundaries are simply preferences.

Third, you practice how to **Manage Discomfort When You Say "No."** You overcome the guilt and fear of conflict that stops you from holding firm.

Fourth, you learn to **Respond Firmly to Boundary Challenges**. You practice reiterating the limit when someone tests your resolve.

Finally, you learn to **Implement Consequences for Repeat Violations**. An unenforced boundary is merely a suggestion. You learn how to protect yourself when the limit is ignored.

This structured approach is essential. When the rules of interaction are clearly defined and enforced, consistency and accountability have a framework within which to operate. This structure is key to paving the way for trust repair.

The Scientific Necessity of Boundaries

Boundaries are not optional. They are necessary for psychological well-being. Psychologists recognize that the absence of healthy boundaries leads directly to negative outcomes like stress and professional burnout.

1. Preventing Burnout: The concept of burnout, famously studied by Christina Maslach, is defined by three dimensions: emotional exhaustion, depersonalization, and reduced personal accomplishment. Lack of boundaries directly contributes to the core dimension: emotional exhaustion. When you fail to set limits on emotional giving and workload, your emotional resources are depleted rapidly. This state makes you highly susceptible to toxic relationships. You become incapable of empathy or patience. Protecting your energy through boundaries is a proactive defense against burnout.

2. Promoting Self-Respect: Healthy boundaries give you a powerful sense of empowerment and self-respect. They clearly separate your wants, needs, thoughts, and feelings from those of others. Boundaries define your autonomy. When you successfully set a limit, you reinforce your self-esteem. You demonstrate to yourself that your needs matter.

3. Autonomy and Codependency: Boundaries are critical for reducing codependent habits. Codependency often involves losing oneself in the drama of tending to someone else's problems, as described by Melody Beattie in her foundational work, *Codependent No More*. Boundaries create the necessary separation. They encourage autonomy. They force you to focus on your own life and responsibilities, rather than attempting to control or fix others. This separation is necessary for genuine psychological health.

Boundaries differ from person to person. They are shaped by culture, personality, and social context. A limit appropriate for a family member may be irrelevant at work. You must clarify your own internal map of acceptable behavior. This clarification is the first step toward living within your clear limits.

CHAPTER 1
DEFINE YOUR PERSONAL AND EMOTIONAL LIMITS

A boundary is not a hostile barrier. It is a necessary edge. A boundary defines you as separate from others. Without this definition, your sense of self merges with the needs, demands, and crises of those around you. This leads to emotional exhaustion.

Healthy boundaries give you a powerful sense of empowerment and self-respect. They clearly separate your wants, needs, thoughts, and feelings from those of others. Before you can communicate a boundary, you must clarify it internally. You must know what you want.

Clarify Your Personal Comfort Levels

Boundaries are individual. What is acceptable to one person may be an invasion for another. Your limits are shaped by your personal history, your culture, and the specific context of the relationship. A limit appropriate for a friend may be irrelevant in a work setting.

You need to know your internal comfort levels regarding three essential areas: physical space, emotional effort, and time commitment.

1. Physical Boundaries (Space and Environment). These limits govern your body, your immediate personal space, and your environment. Violation of these boundaries often triggers an immediate physical reaction.

- **Personal Space:** This involves your distance from others. A violation, such as a "close talker," triggers an automatic step back. Your reaction is an immediate, non-verbal attempt to reset your personal space.

- **Environment:** This covers your tolerance for noise, clutter, and interruption. Examples include the expectation of quiet in your home office or control over the music played in your car.

- **Property:** This covers the use of your possessions. It means setting a limit that people must ask permission before borrowing your car or entering your private room.

You must listen to yourself. Determine what physical space and environmental conditions you need for comfortable functioning. You must learn to recognize when this space is being violated and be prepared to act accordingly.

2. Emotional Boundaries (Feelings and Responsibility). These limits define where your responsibility for another person's feelings ends and where theirs begins. Toxic behavior thrives when emotional boundaries are blurred.

- **Responsibility for Feelings:** Your feelings are yours. The other person's feelings are theirs. You are responsible for managing your anxiety. You are not responsible for managing their disappointment. A boundary means refusing to accept blame for another person's anger or sadness.

- **Emotional Sharing:** This governs how much you are willing to hear and how much you are willing to disclose. A boundary might mean refusing to listen to a friend's constant venting without them committing to seeking professional help. It means refusing to overshare highly personal information with a new acquaintance.

- **Intrusive Questions:** This involves refusing to answer questions about your finances, relationships, or future goals that feel too probing or invasive.

You must be able to separate your emotional experience from the other person's. Healthy boundaries separate your wants, needs, thoughts, and feelings from those of others.

3. Time and Energy Boundaries (Availability). These limits govern how you spend your energy and time. A lack of these boundaries leads directly to burnout.

- **Time Commitment:** This means setting firm limits on your availability. Examples include refusing to take work calls after 7:00 PM or establishing that weekends are reserved entirely for family.

- **Project Completion:** This means refusing to take on tasks that belong to someone else. It means refusing to do another person's homework or clean up their recurring mistakes.

- **Commitment Overload:** This means learning to decline invitations or requests when your schedule is already full.

You must know what you want. Clarify your comfort levels regarding physical space, emotional effort, and time commitment.

The Psychology of Self-Preservation

Setting boundaries is an act of self-preservation and self-respect. Psychologists recognize that awareness of one's own needs, desires, and values is a key aspect of building healthy boundaries.

Self-Awareness: The initial work requires deep self-awareness. You must pay attention to how you feel in different situations and how it affects your well-being. Where do you feel resentment? Where do you feel panic? These feelings are signals that a boundary needs to be established.

Resilience: Once the boundary is defined, you need resilience. This is the ability to remain true to your boundary and confident in your values and needs, even when challenged.

Boundaries and Autonomy

The ability to define your personal limits is foundational to personal autonomy. Autonomy is the capacity to live life according to one's own free will and moral values. Psychological principles, such as those within Transactional Analysis, emphasize the concept of personal autonomy. Self-respect, self-trust, and self-confidence form the foundation of autonomy.

When you fail to set limits, you lose autonomy. You are operating according to someone else's script. You are allowing external demands to dictate your internal state. Establishing boundaries is how you reclaim your own life. This clarity is the first step toward self-improvement and harmonizing relationships.

You must categorize your limits. You must write them down. You must clarify your needs before you attempt to communicate them. An internal map of your boundaries is the only protection against manipulation and emotional exhaustion.

CHAPTER 2
CLEARLY COMMUNICATE EXPECTATIONS AND NEEDS

You have successfully defined your limits internally. You know your personal emotional, time, and physical boundaries. A boundary that is unstated is merely a preference. It is an internal wish with no external power. To be effective, boundaries must be clearly communicated. They must be stated to define expectations for interaction.

Toxic behavior ignores unstated needs. It takes advantage of silence. You must articulate your boundary using the language of assertion you mastered in Book 3. This chapter is about translating your internal map into clear, firm verbal demands for respect.

Boundaries Must Be Stated Clearly

Unstated boundaries are suggestions. They are assumptions that the other person knows your internal map. They do not. You must make the limit explicit. Clarity prevents misinterpretation. It preempts the defense, "You never told me that was a problem."

You must state your boundary clearly and straightforwardly. Do not raise your voice. Do not use aggressive language. You deliver the message in a calm, confident, non-emotional manner. You are simply stating a rule of engagement.

- **Avoid Softening Language:** Do not start with apologies or hesitant phrases like, "I know this is silly, but..." or "Would you mind if..." These softeners signal that the boundary is negotiable and invite challenge.
- **Be Direct:** Use strong, clear words. Example: "I need you to stop interrupting me when I am speaking," or "I cannot answer work emails after 6:00 PM."
- **Use the Assertive Structure:** Employ the XYZ formula (I feel X when you do Y, and I need Z). This frames the boundary as a response to a specific behavior, not a personal attack.

State Your Request Positively

Boundaries are often stated in terms of what you dislike. This frames the boundary negatively. State your request directly in terms of what you *want*, rather than what you dislike.

- **Negative Framing:** "Stop leaving your clothes on the bathroom floor." (Focuses on the problem behavior)
- **Positive Framing:** "I need the bathroom floor completely clear of clothing by 8:00 AM every morning." (Focuses on the desired, measurable outcome)

This positive framing is crucial. It gives the other person a clear target for success. It shows them exactly what action is required. This transforms a complaint into an opportunity for successful compliance.

The Role of Psychological Safety in Expectations

When communicating a boundary, you are defining a new expectation in the relationship. This requires creating a sense of psychological safety for the other person to receive the information without becoming defensive.

Psychological safety, a concept pioneered by Edgar Schein and further researched by Amy Edmondson, is the shared belief within a group that encourages individuals to express themselves without fear of negative consequences. While applied to teams, this concept holds true in personal dialogue. When you state a boundary calmly and respectfully, you demonstrate that the conversation is safe.

Your assertive communication is the tool that creates this safety:

- **Non-Judgmental Tone:** Your calm tone signals that you are setting a limit for self-protection, not to punish. You are opening a dialogue about expectations.
- **Clarity on Consequences (Implied):** The assertion implies that future violation will have a consequence, but the initial statement must be delivered with respect for the other person's ability to choose to comply.

By using the assertive communication skills from Book 3, you articulate your boundary while respecting both your rights and the rights of others.

Clarify Types of Boundaries

You must be precise when defining the nature of the boundary being set.

Boundary Type	Definition and Example
Time Boundary	Setting limits on availability. Example: "I am unavailable for non-emergency calls between 5:00 PM Friday and 9:00 AM Monday."
Physical Boundary	Defining personal space or touch. Example: "Please do not give me advice about my diet or weight."
Emotional Boundary	Clarifying responsibility for feelings. Example: "I can listen to you vent for ten minutes, but I cannot solve this financial problem for you."
Material Boundary	Defining the use of property. Example: "You must ask permission before borrowing my tools, and they must be returned by the end of the day."

The Psychological Impact of Clarity

The psychological benefit of clearly communicating boundaries is immense. Healthy boundaries ensure your physical and emotional comfort. They clarify individual responsibilities in a relationship. They separate your wants, needs, thoughts, and feelings from those of others.

Unclear expectations in a relationship lead to frustration, resentment, and chronic conflict. Clarity, enforced through assertive communication, creates a reliable structure. This structure is essential. When you establish and clearly communicate a boundary, you give yourself a powerful sense of empowerment and self-respect. You are actively protecting your well-being. This is an act of deliberate self-care.

CHAPTER 3
MANAGE DISCOMFORT WHEN YOU SAY "NO"

You have defined your limits. You have clearly communicated those limits using assertive language. The most challenging part is the follow-through. Setting a boundary often causes intense discomfort. You might feel guilt, shame, or fear of conflict. This discomfort is why boundaries fail. You retreat from your stated limit to avoid the feeling.

You must accept the inevitable discomfort that arises. Tolerating the feeling is necessary to maintain the boundary. You are disrupting an old, familiar pattern. This chapter teaches you how to manage the powerful psychological barriers that stop you from holding firm.

Identify the Psychological Barrier

The greatest barrier to assertion is not external. It is internal. It is the fear that enforcing a boundary will damage the relationship or reveal you as a "bad" person. This fear often manifests as the Guilt Cycle.

The Guilt Cycle: Psychologist Zulmaury Saavedra notes that the guilt cycle is an emotional prison. No matter what you do, you end up feeling bad. The cycle has three components: **Should, Action/Inaction, and Guilt.**

1. **The "Should":** This stems from a deep-seated desire to gain or maintain approval from others. You feel you "should" do something for them. This creates a script you feel obligated to follow.

2. **Action/Inaction:** When you take action (saying "yes" when you mean "no"), you follow the script but generate internal resentment. When you choose inaction (saying "no" or holding back), you feel guilty for denying the request.

3. **Guilt:** The guilt is unavoidable in this closed circuit. You are not living life in your own best interest. You are letting someone else control the script.

To break this cycle, you must target the "should." You must recognize that the internal pressure to please is stronger than the external demand. You must choose self-respect over the temporary relief of people-pleasing.

Stop People-Pleasing Behaviors

The feeling of being used, abused, or underappreciated stems directly from failing to assert your preferences and limits. People-pleasing is a submissive behavior. It denies your own rights in favor of others.

You must recognize the comfort you might derive from being a "martyr." You gain a certain kind of approval or identity from being the person who "always helps" or "always sacrifices." This may feel good in the short term, but it poisons your relationships with silent resentment.

The Solution is Self-Compassion: You must approach this discomfort with self-compassion. Self-compassion, as researched by psychologist Kristin Neff, involves three components: self-kindness, recognizing common humanity, and mindfulness. When guilt arises after saying "no," you must:

1. **Acknowledge the Pain (Mindfulness):** Recognize the feeling of guilt without judgment. Say, "I feel guilty right now because I said no to my friend."

2. **Connect to Common Humanity:** Recognize that struggling with boundaries is a universal human experience. You are not alone in this difficulty.

3. **Practice Self-Kindness:** Respond to yourself with warmth and care, instead of criticism. Reiterate: "I have a right to my time. Saying 'no' was an act of self-respect, not a failure."

This gentle but firm internal response is how you tolerate the discomfort. You choose to accept the guilt instead of retreating from your stated limit.

Asserting Boundaries with Confidence

When you deliver a boundary, your language must convey internal conviction. This confidence is the external expression of your commitment to self-respect.

1. Use Firm, Simple Language: Do not over-explain. Do not justify. Justify means apologize. A simple "no" is complete. If the person insists, you can use a technique called **Fogging** (developed by Manuel J. Smith in *When I Say No, I Feel Guilty*). This involves acknowledging the truth in their statement without changing your position.

- **Boundary:** "I cannot work late tonight."
- **Challenge:** "But if you do not stay, the team will be disappointed."
- **Fogging Response:** "I understand the team will be disappointed. I still cannot work late tonight."

You acknowledge their emotion or perspective without taking responsibility for it. This defuses the challenge without giving ground.

2. Recognize the Relationship Test: Recognize that setting limits will not disrupt a healthy relationship. Healthy relationships respect limits. If the relationship falls apart because you assert your needs, it was not based on mutual respect. It was based on your compliance and submission. You use the boundary as a test. The person's reaction to your limit tells you everything you need to know about the nature of the relationship.

Building Resilience: The Scientific View

The ability to maintain a boundary despite discomfort is called psychological resilience. Resilience is the ability to remain true to your boundary and confident in your values and needs, even when challenged. This is not simply about standing firm in the moment. It is about a consistent internal conviction.

The fear of conflict often leads to silence. You avoid confrontation, but you accumulate resentment. This resentment is toxic. Assertiveness is the antidote. It allows you to address the conflict directly, cleanly, and respectfully.

You must develop a support system of people who respect your right to set limits. Distance yourself from toxic individuals who actively seek to manipulate or control you. This is an act of proactive self-care. It reinforces the idea that your needs are valid.

By managing the discomfort of saying "no," you replace the destructive cycle of guilt and resentment with a productive cycle of self-respect and honest communication. This is a deliberate, daily choice for freedom.

CHAPTER 4
RESPOND FIRMLY TO BOUNDARY CHALLENGES

You have successfully defined and stated a boundary. You have managed your initial discomfort and guilt. The next challenge is external. You must learn how to respond when someone challenges, tests, or attempts to negotiate your new limits. If you allow a challenge to succeed, the boundary erodes immediately. The other person learns that persistence pays off.

Toxic individuals, especially those accustomed to your previous lack of limits, will frequently test the new boundaries. They will try to pull you back into the old pattern of compliance. Your response must be firm, simple, and consistent. This chapter provides the psychological strategies and practical scripts for maintaining your limit.

Recognize the Boundary Test

A boundary challenge often looks like confusion, frustration, or even emotional manipulation. The person may not intend to be malicious. They may simply be reacting to the sudden shift in the relationship dynamic. You must recognize the test and prepare to maintain your position.

Common Challenges:

- **Guilt Induction:** "I guess you do not care about me since you will not help with this."
- **Negotiation:** "Can you just do it this one time? I promise it will never happen again."
- **Feigned Confusion:** "I do not understand why this is a problem now. It was never a problem before."
- **Anger or Sulking:** The person responds to your limit with silence, withdrawal, or an aggressive outburst.

Your response must communicate two things: respect for the other person's feelings, and unwavering commitment to your limit.

Reiterate the Boundary Simply and Firmly

When challenged, you must not justify or over-explain. Justification invites debate. If you offer a reason, the other person will try to argue against the reason. This pulls you into a power struggle.

Reiterate the boundary simply. Use short, firm sentences. This technique is often called the "broken record" technique in assertiveness training. You repeat your request or refusal calmly, without changing your stance or tone.

- **The Script:**
    - **Boundary:** "I cannot work on your project with you this weekend."
    - **Challenge:** "But I really need your help! I thought we were friends."
    - **Firm Reiteration:** "I understand you need help. I still cannot work on your project this weekend."
    - **Second Challenge:** "But the deadline is Monday! Are you just going to leave me hanging?"
    - **Final Reiteration:** "I hear how stressed you are. I still cannot work on your project this weekend."

You acknowledge their feeling without taking responsibility for fixing it. This demonstrates the core of assertion: your rights are equal to theirs. You have listened and validated their stress, but your boundary remains fixed.

Strategize Difficult Conversations in Advance

Dealing with persistent challenges requires pre-planning. You must structure the conversation in advance, knowing that the person will likely push back. This helps you remain calm and non-emotional during the process.

Structured Conversation Approach (Three Parts):

1. **State the Violation Factually:** Use the XYZ formula to state the specific violation and your feeling about it. Example: "I felt frustrated when I saw you used my laptop without asking me first this morning."

2. **Listen and Empathize:** Listen to their perspective without defense. Use the empathy skills from Book 2. Validate their feeling, but not their behavior. Example: "I hear that you were in a rush and felt panicked, and I accept that feeling."

3. **Propose Resolution and Reiterate Limit:** Clearly restate the boundary and the expectation for the future. Example: "For the future, the rule is that you must always ask me before using my laptop. I need you to agree to that."

This structure, often used in professional settings, helps keep the discussion focused on the necessary resolution. Do not get overly emotional during the process. Your calm delivery is proof of your conviction.

Accountability for Overstepping: Apologize Sincerely

You are human. You will occasionally overstep someone else's boundary. When this happens, you must own the mistake immediately. Apologize sincerely.

The Sincere Apology:

1. **Acknowledge the Mistake:** State clearly what you did. Example: "I realize I overstepped your boundary by giving you advice about your job when you only asked me to listen."

2. **Validate Their Reaction:** Acknowledge their right to feel upset. Example: "I understand why that frustrated you."

3. **Ask for Clarity:** If you need it, ask for clarity so you can avoid the mistake again. Example: "What can I do differently next time you need to vent?"

Be humble enough to acknowledge the mistake. This models the exact behavior you expect from others when they violate your limits. This accountability reinforces the idea that boundaries are mutually respected rules of engagement, not one-sided demands.

The Psychology of Distress Tolerance

The ability to maintain a boundary despite the other person's negative reaction—their anger, guilt-tripping, or sadness—is rooted in a concept called **Distress Tolerance (DT)**.

Distress Tolerance is the capacity to endure negative emotional states. It is the ability to withstand uncomfortable feelings without engaging in destructive behaviors to make the feeling stop. When the person you set a boundary with becomes angry, that anger creates distress in you. Your old toxic pattern was to immediately give in to the boundary challenge to make the distress (the guilt or the conflict) go away.

Research consistently links low distress tolerance to various psychological symptoms. Studies show that a greater capacity to tolerate emotional distress is inversely correlated with the presence of psychopathological symptoms and general distress. This means the better you are at enduring emotional discomfort, the lower your general stress levels are.

When you maintain your boundary, you are actively increasing your distress tolerance. You are choosing to endure the temporary pain of conflict. You are choosing to accept the other person's disappointment. You are doing this because you know the long-term cost of retreat is greater. Tolerating their anger for five minutes prevents months of internal resentment and burnout. This resilience is the true power of an enforced boundary.

CHAPTER 5
IMPLEMENT CONSEQUENCES FOR REPEAT VIOLATIONS

You have established the boundary. You communicated it clearly. You responded firmly to the initial challenge. Now you must address the critical final step: the repeat violation. When a person violates a clearly expressed boundary repeatedly, you must implement consequences.

An unenforced boundary is not a limit. It is a suggestion. It tells the other person that your needs are optional. If you allow challenges to succeed, the boundary erodes immediately. This chapter focuses on the necessary, operational steps to implement consequences. Consequences serve to protect you. They are not intended to control the other person.

The Psychology of Compliance: Pain is a Motivator

The unfortunate truth about human behavior is that change is often motivated by loss. When behavior that has been previously reinforced no longer produces reinforcing consequences, the behavior decreases. This is a core principle of operant conditioning known as extinction.

A consequence for a boundary violation often involves inflicting psychological or practical "pain." This typically means removing your effort, your time, or your presence from the interaction. The other person feels the loss of your service or attention. This feeling of loss is frequently the strongest motivator for behavioral change in others.

It is crucial to understand that setting consequences is about self-protection. You are not punishing the other person. You are protecting yourself from further emotional exhaustion, resentment, and manipulation. You are ensuring you are not trampling over your own limits. If you do not enforce the consequence, you continue having the same fights. You continue to feel unheard and trampled over. This is entirely avoidable.

Define Consequences in Advance

You cannot invent a consequence in the heat of the moment. Consequences must be defined and articulated in advance. They need to be clear, measurable, and enforceable by **you alone**. You must ensure you have the internal conviction to follow through.

A good consequence focuses on removing your contribution or presence:

- **Boundary:** "I cannot lend money for non-emergencies."
- **Consequence:** "If you ask me to lend you money outside of a genuine medical emergency, I will end the phone call immediately." (You control the call, not their asking.)
- **Boundary:** "Do not interrupt me when I am working in the home office between 9:00 AM and 1:00 PM."
- **Consequence:** "If you interrupt me again during those hours, I will leave the office for the rest of the day and finish my work at a coffee shop." (You control your location and effort.)

Avoid Consequences You Cannot Enforce: Never set a limit that relies on the other person changing or that requires huge, punishing effort from you. For example, do not say, "If you yell at me again, I will leave you forever." That is an unpredictable, aggressive threat. Instead, say, "If you raise your voice at me, I will leave the room and not re-engage for one hour." This is measurable. You control the action.

The Extinction Burst: Prepare for Escalation

When you consistently remove the reward for a behavior, the person may try harder to get the old result. This phenomenon is known as the **extinction burst.**

The extinction burst is a temporary, but intense, increase in the frequency and intensity of the unwanted behavior.

- **Example:** A child cries to get attention. When the parent stops giving attention (extinction), the child first cries **louder** and **longer** (extinction burst) before the behavior finally decreases.

When you enforce a boundary, the other person's challenges may become more intense. They may become angrier. They may resort to more significant guilt induction or passive-aggressive tactics. They are testing the new rule. This escalation signals that the boundary is working. You must anticipate this burst and remain unwaveringly consistent. If you give in during the extinction burst, you teach the person that they simply need to escalate their efforts to regain control.

The Process of Implementation

When the boundary is violated repeatedly, you follow these steps:

1. **Reiterate the Limit and State the Consequence (Before Violation):** State explicitly, "We agreed that I cannot work after 6:00 PM. If you send me another non-emergency email after that time, I will not respond until 9:00 AM the next morning."

2. **Follow Through Consistently (After Violation):** When the violation occurs, you act immediately and without emotion. Do not lecture. Do not argue. Simply implement the defined consequence. If they send the email at 7:00 PM, you ignore it.

3. **Use Silence and Action:** The power lies in your disciplined inaction. If you promised to leave the room, you leave the room. If you promised to end the call, you end the call. The pain felt as the loss of your presence or service is the motivator for them to respect the limit.

If you fail to enforce the consequence, the boundary loses all credibility. The cycle of feeling unheard continues. Following through is difficult, but it is necessary for achieving self-respect and lasting change.

It is critical to distinguish between control and self-protection.

Control: An attempt to dictate another person's feelings or choices. Example: "You must stop being angry at me." (You cannot control their feelings.)

Self-Protection (Consequence): An action you take to protect your space and well-being. Example: "Because you are angry, I am choosing to leave the room." (You control your presence.)

Your consequences must be about your behavior. They are not threats. They are clear statements of what you will do to protect your limits. This shift in focus, from controlling them to protecting yourself, is the definition of maturity and autonomy. It moves you out of the toxic cycle and into self-respect.

CHAPTER 6

BOOK 4 CONCLUSION:
LIVE WITHIN YOUR CLEAR LIMITS

You have completed the essential work of defining and defending your personal space. You moved from the internal acknowledgment of your limits to the external, consistent enforcement of those limits. Boundary setting establishes the necessary framework for healthy relationships. This structure is essential.

Without boundaries, the other foundational skills, anger control, empathy, and assertion, break down. If you do not protect your time, you become exhausted and impatient. You regress to toxic anger. If you do not enforce your emotional limits, resentment builds, silencing your assertive voice. Boundaries are the operational defense system for your non-toxic life.

Your new structure for living within your limits is built on five necessary, consistent actions. This work is about translating self-respect into repeatable behavior.

Pillar One: Define Your Personal and Emotional Limits. You clarified your internal map of acceptable behavior. You separated your needs from the needs of others. You categorized your limits: physical space, emotional effort, and time commitment. You acknowledge that your feelings are yours, and the other person's feelings are theirs. This self-awareness, including resilience, is a key aspect of building healthy boundaries. You must know what you are defending before you can defend it.

Pillar Two: Clearly Communicate Expectations and Needs. A boundary must be stated explicitly. Unstated boundaries are simply wishes. You state your boundary clearly, straightforwardly, and with a calm, assertive tone. You use the assertive structure you mastered. You state your request in terms of what you *want* (a positive outcome), rather than what you dislike (a negative behavior). This positive framing gives the other person a clear, manageable target for compliance.

Pillar Three: Manage Discomfort When You Say "No." You overcome the psychological barrier of guilt and fear of conflict. You accept the inevitable discomfort that arises when you say "no." This pain is temporary. You recognize that saying "no" is an act of self-respect, not a failure. You stop people-pleasing behaviors that stem from the Guilt Cycle. You practice self-compassion to tolerate the distress. Setting limits will not disrupt a healthy relationship. It only tests its existing structural integrity.

Pillar Four: Respond Firmly to Boundary Challenges. You must defend your limit when it is tested. You do not justify or over-explain. Justification invites debate. When challenged, you reiterate the boundary simply, using the "broken record" technique. You acknowledge the other person's feeling, but not their right to violate your limit. You strategize difficult conversations in advance, knowing that your calm delivery is proof of your conviction. This maintenance ensures the boundary does not erode.

Pillar Five: Implement Consequences for Repeat Violations. An unenforced boundary is a suggestion. When the limit is violated repeatedly, you implement a predefined consequence. This consequence must be clear, measurable, and enforceable by **you alone.**

You are not punishing the other person. You are protecting yourself by removing your effort, time, or presence from the interaction. You understand the extinction burst, which is the temporary escalation of their demanding behavior. You remain consistently firm. The loss of your service or attention is often the necessary motivator for their behavioral change. This act of disciplined follow-through is the definition of self-protection.

The Autonomy and Resilience of Clear Limits

By defining your limits and consistently applying consequences for violations, you model profound respect for yourself. This consistent action has far-reaching psychological benefits.

Autonomy: Boundaries are fundamental to personal autonomy. Autonomy is the capacity to live life according to your own free will and moral values. When you fail to set limits, you lose this autonomy. You are operating according to external demands. The work of Transactional Analysis emphasizes that self-respect, self-trust, and self-confidence form the foundation of autonomy. Establishing boundaries is the direct action you take to reclaim your life. This action separates you from the drama and demands of others.

Distress Tolerance: The ability to maintain a boundary despite the other person's negative reaction, their anger or emotional manipulation, is rooted in Distress Tolerance. Distress Tolerance is the capacity to endure negative emotional states without resorting to destructive behavior to make the feeling stop. Research confirms that the greater your capacity to tolerate emotional distress, the lower your general stress levels are. When you stand firm against a challenge, you are actively increasing your resilience. You are choosing to endure temporary pain for long-term health.

Relational Accountability: When the basic rules of interaction are clearly defined and enforced, consistency and accountability have a clear framework within which to operate. This structure is key. It eliminates the ambiguity that toxic relationships thrive on. You are creating a predictable, reliable environment. This consistent, predictable structure is the final step necessary for repairing broken trust, which is the focus of Book 5. Trust cannot be rebuilt unless the relationship has clearly defined rules that are respected by both parties.

Your commitment to clear limits demonstrates an unwavering loyalty to your own well-being. This is a deliberate, daily choice for self-respect. You are choosing to live within your clear limits, defending your emotional space, and building the stable platform required for deeper connection. The toxic habits of submission and aggression are replaced by confidence and clarity.

Reflection Questions

1. Identify one boundary you successfully enforced this week. What was the specific limit, and what emotion (guilt, shame, or fear) did you tolerate to maintain it?

2. Draft the precise consequence you will implement the next time a specific boundary is violated. Ensure this consequence is measurable and enforceable by you alone.

3. Name one physical boundary and one emotional boundary you will clearly communicate this week. State the request in positive terms (what you want, not what you dislike).

4. Describe a moment when someone attempted a guilt induction or negotiation to challenge your boundary. How could you have used the "broken record" technique to maintain your limit simply and calmly?

5. How does your choice to enforce boundaries actively contribute to your sense of autonomy and self-respect?

CHECKLIST
LIVING WITHIN YOUR CLEAR LIMITS

This is your practical guide from Book 4: Set Boundaries. It helps you turn your inner self-respect into a consistent, everyday defense around your emotional and physical space.

I. Defining Your Limits: Being Clear with Yourself

Before chatting with anyone, you need to be crystal clear on your personal and emotional limits. A boundary you don't speak up about is just a wish. This part is about honest self-awareness.

Did you take time this week to get clear on these?

- Know where your responsibility stops for others' feelings. Their anger or sadness? That's on them, not you. Did you refuse to take blame for their overreactions? Healthy boundaries mean separating your feelings from theirs.

- Figure out exactly how much time you need for yourself. Did you carve out some "me time" that's off-limits? Maybe no work calls after 7 p.m., or whole Sunday mornings just for you. These boundaries fight burnout.

- Understand your physical comfort zone. What about noise, space, or your environment keeps you feeling okay? Did you notice a quick flinch or step back when someone got too close?

- Catch those "should" thoughts like "I should help even when tired." That pressure comes from wanting approval, trapping you in a guilt cycle. Choose self-respect instead.

- Remind yourself your needs matter as much as anyone's. Setting limits is self-care, it's not negotiable.

II. Speaking Up: Saying Your Needs Clearly

A boundary needs to be said out loud, loud and clear. Soft words mean soft boundaries.

When stating a boundary, did you:

- Speak calmly and confidently? Avoid weak phrases like "I know this sounds silly, but..." or "Would you mind if..." Use clear, strong words to stop confusion.

- Frame your requests positively, focusing on what you want rather than what you don't. For example, say "Please keep the kitchen counter clear," not "Stop leaving your mess."

- Use a structured way (like the XYZ formula) to state your boundary. Focus on behavior, not attacking the person, respecting both sides.

- Make clear this is a rule, not a question. Unsaid limits are just suggestions. Your tone should prove you mean business.

- Say "No" firmly but politely. No "I'm too busy" or "I guess I can." Just a simple "No." And don't over-explain your reasons, you don't owe anyone that.

III. Defending Your Boundary: Handling Pushback

Setting a boundary gets tested. If guilt or fear break you down, the boundary fails. This stage is all about building resilience.

When your limits got pushed, did you:

- Sit with the guilt and not back down? That discomfort is normal—you're breaking the old people-pleasing cycle.

- Repeat your boundary calmly and firmly, like a broken record. No changing your stance or adding new justifications, keep it simple.

- Avoid explaining too much. Just state your limit. For example, say, "I can't lend money," not, "I can't because my bank account is low."

- Acknowledge their feelings without bending your boundary. If they're upset, say, "I understand you're disappointed," but hold your ground.

- Apologize quickly and sincerely if you slip up and cross their line. Ask how to improve, showing respect both ways.

IV. Enforcing Limits: Consequences for Repeat Offenses

Boundaries mean nothing without follow-through. This last step is all about protecting yourself with consequences you control.

For repeat boundary crossers, did you:

- Decide consequences ahead of time? Make sure they're clear and you can do them yourself. For example, "If this happens, I will leave the room."

- Focus consequences on removing your involvement, your time, effort, or presence. Don't try to control their feelings or actions.

- Stay calm through the "extinction burst", when pushback gets louder or nastier. It's a sign your boundary is working. Stand firm.

- Act immediately when boundaries are broken. No lectures, just quiet action. Walk away or ignore the text. Not following through ruins your boundary.

- Remember it's self-protection, not punishment. You're choosing peace for yourself, not trying to make them behave.

BOOK FIVE

FIX BROKEN TRUST:
REBUILD SECURITY THROUGH CONSISTENCY

INTRODUCTION

You have achieved the prerequisite skills for a healthy relationship. You established internal control. You mastered external empathy. You communicate with assertive clarity. You defined and defended your boundaries. These four books established a platform of predictability. Now you must address the ultimate challenge: restoring trust after betrayal.

Trust is the single cornerstone of all intimate relationships. Without it, the relationship becomes a constant source of anxiety and vigilance. When trust is broken, whether by lying, infidelity, or consistent violation of core boundaries, words alone are insufficient to fix the damage. The damage is not merely factual. It is neurological. It erodes the sense of safety the relationship was supposed to provide.

You are not aiming to return to the way things were. That old relationship is gone. Once trust has been broken, the old relationship cannot exist anymore. You are now creating a **new** relationship with your partner. This new foundation must be built on improved communication skills, deeper vulnerability, and radical, visible accountability.

This book provides the structured path to rebuilding that security. Trust must be earned back through sustained consistency and measurable behavioral change.

The Psychological Cost of Betrayal

Betrayal is a profound violation of psychological safety. The injured party loses their sense of reality. They question their own judgment. They enter a state of emotional trauma. They require tangible, repeated evidence that the threat is gone.

The healing process is necessarily long. It requires unwavering commitment from the person who caused the damage. It demands accountability, not excuses. Explanations and excuses can worsen the damage. The healing process demands immediate, comprehensive ownership of the damage caused.

The Scientific Framework for Repair

Trust repair is an active construction project. It follows a predictable psychological pattern. The process model for trust repair emphasizes the temporal nature of the recovery. It does not happen overnight. It requires sustained, positive behavior over time.

This book guides you through five essential stages of repair:

First, you learn to **Take Full Accountability for Your Actions**. This is immediate, comprehensive ownership of the mistake without sidestepping the issue or shifting blame.

Second, you practice offering a **Meaningful, Non-Defensive Apology**. You listen to the other person's anger and hurt without defense or excuse.

Third, you learn to **Practice Radical Transparency and Openness**. You eliminate secrecy. You answer all questions openly, even if the truth causes you discomfort.

Fourth, you learn to **Establish Consistent Trust-Building Behaviors**. You rebuild security through observable action, not promises. You follow through with every commitment, large or small.

Finally, you learn to **Stay Loyal to the Healing Process**. You accept the injured party's timeline. You hold space for their ongoing hurt, demonstrating unwavering loyalty to the process of change.

The Role of Attachment and Vulnerability

This repair work relies heavily on principles of attachment theory. Psychologists Susan M. Johnson and Leslie S. Greenberg developed Emotionally Focused Therapy (EFT) based on these principles. EFT emphasizes the importance of emotional bonds in healthy relationships. EFT is designed to enhance emotional connections and resolve relationship distress, including issues of trust and trauma.

When trust is broken, the core attachment bond is ruptured. The injured party experiences profound fear of abandonment or loneliness. The repair process must facilitate the open communication of these fears. It must foster a more positive and resilient relational environment. You achieve this by working on deeper vulnerability and improving communication skills.

You must commit to building security through consistency. You are creating a new, stronger relationship that survives the betrayal by adhering to clear, predictable rules of engagement. This disciplined, transparent approach is the only way to replace the relationship's fear and vigilance with genuine security.

CHAPTER 1
TAKE FULL ACCOUNTABILITY FOR YOUR ACTIONS

Trust is gone. That is the stark, undeniable reality you must face. The relationship is operating on fear. The person you hurt is vigilant. They are anxious. They are waiting for the next violation. You have established calm control and clear boundaries. That foundational work prepared you for this moment. This chapter addresses the absolute first step in trust repair: immediate, comprehensive ownership of the mistake.

Trust repair demands accountability. It is not an option. It is the price of admission to the new relationship. You must take full responsibility for your actions. Do not attempt to sidestep the issue. Do not try to shift blame to the other person. This ownership must be absolute.

The Problem with Excuses

When a violation occurs, the instinct is to explain. You want to offer context. You want to show that external factors, stress, fatigue, misunderstanding, played a role. Stop this instinct immediately.

In the early stages of repair, explanations are excuses. They are heard as deflection. Explanations and excuses can actually worsen the damage done to the relationship. Your partner is not listening for context. They are listening for a confession of ownership. Any attempt to minimize your role is heard as further evidence that you have not truly changed. It reinforces the fear that you will repeat the behavior.

You are responsible for your actions. You are responsible for the subsequent damage. You must communicate this responsibility clearly. Accountability means the following:

- **No Sidestepping:** You do not mention what the other person did to contribute to the conflict. The focus remains only on your specific, destructive behavior.

- **No Minimization:** You do not downplay the gravity of the betrayal. You acknowledge the seriousness of the damage you caused.

- **No Rationalization:** You do not use stress, job pressure, or tiredness as a reason for your actions. You simply state that you made the choice.

You are creating a new relationship with your partner. The foundation of this new relationship is honesty. Honesty begins with an honest assessment of your own actions.

The Science of Attribution in Trust Repair

To understand why accountability must be absolute, you need to understand how the injured party processes the betrayal. Trust is a product of both reason and emotion. The listener's brain is performing an intense calculation. It is determining whether to take the risk of trusting you again.

Psychological models of trust repair rely heavily on Attribution Theory. This theory, applied to trust repair by researchers like Schoorman, Mayer, and Davis, suggests that after a negative event, the injured party automatically determines the cause of the transgression. The cause is usually attributed to one of four areas:

1. **Ability:** The transgression happened because you lacked the necessary skill. (Example: You failed to complete a task because you did not know how.)

2. **Kindness (Benevolence):** The transgression happened because you did not care about the relationship. (Example: You missed an important event because you prioritized a casual outing with friends.)

3. **Integrity (Character):** The transgression happened because you lied, manipulated, or violated a core moral value. (Example: You lied about your actions or kept a secret.)

4. **External Reasons:** The transgression was caused by factors outside your control. (Example: A car crash caused you to be late.)

Toxic behavior is rarely attributed to "External Reasons." It is usually a violation of **Integrity** or **Kindness**.

When the injured party attributes the cause to a lack of **Integrity** (character, honesty, moral fiber), trust repair is significantly harder. Integrity violations, like lying or deliberate boundary breaking, require immediate, comprehensive ownership of the action. You must show the injured person that you understand your action reflects negatively on your entire character. You must prove the flaw lies in a learned behavior, not a permanent moral defect. Full accountability is the first evidence of this internal shift.

The Operational Language of Accountability

Taking accountability is an action. It is delivered through specific, clean language. You use the "I" statements you mastered in Book 3, but the focus shifts entirely from asserting a need to asserting an acceptance of error.

Accountability is not merely saying, "I apologize if I hurt your feelings." That is submissive language. It is a soft apology that questions the reality of the injured party's pain. Accountability means owning the action and the resulting damage.

The Accountability Script:

1. **Own the Action:** State clearly, using the first person, what you did. Example: "I kept the debt secret from you for six months."

2. **Own the Impact:** Acknowledge the known damage, without qualification. Example: "I understand that my action caused intense fear and a complete loss of security for you."

3. **Own the Cause (Internal):** State that the cause was your choice, not an external factor. Example: "I did this because I chose to prioritize my comfort over our security. That was a selfish choice, and it was wrong."

This direct, unequivocal language transfers the responsibility fully to you. You separate the problem from the context and anchor it in your choice. You are proving that you are operating from an Internal Locus of

Control. You are demonstrating that your behavior is guided by your decisions, not external fate. This is the first verifiable step in rebuilding trust.

Eliminating the Toxic Habits of Deflection

Toxic individuals rely on deflection to avoid ownership. You must identify and eliminate these habits instantly.

1. Minimization: This involves reducing the perceived severity of the damage. Example: "It was just a small lie," or "Why are you still talking about this three weeks later?" Minimization tells the injured party that their emotional response is disproportionate. It is a secondary betrayal. Stop minimizing. Listen to the perceived severity of the damage. You must accept their feeling as valid.

2. Justification: This involves explaining the circumstances that forced your hand. Example: "I only lied because I was afraid you would be angry." While this may be factually true, it uses fear as an excuse. It shifts the cause of the lie onto the injured party's potential reaction. This is blame-shifting. Stop justifying. Simply state the action was wrong and accept the full responsibility for the choice.

3. Blame Shifting: This is the most damaging habit. You introduce past grievances or the partner's flaws. Example: "If you were not always checking up on me, I would not have felt the need to lie." This instantly contaminates the discussion. It moves the focus away from your transgression and onto the partner's behavior. You must maintain present focus. You are only addressing your specific violation.

The conversation about your partner's flaws can happen later. It must happen only after the full trust repair process is well underway. First, you must prove you are safe.

The Initial Difficult Conversation

The initial conversation where you take full accountability is a crucial conversation. These discussions involve high stakes and high emotions, and the authors of *Crucial Conversations* provide principles that apply directly to this repair work.

1. Start with Heart (Your Intention): Before the conversation, be clear with yourself about what you really want. Your intention must be repair, not personal relief. You are not seeking forgiveness. You are seeking to lay the foundation for honesty. You must maintain composure when feeling anxious or defensive.

2. Make It Safe: You must create an environment where the injured party can express anger and hurt without fear of consequence or defensiveness from you. Your calm, assertive posture (Book 3) and non-defensive listening (Book 2) are mandatory here. Your silence and attending skills provide the safety.

3. State Your Path (The Accountability): You share your strong ownership without shutting down the other person's viewpoint. You must use the Accountability Script. You state, "I am responsible for this. I did this. I caused the pain." This clear statement is the only way to move the conversation forward constructively.

Accountability is an action that precedes the apology. It is the necessary bridge to the new relationship. You are showing you are willing to endure the discomfort of being wrong. You are demonstrating that your commitment to integrity is stronger than your commitment to your ego. This sustained, transparent effort is the only currency for rebuilding trust.

CHAPTER 2
OFFER A MEANINGFUL, NON-DEFENSIVE APOLOGY

You have successfully taken full accountability for your actions. You owned the choice. You acknowledged the severity of the damage. This necessary step precedes the apology. Accountability validates the facts. The apology validates the feelings.

A sincere apology is only the beginning of the repair process. It is a necessary ritual, not a finish line. The apology must acknowledge the depth of the pain caused. It must be delivered without defense or excuse. This chapter teaches you how to transition from owning the action to validating the subsequent emotional experience.

The Anatomy of a Sincere Apology

A meaningful apology is structured. It is a deliberate communication that centers the injured party's experience. A sincere apology requires two core elements: expression of genuine regret and commitment to listening without defense.

1. Express Genuine Regret: You must communicate that you understand the gravity of the betrayal. Do not apologize "if" they were hurt. Apologize "for" the action you committed.

- **Weak Apology (Conditional):** "I apologize if my comments upset you." (This questions the reality of their feeling.)
- **Sincere Apology (Acceptance):** "I am deeply sorry that I violated your trust by lying about the finances. I know my actions caused you fear and instability."

You acknowledge the mistake openly. You recognize the gravity of the betrayal without deflecting or rationalizing. Trust begins with honesty and integrity.

2. Be Prepared to Apologize Repeatedly: The injured party is working through emotional trauma. They will experience the pain in cycles. They may need to talk about the betrayal many times. You must be prepared to offer the apology repeatedly, acknowledging the partner's ongoing hurt. The pain is not linear. Your consistency must match their timeline. You cannot pressure them to "move on."

Commitment to Listening Without Defending

This is the hardest part of the apology. You must listen to the other person's anger and hurt feelings without defense or excuse. The injured party needs to process their pain out loud. They need to express their frustration, sadness, and anger in a safe space. Your job is to provide that safety.

- **Non-Defensive Posture:** Use the empathy skills learned in Book 2. Maintain an open, non-defensive posture. Your non-verbal signals must convey acceptance, not impatience.
- **Validate the Feeling:** Use reflective listening. Do not argue against the feelings. Simply validate them. Example: "I hear how much disappointment this has caused you," or "Your anger makes complete sense to me." Validation is acceptance of their emotional reality. It does not require agreement with their every conclusion.

Commitment to listening without defending is a powerful action. It shows the injured party that your desire for their healing is stronger than your need to protect your ego. Every time you refrain from offering an excuse, you reinforce the safety of the new relationship.

The Scientific Necessity of Emotional Validation

The emotional stage of trust repair is critical. The injured party is operating from a place of intense emotional distress. Emotional validation is not simply being nice. It is a scientifically necessary component of emotional regulation.

Emotionally Focused Therapy (EFT), developed by Susan M. Johnson and Leslie S. Greenberg, emphasizes the importance of emotional bonds and the need for emotional safety in repair. When trust is broken, the core attachment bond is ruptured. The injured party feels existential fear.

Validation, the act of confirming that the other person's emotions are real and understandable, helps regulate these intense feelings. When feelings are validated, the emotional intensity decreases. This allows the injured party to move out of the reactive, defensive posture and into a more vulnerable, honest space. This is necessary for the conversation to move from conflict to constructive dialogue.

If you block their expression of anger with an excuse, you force them back into isolation. You tell them their pain is too much for you to handle. You must accept their perspective and feelings as valid.

Preparing for Vulnerability

The apology and the act of non-defensive listening are your primary actions of vulnerability in this stage. Vulnerability, as researched by Brené Brown, is not weakness. It is emotional risk.

- **Risk:** You risk hearing harsh, painful truths about yourself and your behavior.
- **Necessity:** This risk is necessary for building the confidence needed to express thoughts and emotions genuinely. By embracing the discomfort of hearing their pain, you prove your commitment to integrity.

This demonstrated commitment, showing up consistently and calmly to hear the pain, is the verifiable evidence of change. It signals to the injured party that you are now a safe presence. Your honesty and willingness to endure their anger lay the groundwork for transparency, which is the next crucial step.

CHAPTER 3
PRACTICE RADICAL TRANSPARENCY AND OPENNESS

You have established the two foundation stones of repair: accountability for the action and a non-defensive apology for the emotion. These steps clear the past. The next stage is building the future. Trust cannot be rebuilt in secrecy. Openness is the necessary currency.

Betrayal introduces fear and uncertainty. The injured party loses their sense of safety and reality. They question their own judgment. Transparency counters this fear directly. It is the action that proves the threat of secrecy is gone. You must engage in complete honesty and open communication. This involves answering all questions openly. You must avoid any form of secrecy. This is radical transparency.

After a trust violation, the injured party's brain enters a state of hypervigilance. They become obsessed with finding "proof" that the transgression is truly over. The natural human tendency is to seek certainty. Since trust is based on positive expectations of the other person's behavior, that expectation must be restored through verifiable evidence.

Your radical transparency provides that verifiable evidence. Every answer you give openly diminishes the fear. Every secret you eliminate rebuilds the psychological safety.

1. Eliminating the Information Gap: Secrecy creates an information gap. The injured party fills this gap with worst-case scenarios and hostile assumptions. Complete openness eliminates this gap. It gives the injured person the factual data they need to start regulating their anxiety.

2. Countering Gaslighting: Often, toxic behavior involves persistent denial of events or shifting reality. This tactic, known as gaslighting, makes the victim question their own reality and judgment. Radical transparency is the complete antidote. You validate their memory. You confirm the facts. You eliminate the ability of manipulation to take root. You are restoring their perception of reality.

Engaging in Radical Transparency

Radical transparency means providing access to information, even if the truth causes you discomfort. You must be willing to endure discomfort as you reveal the truth. This is part of the cost of repair.

1. Answer All Questions Openly: Be prepared for probing, uncomfortable questions. You must answer them fully, honestly, and without impatience. If you dodge a question or give a vague response, you instantly reintroduce secrecy. You trigger the hypervigilance response.

2. Avoid the Defense of Privacy: In the past, you may have claimed certain areas were private. After a major trust violation, the injured party has a temporary right to increased access. This may include sharing access to communication channels or explaining your schedule in detail. This transparency is a temporary tool for safety, not a permanent invasion. You are demonstrating that you have nothing left to hide.

3. Separate Honesty from Detail Overload: Honesty is essential, but you must avoid providing unnecessary, excessive details that could create new, vivid images of the betrayal. This is especially true in cases of infidelity. You must clarify the facts without creating new trauma. If a detail is requested, you provide it honestly. You do not volunteer unnecessary, graphic details.

Asking for Future Boundaries and Expectations

Once you have opened the communication, you transition to setting clear expectations for the new relationship. Trust repair is about preventing recurrence.

You must ask what is needed to prevent the recurrence of the specific violation. This transfers some psychological control back to the injured party, helping them establish emotional safety.

- **Clarifying Boundaries:** Ask, "What new boundaries do you need me to commit to for you to feel safe?" This may involve a new boundary on phone use, alone time, or financial reporting. You must commit to keeping these new, specific limits.

- **Defining Acceptable Behavior:** Ask, "What specific behavior from me will show you that I am committed to honesty?" This helps the injured person define measurable, observable actions they can look for. This moves them from vague fear to measurable verification.

The Role of Psychological Safety in Repair

The framework for this open dialogue is Psychological Safety. Psychological safety is the shared belief that encourages individuals to express themselves without fear of negative consequences. While studied in teams, this concept applies profoundly to relationship repair.

The work of Amy Edmondson on psychological safety emphasizes that fostering open communication is essential for learning and performance. In the context of trust repair, psychological safety is the guarantee that the injured party can express their raw fear and anger without you withdrawing or retaliating. Your calm, non-defensive transparency creates this safety. It allows the injured party to speak without fear of being re-traumatized by your defensiveness.

By offering radical transparency and clarifying future expectations, you demonstrate that your commitment to integrity is paramount. You are proving that your behavior is now predictable and safe. This sustained action lays the foundation for consistency.

CHAPTER 4

ESTABLISH CONSISTENT TRUST-BUILDING BEHAVIORS

You have cleared the psychological wreckage. You took full accountability. You offered a non-defensive apology. You committed to radical transparency. Now you move to the core of lasting repair. Trust is fixed by observable action, not by promises.

The injured party is no longer listening to your words. They are watching your feet. You must consistently show up with reliability and honesty. This chapter outlines the necessary actions for establishing consistent, verifiable trust-building behaviors. You are creating a new, predictable history.

The Problem with Promises

Promises are verbal statements of future intent. After a betrayal, promises are meaningless. They are simply words. The trust violation proved that your past words could not be relied upon. Trust must be rebuilt by observable evidence that your present behavior aligns with your stated future intent.

Your commitment must be demonstrated through small, consistent, measurable actions. You must rebuild security through predictability.

Trust is fragile. Once broken, consistent follow-through on even small commitments is essential for demonstrating reliability. This relentless focus on detail proves your integrity is restored.

1. Follow Through with Every Commitment: Be true to your word. You must follow through with every commitment, large or small. If you say you will call at 7:00 PM, you call at 7:00 PM. If you say you will handle the grocery shopping, you handle the grocery shopping. There is no room for excuses or forgetfulness in this phase. The smallest lapse can re-trigger anxiety and hypervigilance.

2. Consistent Honesty in Low-Stakes Moments: Practice radical transparency in every interaction, even when the truth is inconvenient. If you are five minutes late, you state the fact clearly: "I am five minutes late because I forgot to check the time." Do not invent a complex reason. This consistency in low-stakes moments allows the injured partner to observe your efforts and build confidence in your new honesty.

3. Offer a Clear, Measurable Act of Accountability: The injured party requires tangible evidence of change. This must be an action that addresses the nature of the specific betrayal.

- **If the betrayal was financial:** You commit to automatic weekly budget updates or shared access to accounts.

- **If the betrayal was lying/secrecy:** You commit to weekly, uninterrupted check-in conversations where you ask your partner for their assessment of your honesty.

This measurable act of accountability is a specific, tangible action that transfers some verifiable control to the injured party.

Trust-building rituals are consistent habits that reinforce security in the relationship. They are predictable actions that signal safety and foster reconnection. These rituals must be deliberately planned and maintained. They should focus on appreciation and positive effort, rather than past mistakes.

- **Meaningful Conversation Time:** Commit to setting aside time each week for a meaningful conversation. This time is reserved exclusively for connection, using the empathy skills from Book 2. It is not for arguing or scheduling.

- **Positive Appreciation:** Create a culture of appreciation. Focus on present efforts to reconnect, rather than past betrayals. Make it a ritual to acknowledge specific, positive things your partner did today. For example, "Thank you for getting the house ready this morning. I appreciate your effort." This focuses the energy on the positive future you are building.

- **Predictable Check-ins:** Establish daily check-in habits. These small rituals—a text upon arriving at work, a defined time for dinner—establish predictable reliability. Predictability is the antidote to the anxiety betrayal creates.

The Role of Behavior Modification in Trust

The repair process relies on principles of behavior modification. You are actively conditioning the injured party to associate your presence with safety and honesty, replacing the old association with fear and dishonesty.

1. Operant Conditioning and Reinforcement: When you consistently follow through on a commitment, you reinforce the belief that you are reliable. This positive outcome strengthens the desired behavior (trusting you). The inverse is also true: any lapse in honesty is a punishment that weakens the positive association you are trying to build.

2. Loss Aversion: Behavioral economics, particularly the research of Daniel Kahneman and Amos Tversky on Loss Aversion, shows that the pain of a loss is psychologically twice as powerful as the equivalent gain. This means a single instance of dishonesty or a repeated violation of a boundary will have a significantly greater negative impact than multiple acts of honesty have a positive one. You must be aggressively consistent because the brain is wired to focus on potential loss. This understanding mandates flawless follow-through in the early stages of repair.

3. Behavioral Contracting: In therapeutic settings, behavioral contracting is often used to solidify commitments. This involves making explicit, written agreements about specific, measurable behaviors and consequences. This formalizes your commitment to the agreed-upon new boundaries. Your measurable act of accountability is a form of behavioral contract. It ensures that the path to repair is defined by actions that are clear, observable, and specific.

Maintaining Integrity Under Pressure

This phase requires you to maintain integrity even when it is inconvenient. The commitment must be unwavering. You must choose to stay the course and hold space for your partner's needs, even when forgiveness does not unfold in the timeline you want.

You are providing tangible, consistent proof that you are safe. This is an act of deep humility and commitment. This consistent action is the only currency strong enough to rebuild security and move the relationship toward a resilient future.

CHAPTER 5

STAY LOYAL TO THE HEALING PROCESS

You have completed the actionable steps of repair. You took full accountability. You proved consistency in small actions. Trust is now stabilized. It is not, however, fully restored. Trust rebuilding is not a quick fix. It is an enduring commitment to the healing process.

The betrayal created trauma. Healing from trauma takes time. The process is not linear. You must demonstrate unwavering loyalty to the injured party's timeline. You must accept that forgiveness will not unfold according to your desired schedule. This chapter focuses on the necessary long-term commitment. It requires the psychological resilience necessary to secure the new relationship.

The Problem with the Timeline

The greatest obstacle in this phase is your own impatience. The person who caused the damage naturally wants the discomfort to end quickly. You want the relationship to return to stability. This desire for immediate relief often translates into subtle pressure on the injured party to forgive and "move on."

You must recognize this pressure as another form of self-centeredness. You are asserting your need (for personal relief) over their need (for psychological safety). This impatience can feel like a secondary violation.

You must accept the injured party's timeline. You must hold space for their ongoing hurt. You must be prepared for pain to resurface unexpectedly. Traumatic events, like a trust violation, create a failure to extinguish conditioned fear. The brain does not simply erase the memory of the betrayal. It creates a new "safety memory" that inhibits the fear response. This new memory is fragile. If a small trigger occurs, the fear memory can resurface instantly.

Your job is to remain calm, consistent, and non-defensive when the pain resurfaces. You demonstrate unwavering loyalty to the healing process.

Commitment Through Sustained Vulnerability

Rebuilding trust requires creating a new relationship built on improved communication skills and deeper vulnerability. You must accept that the old relationship cannot exist anymore. You are building the foundation together.

1. Continuously Work on Deeper Vulnerability: Vulnerability is not weakness. It is emotional risk. You must continue to share your internal struggles and fears openly, even when it feels uncomfortable. You share your fears about the relationship failing. You share your progress and your setbacks. This consistent openness prevents the reintroduction of secrecy. It demonstrates your commitment to living with integrity. Brené Brown's research on vulnerability emphasizes that embracing emotional risk allows individuals to become more authentic. This builds the confidence needed to express emotions genuinely.

2. Practice Relational Mindfulness: You must remain present in your interactions. Mindfulness, the practice of non-judgmental present awareness, is a powerful tool for relational stability. Research confirms the benefits of mindfulness in relationships. Greater mindfulness practice on a given day is associated with improved relationship happiness and reduced relationship stress on subsequent days. Mindfulness helps you stay present with your partner's current emotional state. It helps you notice when you are slipping into defensive patterns or contaminating the present with past anger.

3. Separate Forgiveness from Trust: You must understand the difference. Forgiveness is a personal, emotional process that the injured party must undertake for themselves. It is the release of personal anger and resentment. Trust is a behavioral process. It is your confidence in your partner's future actions. You cannot force forgiveness. You can only earn back trust through your consistent actions. You focus only on the behavior you control.

Fostering Positive Interactions

The long-term goal is to shift the emotional tone of the relationship away from anxiety and toward positivity. This requires deliberate action focused on the present.

1. Focus on Small Positive Moments: Appreciate consistent efforts to rebuild trust over time. Look for and acknowledge the small, positive moments of connection. This acts as positive reinforcement.

2. Create a Culture of Appreciation: John M. Gottman's extensive research on marriage stability emphasizes that successful relationships maintain a high ratio of positive to negative interactions. You must actively create a culture of appreciation. Focus on present efforts to reconnect, rather than dwelling on past betrayals. This positive reinforcement helps strengthen the new relationship dynamic. It creates moments of emotional gain that slowly outweigh the past loss.

The Science of Psychological Flexibility (ACT)

Staying loyal to a difficult, non-linear healing process requires robust psychological resilience. Acceptance and Commitment Therapy (ACT) provides the framework for this endurance. ACT focuses on fostering **Psychological Flexibility**—the ability to accept difficult emotions while committing to meaningful, value-driven actions.

- **Acceptance:** You accept the reality of the lingering pain. You accept the lack of immediate forgiveness. You stop fighting the reality of the situation.

- **Committed Action:** You commit to the values of honesty, consistency, and respect. You maintain your positive behavior regardless of whether your partner is currently rewarding you with relief or forgiveness. Your behavior is guided by your values, not your desire to end your discomfort.

This ACT approach helps individuals manage stress and emotional challenges by embracing life's difficulties with openness. You are choosing to endure the discomfort of the repair process. You are doing this because your value—the restoration of safety and integrity—is more important than your immediate emotional relief.

This unwavering commitment, demonstrated through sustained positive action and radical transparency, is the only way to secure the new relationship. You are building structural integrity brick by predictable brick.

CHAPTER 6
BOOK 5 CONCLUSION:
SECURE YOUR NEW RELATIONSHIP

You have successfully navigated the most difficult phase of your self-improvement: the repair of broken trust. This work required the consistent application of every skill learned in the previous four books. You established internal control. You employed empathy to hear the pain. You used assertive language for clarity. You defended new boundaries for security.

Rebuilding trust is an active construction project. It requires time, radical accountability, and the sustained consistency of small, positive actions. The foundation of your new relationship is transparency and an unwavering loyalty to the healing process.

Your commitment to securing the new relationship relies on executing these five steps without fail.

Pillar One: Take Full Accountability for Your Actions. You accepted absolute, comprehensive ownership of the mistake. You owned the action. You owned the resulting damage. You separated your choice from external excuses or blame-shifting. You proved the flaw lay in a learned behavior, not a fixed moral defect. This full accountability is the first evidence of integrity.

Pillar Two: Offer a Meaningful, Non-Defensive Apology. You followed accountability with emotional validation. You offered a sincere apology expressing genuine regret. You committed to listening without defense or excuse. You used the empathy skills from Book 2 to accept the injured party's perspective and feelings as valid. This commitment to hearing the pain reinforces psychological safety. Research confirms that validation is a necessary component of emotional regulation.

Pillar Three: Practice Radical Transparency and Openness. You eliminated secrecy entirely. You committed to complete honesty in all areas. You answered all questions openly, enduring the discomfort of revealing the truth. This radical transparency eliminates the information gap that fuels fear and anxiety in the injured party. You clarify expectations and set clear boundaries for the new relationship. This openness is the necessary antidote to the shame and denial of the toxic past.

Pillar Four: Establish Consistent Trust-Building Behaviors. Trust is fixed by observable, measurable action, not by promises. You consistently showed up with reliability. You followed through with every commitment, large or small. You understood that due to the psychological principle of loss aversion, a single lapse in honesty has twice the negative impact of an equivalent positive action. You created trust-building rituals. This consistent action proves that your behavior is now predictable and safe.

Pillar Five: Stay Loyal to the Healing Process. You accepted the injured party's non-linear timeline for healing. You were prepared for their pain to resurface unexpectedly. You remained non-defensive when anger returned. You committed to sustained vulnerability. You recognized that you are building a new relationship, one that relies on continuous openness. You focused on fostering small, positive moments, actively creating a positive emotional tone to outweigh the past loss.

Securing the New Foundation

The cornerstone of the new relationship is predictability and integrity. By adopting assertive communication and firm boundaries, you provide the structural integrity needed to make the new relationship stronger than the old one.

Integration of Skills: The success of this book is the integration of skills from the previous four. The boundaries you set (Book 4) become the new rules of the relationship. Your assertive language (Book 3) is used to maintain transparency. Your calm control (Book 1) allows you to endure the pain of the apology without deflection. This integration is the definition of a non-toxic life.

The Role of Psychological Flexibility: Maintaining trust and stability requires psychological flexibility. This is the capacity to accept the reality of difficult emotions—your own fear, their lingering anxiety—while staying committed to your values of integrity and openness. You do not fight reality. You live by your values. This approach, central to Acceptance and Commitment Therapy, gives you the resilience to maintain the repair long-term.

The Enduring Commitment: The old relationship, based on compliance or control, is gone. You are now partners in maintenance. You must keep focusing on consistent actions. Trust is maintained daily. Your willingness to choose integrity over ego, transparency over comfort, and safety over speed, defines your new, secure relationship. This is not the end of the work. It is the beginning of a truly honest life.

Reflection Questions

1. Identify one measurable act of accountability you committed to implementing this week. Did you achieve it? Why or why not?

2. What is one new, specific boundary you discussed and implemented for the **new** relationship moving forward? How does this boundary directly prevent the specific betrayal from recurring?

3. List three commitments you upheld consistently this past week, no matter how small they were. How did following through on these small actions reduce your partner's anxiety?

4. Describe a moment where you listened to your partner's hurt without becoming defensive. What specific empathy skill (e.g., validation, silence) helped you most to endure that discomfort?

5. What steps are you taking to increase vulnerability in the new relationship structure? How are you sharing your internal struggles and fears without shifting blame?

CHECKLIST
SECURE YOUR NEW RELATIONSHIP

You are not seeking forgiveness right now. You are seeking to lay the foundation for safety. This requires focused action across five crucial stages. You must execute these steps sequentially and without exception.

I. Stage 1: Absolute Accountability for the Action

The first step is total ownership. Before any repair can happen, the psychological wreckage must be cleared. You must acknowledge the precise damage you caused. Any excuse, minimization, or deflection is heard as a secondary betrayal.

Did you commit to the following actions this week?

- **Owned the Action Unequivocally:** Did you use clear, first-person language to state exactly what you did? You must state the action without sidestepping the issue. Example: "I kept the debt secret from you for six months." You are the cause. You must own that fact. This separation of action from external context proves integrity.

- **Refused to Offer Excuses or Explanations:** Did you completely suppress the instinct to explain *why* you did it? You must understand that explanations—stress, fatigue, childhood history—are heard as deflection in this phase. Explanations can actually worsen the damage. Your only acceptable cause must be, "I made the choice, and it was wrong."

- **Acknowledged the Known Damage:** Did you acknowledge the severity of the betrayal without minimizing it? You must validate the impact. Example: "I know my action caused you intense fear and a complete loss of security." You must recognize the gravity of the betrayal. You must stop trying to make the pain smaller.

- **Maintained Present Focus on Your Transgression:** Did you avoid contaminating the discussion with old grievances? Did you stop introducing your partner's flaws or past mistakes? You must maintain the focus entirely on your specific violation. The other conversation can only happen much later, after safety is fully restored.

- **Identified the Attribution Type (Internal Check):** Did you reflect on why your action was wrong? Was it a violation of **Kindness** (you did not care) or **Integrity** (you lied or manipulated)? You must prove the flaw lies in a changeable behavior, not a permanent lack of character. Accountability is the first piece of evidence for this change.

- **Troubleshooting Accountability:** If you feel defensive, immediately take a tactical timeout (Book 1) and use self-talk. Say: "My job is to provide safety, not to feel comfortable right now." You are choosing commitment over your ego.

II. Stage 2: Offer a Meaningful, Non-Defensive Apology

Accountability clears the facts. The apology validates the feelings. This commitment to listening without defense is the most powerful action of vulnerability you can offer.

Did you ensure your apology was sincere and non-defensive?

- **Delivered a Sincere, Unconditional Apology:** Did you apologize **for** the action you committed? You must avoid using the conditional "if." You must not say, "I apologize *if* I hurt your feelings." Say: "I am deeply sorry that I violated your trust by lying about the finances. I know I caused you fear." You must accept their feeling as real.

- **Committed to Listening Without Defending:** Did you sit and actively listen to your partner's anger, sadness, and frustration without offering a single excuse? This is difficult. You must provide a safe space for them to process their pain out loud. Your silence and non-defensive posture are mandatory here.

- **Validated Their Emotional Reality:** Did you use reflective listening (Book 2) to validate their anger? Example: "I hear how much disappointment this has caused you. Your anger makes complete sense to me." You validate the feeling. You do not argue against the feeling. This acceptance is necessary for emotional regulation.

- **Prepared to Apologize Repeatedly:** Did you accept that they will experience pain in cycles? You must be prepared to offer the sincere apology whenever the pain resurfaces, acknowledging their ongoing hurt without impatience. You cannot pressure them to "move on."

- **Used Vulnerability as a Tool:** Did you consciously choose to endure the discomfort of hearing the painful truths about your behavior? This demonstrated commitment—showing up consistently and calmly to hear the pain—is the verifiable evidence of your change. This proves your commitment to integrity is stronger than your ego.

III. Stage 3: Practice Radical Transparency and Openness

Trust cannot be rebuilt in secrecy. Transparency is the action that proves the threat of denial is gone. You must eliminate the information gap that fuels fear and anxiety in the injured party.

Did you commit to the following acts of transparency this week?

- **Answered All Questions Fully and Honestly:** Were you prepared for probing, uncomfortable questions? You must answer them completely, honestly, and without showing impatience. Dodging a question or giving a vague response instantly reintroduces secrecy and triggers hypervigilance.

- **Eliminated the Defense of Privacy (Temporarily):** Did you accept the temporary loss of personal privacy? This may involve sharing access to communication channels or explaining your schedule in detail. You must offer this access as a **tool for safety**, not a punishment. This openness demonstrates that you have nothing left to hide.

- **Proactively Shared Information:** Did you wait for your partner to ask, or did you proactively offer information about your schedule or whereabouts? You must communicate openly to counter their hypervigilance. A proactive update signals that you are thinking about their safety, not hiding.

- **Avoided Creating New Trauma:** Did you provide clarity without offering unnecessary, excessive details? Honesty is essential, but you must avoid providing graphic details that could create new, unnecessary trauma. If a detail is requested, you provide it honestly. You do not volunteer painful information.

- **Asked for Future Verification Needs:** Did you ask what verifiable steps or boundaries are needed to prevent recurrence? Example: "What new boundary do you need me to commit to for you to feel safe regarding the finances?" This inquiry transfers some control back to the injured party, helping them establish emotional safety.

IV. Stage 4: Establish Consistent Trust-Building Behaviors

Trust is fixed by observable action, not by promises. Your long-term security relies on creating a new, predictable history. You must be relentlessly consistent.

Did you perform these actions with flawless consistency this week?

- **Flawless Follow Through on Every Commitment:** Did you keep every promise, large or small? If you said you would call at 7:00 PM, did you call at 7:00 PM? There is no room for forgetfulness in this phase. The smallest lapse can re-trigger anxiety. You must understand the principle of **Loss Aversion**: the pain of a failure is twice as powerful as the equivalent gain, meaning your consistency must be aggressively maintained.

- **Used Consistent Honesty in Low-Stakes Moments:** Did you practice radical transparency even when the truth was inconvenient or embarrassing? If you forgot to take out the trash, did you state the fact clearly without making excuses? This consistency in small, low-stakes moments is how the injured partner verifies your integrity.

- **Delivered a Measurable Act of Accountability:** Did you follow through on the specific, measurable action that directly counters the specific betrayal? Example: If the issue was lying about friends, you must commit to a verifiable action regarding your time with those friends. This measurable act provides tangible evidence of your change.

- **Established Predictable Trust-Building Rituals:** Did you deliberately maintain consistent habits that reinforce security? Did you set aside time each week for a meaningful, uninterrupted conversation? Did you maintain predictable check-in times? Predictability is the antidote to the anxiety betrayal creates.

- **Practiced Emotional Self-Regulation Under Pressure:** Did you maintain your consistency even when tired or stressed? You must commit to your values of honesty and reliability, regardless of internal or external pressure. Your consistent action conditions the injured party to associate your presence with safety, replacing the old association with fear.

V. Stage 5: Stay Loyal to the Healing Process

You must accept the reality that healing is non-linear. You are securing the new relationship by committing to the long-term process, not by demanding immediate relief.

Did you demonstrate unwavering loyalty to the healing process this week?

- **Accepted the Non-Linear Timeline:** Did you recognize that forgiveness will not unfold according to your desired schedule? You must hold space for your partner's ongoing hurt without applying subtle pressure to "move on." You choose loyalty to their process over your immediate comfort.

- **Remained Non-Defensive During Pain Resurfacing:** When your partner's pain resurfaced unexpectedly, did you remain calm and non-defensive? You must not view their resurfaced anger as a personal attack. You must view it as a symptom of trauma. Your job is to calmly endure the expression of that pain.

- **Focused on Fostering Positive Interactions:** Did you actively look for and appreciate small positive moments of connection? You must create a high ratio of positive to negative interactions. You focus on present efforts to reconnect, rather than dwelling on past betrayals. This acts as positive reinforcement for the new dynamic.

- **Practiced Psychological Flexibility (Acceptance):** Did you accept the reality of the lingering pain and the temporary lack of full trust? You must stop fighting reality. You are guided by the principles of **Acceptance and Commitment Therapy (ACT):** you accept difficult emotions while staying committed to your values of integrity and openness.

- **Committed to Sustained Vulnerability:** Did you continue to share your internal struggles and fears openly, without shifting blame? This continued emotional risk is necessary for building confidence and prevents the reintroduction of secrecy. This demonstrates that your commitment to integrity is paramount.

OVERALL CONCLUSION:
MAINTAIN YOUR NEW PATH

You have journeyed through five essential skill sets. You began with a toxic, reactive identity defined by explosive anger and denial. You end this collection as a person defined by deliberate action, emotional competence, and unwavering integrity.

Your transformation is not a promise. It is an operational reality built through consistent, measurable choices. You have replaced harmful, automatic reactions with deliberate, respectful responses. You understand that toxicity is not a fixed personality trait. It is a set of learned behavioral responses rooted in poor emotional management. You have installed the foundational skills necessary to maintain stability and repair deep relational damage.

The Five-Part Blueprint for Stability

Your stable life relies on the daily, integrated use of all five books. These skills do not operate in isolation. They form a unified system of self-control and relational integrity.

1. Control Anger (Internal Management): You established the internal structure. You learned that anger is a normal signal, not a mandate for attack. You mastered **Interception**. You recognized the physical warning signs—the racing heart, the clenched jaw—that signal the neurological takeover by the amygdala. You deployed **Physical De-escalation** (timeouts, controlled breathing) to restore rational thought. You conquered hostile thinking through **Cognitive Restructuring**. This process of gathering evidence against your own assumptions reduces hostility, a result consistently supported by clinical research. You redirected the energy of anger toward **Problem-Solving**, making challenges manageable instead of catastrophic.

2. Build Empathy (External Connection): You shifted your focus from self-preoccupation to genuine connection. You mastered **Attending Skills**—open posture, non-verbal feedback—to prove you are present. You avoided the illusion of understanding by **Rephrasing Content** and **Reflecting Feelings**. This act of emotional validation is crucial for regulating intense emotions in the speaker. You learned that non-judgmental acceptance of a person's reality creates psychological safety, allowing them to process pain without defense.

3. Talk with Respect (Assertive Clarity): You replaced blame with responsibility. You mastered the **XYZ Formula** (I feel X when you do Y, and I need Z). This assertive structure ensures your needs are stated clearly, respectfully, and without resorting to accusations. You learned that this language is necessary for relationship health. You understood that **Congruence** matters most. Your calm, low-pitched tone must align with your words, as non-verbal cues carry the majority of emotional weight in communication. You gained **Self-Respect** by stating your needs directly, without apology or guilt.

4. Set Boundaries (Structural Defense): You protected your time, space, and emotional energy. Boundaries are the operational defense system for your non-toxic life. You **Defined Limits** (physical, emotional, time) and recognized that these limits are essential for **Autonomy**. You learned to **Manage Discomfort**, tolerating the guilt that arises when you say "no," understanding that this discomfort is temporary. You learned that an unenforced boundary is merely a suggestion. You committed to **Implementing Consequences** (removable of your effort or presence) when limits are violated, understanding that this follow-through is an act of self-protection. This resilience is crucial for reducing burnout and maintaining self-respect.

5. Fix Broken Trust (Relational Integrity): You mastered the ultimate skill: rebuilding security after betrayal. You provided **Radical Accountability**, owning the action and the damage without excuse. You committed to **Consistent Trust-Building Behaviors**. This means following through on small commitments daily, creating a predictable history. You understood that trust repair is an exercise in **Psychological Flexibility**—accepting the injured party's timeline and pain without demanding immediate relief. By adhering to this disciplined, transparent path, you secure the new relationship foundation.

Action Plan Guide for the Road Ahead

Your continued success depends on daily maintenance and structured self-correction. Use this plan to govern your behavior moving forward.

Phase	Action Focus	Daily Maintenance Task	Quarterly Review Goal
I. Interception (Internal)	**Stop the Cycle**	**Check-in:** At noon and 4 PM, check your body for physical warning signs (tension, rapid breath). Deploy a 6-second controlled breathing exercise immediately if signs appear.	Review Anger Log. Ensure 80% of identified triggers resulted in a successful timeout or cognitive restructuring response.
II. Assertion (External)	**Clean Communication**	**XYZ Formula:** Use the complete "I" statement structure (X-Y-Z-Resolution) at least once daily when expressing a need or frustration.	Audit conversations for Contamination (using "always" or "never"). Ensure you addressed one issue at a time in all conflict dialogues.
III. Boundaries (Defense)	**Protecting Space**	**Refusal:** Practice saying "no" politely but firmly to one small, non-essential request per day (internal or external) without apologizing or justifying.	Verify Consequences. Check that the consequences for three key boundaries were implemented immediately and calmly when challenged.
IV. Empathy (Connection)	**Active Listening**	**Validation:** In your primary relationship, use Stage 3 listening (reflect feelings) once daily. Example: "It sounds like you are feeling overwhelmed because of X."	Review relationship happiness. Ensure you actively listened and validated feelings during all difficult conversations before offering solutions.

Phase	Action Focus	Daily Maintenance Task	Quarterly Review Goal
V. Trust (Integrity)	Building Security	**Small Commitment:** Maintain flawless follow-through on one small, specific commitment (e.g., calling at an exact time, specific chore) to build reliability.	Assess Transparency. Ensure no new secrets or half-truths were kept, and that you proactively initiated vulnerability once per month.

The Roadblocks to Anticipate:

1. **The Lapse:** You will lose your temper. You will violate a boundary. A lapse is not a collapse. Do not punish yourself. Immediately engage in **Self-Correction**. Return to your log. Analyze the failure point. What skill failed first? Re-engage the issue assertively.

2. **The Extinction Burst:** When you enforce a boundary or refuse to engage in an old toxic pattern, the other person's challenges may escalate temporarily. They may increase anger or guilt induction. You must anticipate this and remain **Unwavering**. Do not give in to the escalation. Consistency during the burst is the only way to solidify the new boundary.

3. **Impatience for Forgiveness:** You will want the pain to end. You will want your partner to forgive you immediately. You must accept that this is their process. Your job is sustained, humble commitment. You focus on controlling your own behavior, not their feelings. You choose loyalty to the healing process.

Your consistent commitment to these deliberate actions defines your new, non-toxic path. You are not defined by your past reactions. You are defined by your present choices.

APPENDIX:
CONFLICT RESOLUTION SCENARIOS

This appendix provides ten common conflict scenarios. The correct response applies the integrated skills from this collection: Control Anger (calm), Build Empathy (validate), Talk with Respect (assert), and Set Boundaries (enforce).

Scenario 1: The Interrupting Colleague

The Conflict: During a critical work meeting, a colleague, accustomed to dominating the conversation, repeatedly cuts you off mid-sentence, dismissing your ideas. You feel extreme frustration rising.

Skill Used	Action/Script	Principle Applied
Control Anger (Interception)	**Action:** You feel heat rising. Take a 6-second breath, focusing on the slow exhale. **Goal:** Prevent the aggressive outburst.	Interrupts the neurological cascade (amygdala hijack) and restores cognitive control.
Talk with Respect (Assertion)	**Script (XYZ):** "I feel **frustrated** [X] when I am **interrupted mid-sentence** during the meeting [Z]. I need you to **let me finish my thought** before you respond."	States need assertively without attacking character. Focuses on observable behavior.
Set Boundaries (Defense)	**Enforcement:** If they interrupt again, gently raise your hand to stop them, and repeat: "Please wait. I am finishing my thought now."	Reiteration without justification maintains the limit.

The Conflict: Your close friend is habitually 20 minutes late to social engagements. You feel angry because you perceive this as disrespect for your time. You have previously just sulked or made passive-aggressive comments.

Skill Used	Action/Script	Principle Applied
Control Anger (Cognitive Restructuring)	**Challenge Hostile Thought:** Stop thinking, "They are late because they do not value me." **New Thought:** "They are late because they struggle with time management."	Separates the action from malicious intent, reducing anger and hostility.
Talk with Respect (Assertion)	**Script (XYZ):** "I feel **disrespected [X]** when you **arrive twenty minutes late** to our plans [Z]. I need you to **send a text ten minutes before** if you are delayed."	Provides a measurable, positive path for compliance. [9]
Set Boundaries (Consequence)	**Consequence:** If they violate the limit repeatedly, state in advance: "If you are more than ten minutes late without warning, I will order my food without you."	Implements a consequence enforceable by you alone, protecting your time.

The Conflict: A family member calls you every evening to vent for an hour about the same unresolved job issues. You feel emotionally exhausted and drained, but feel guilty saying no.

Skill Used	Action/Script	Principle Applied
Set Boundaries (Define Limits)	**Internal Clarity:** Acknowledge your emotional limit. You are responsible for listening, not for solving or being drained by their problem.	Defines the emotional edge and prevents burnout (emotional exhaustion).
Talk with Respect (Assertion)	**Script (Time Limit):** "I have twenty minutes to talk right now, and then I have to go."	States a time boundary clearly and firmly, without using softening language or excuses.
Set Boundaries (Manage Discomfort)	**Self-Talk:** When the guilt arises, acknowledge it, but reaffirm: "I am choosing self-kindness. Saying 'no' is an act of self-respect, not a selfish act."	Tolerates the discomfort (guilt) to maintain the boundary, breaking the Guilt Cycle.

The Conflict: Your boss harshly criticizes your work, using generalizations like, "You always miss the key deadlines," even when your record is largely strong. You feel defensive and angry.

Skill Used	Action/Script	Principle Applied
Control Anger (Cooling Strategy)	**Action:** Do not respond immediately. Take a time-out. State: "I need to review those notes. I will come back to discuss this with you in ten minutes."	Creates distance to clear adrenaline and engage the rational prefrontal cortex.
Talk with Respect (Assertion)	**Challenge Absolute Language:** Do not argue the feeling. Focus on the facts. Ask: "Can you point to the specific deadline I missed this month, so I can review my tracking system?"	Eliminates absolute language ("always") and moves the discussion back to specific, observable facts.
Build Empathy (Reflect Content)	**Reflection:** "So, what I hear you saying is that the overall project felt delayed, even if my individual part was on time. Did I get that right?"	Checks accuracy and demonstrates listening, which de-escalates potential conflict.

The Conflict: You have committed a betrayal (e.g., financial secrecy). You offer a sincere apology, but your partner is still angry and attacks your character: "You are just saying that because you got caught. You are inherently dishonest."

Skill Used	Action/Script	Principle Applied
Fix Broken Trust (Accountability)	**Action:** Do not defend your character. Own the action that proved their perception. **Script:** "I understand why you feel that way. My choice to keep the debt secret *was* dishonest, and I am responsible for the pain that caused."	Takes full accountability and validates the perception, bypassing the defense mechanism.
Build Empathy (Non-Defensive Listening)	**Action:** Maintain open posture. Use reflective listening. **Script:** "I hear how angry and betrayed you are. Tell me more about what you need to feel safe right now."	Commitment to hearing pain without defense is the powerful action that rebuilds safety.
Fix Broken Trust (Transparency)	**Action:** Focus on the future structure. **Script:** "What one new boundary or verification step do you need me to commit to right now to prevent this specific issue from recurring?"	Transfers control and establishes clear expectation for the new relationship.

The Conflict: Your neighbor frequently shows up unannounced and stays for over an hour, disrupting your dinner routine. You have never said anything.

Skill Used	Action/Script	Principle Applied
Set Boundaries (Define Limits)	**Internal Clarity:** Acknowledge your need for predictable, protected time for dinner and family.	Defining your autonomy and setting expectations for mutual respect.
Talk with Respect (Assertion)	**Script (Positive Framing):** "I feel happy to chat, but I need our dinner hour (6:00 PM - 7:00 PM) to be protected family time. Please call me before you stop by, so I can give you my full attention."	States the request clearly and positively, giving a clear path for success.
Set Boundaries (Consequence)	**Enforcement:** If they show up unannounced again, use the physical boundary: "It is great to see you, but we are in family dinner time now. I have to let you go. I will text you later this evening."	Follows through consistently, reinforcing the limit with action.

The Conflict: Your spouse says, "You **never** listen to me. I **always** have to tell you three times."

Skill Used	Action/Script	Principle Applied
Control Anger (Cognitive Restructuring)	**Challenge Thought:** Do not focus on defending the "never." Focus on the feeling. **Script:** "I need a moment to process this. I feel attacked when you use the word 'never.'"	Avoids arguing the generalization and keeps the focus on the current emotional state.
Build Empathy (Reflect Feelings)	**Reflection:** "I hear that you feel **unheard** and **frustrated** right now. Is that correct?"	Validates their underlying emotion, which de-escalates the tension immediately.
Talk with Respect (Assertion)	**Script (Present Focus):** "I want to hear you fully right now. Can we talk about the **specific thing** I failed to listen to this morning, so I can fix it?"	Pulls the conversation back to one, manageable, present issue, avoiding contamination.

The Conflict: Your mother says, "If you loved me, you would come over to help me with the garden this weekend, even though you have a deadline." You feel immense guilt.

Skill Used	Action/Script	Principle Applied
Set Boundaries (Manage Discomfort)	**Internal Self-Talk:** Acknowledge the guilt, but reframe it. "This is the Guilt Cycle. I choose self-respect over fear of disapproval. My deadline is necessary."	Breaks the guilt cycle by acknowledging the "should" but choosing self-respect.
Talk with Respect (Assertion)	**Script (Firm Refusal):** "I understand you need help this weekend. I cannot come over this weekend, as I have a firm work commitment. I am available next Saturday."	Uses simple, firm language. Refuses to justify or apologize for the refusal.
Set Boundaries (Defense)	**Reiteration (Fogging):** If she presses, "But the garden will die," you respond: "I understand the garden is important to you. I still cannot come this weekend."	Acknowledges her reality without taking responsibility for the consequence.

The Conflict: Your partner, after an infidelity, asks you about your whereabouts and phone use several times a day. You feel annoyed by the constant questioning, but you know you must endure it.

Skill Used	Action/Script	Principle Applied
Fix Broken Trust (Transparency)	**Action:** Provide the information immediately and calmly. Do not show annoyance. **Script:** "I appreciate you checking in. I am at the library now and will be home at 5:30 PM. Did you need anything else?"	Provides verifiable evidence of safety and counters the fear of secrecy.
Fix Broken Trust (Loyalty to Process)	**Self-Talk:** Recognize that their anxiety is a natural response to the trauma you caused. Your annoyance is irrelevant. Hold space for their timeline.	Demonstrates unwavering loyalty to the healing process, accepting the non-linear path to repair.
Build Empathy (Validation)	**Reflection:** "I know these questions are hard for you to ask, but I am committed to answering them to help you feel safe."	Validates the need for vigilance, showing the cost of the repair is accepted by you.

The Conflict: You and your partner are arguing about how to handle a complex joint financial problem. Emotions are high, and you are generating poor solutions.

Skill Used	Action/Script	Principle Applied
Control Anger (Physical De-escalation)	**Action:** State a definitive timeout. "We are both too heated to solve this. I need a twenty-minute break to cool down. We will use that time to individually write down three possible solutions."	Separates problem-solving from peak emotion. Restores cognitive function before planning.
Control Anger (Structured Problem-Solving)	**Action:** After cooling, use the structure: Define Problem, Generate Solutions (Three each), Evaluate objectively.	Replaces the destructive cycle of chronic anger with a productive resolution cycle.
Build Empathy (Reflect Content)	**Action:** Before arguing solutions, use rephrasing: "So, your priority is paying down the credit card debt first, even if it delays the car payment. Is that correct?"	Ensures factual accuracy and confirms understanding of their solution priority before negotiation.

PART 2: HOW TO STOP BEING NEGATIVE, RUDE, AND HURTFUL 5-IN-1

The Complete Guide to Boost Positivity, Calm Anger, Speak with Kindness, Practice Gratitude, and Spread Respect

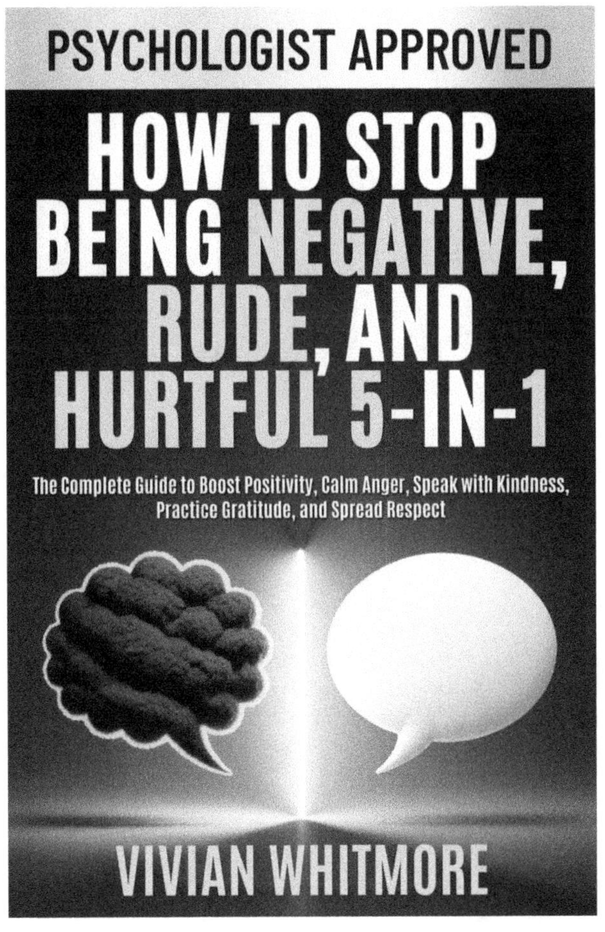

How to Stop Being Negative, Rude and Hurtful 5-in-1: The Complete Guide to Boost Productivity, Calm Anger, Speak with Kindness, Practice Gratitude, and Spread Respect

By: Carolina Estevez, Psy.D., Licensed Psychologist

How to Stop Being Negative, Rude and Hurtful 5-in-1: The Complete Guide to Boost Productivity, Calm Anger, Speak with Kindness, Practice Gratitude, and Spread Respect is an excellent multi-volume collection offering a thoughtful, well-structured, and clinically informed roadmap for personal growth, emotional regulation, and healthier interpersonal functioning. As a psychologist, I appreciate the author's clear integration of evidence-based techniques across cognitive-behavioral therapy, mindfulness, interpersonal effectiveness skills, and positive psychology. The five-book structure allows readers to explore change through multiple dimensions—thought patterns, emotional regulation, communication, gratitude, and respect— each reinforcing the others in meaningful ways.

Book 1, which focuses on rewiring negative thinking patterns, provides an accessible introduction to cognitive distortions, behavioral experiments, and attentional training. The incorporation of the HEAL method and emphasis on building agency align with current neuroscience findings on neuroplasticity and emotional learning. This section is an excellent resource for readers seeking practical steps to interrupt habitual negativity and establish healthier mental habits.

Anger regulation with a clinically grounded understanding of anger as both a biological response and an informational signal is discussed in Book 2. The chapters on breathwork, rumination interruption, problem-solving, and HRV tracking reflect modern approaches to physiological and psychological regulation. I found the discussion of hostile attribution bias particularly valuable; it is a common yet often overlooked contributor to chronic anger. The book's focus on reshaping the internal narrative around anger will resonate with many individuals seeking more adaptive coping strategies.

Book 3 shifts toward interpersonal communication, offering practical and research-supported techniques for speaking with clarity and compassion. The inclusion of Nonviolent Communication, assertiveness training through the DESC script, empathy development, and conflict repair provides a comprehensive interpersonal toolkit. This section is especially useful for individuals seeking to improve relationship satisfaction, as it captures both the mechanics of communication and the emotional attunement necessary for meaningful connection.

Gratitude, not as a superficial exercise, but as a clinically significant intervention with measurable benefits on stress, mood, and overall well-being is covered in Book 4. The emphasis on journaling, relational appreciation, and resilience-building is consistent with the positive psychology literature and offers readers structured ways to deepen their sense of meaning.

Finally, Book 5 offers a strong exploration of boundaries, fairness, respect, and values-based living. This book stands out for its clarity in explaining the reciprocal nature of respect and the psychological importance of healthy limits. The boundary scripts and reflections on integrity provide readers with actionable guidance for building healthier relationships rooted in mutual regard.

Overall, this collection is insightful, practical, and grounded in psychological science. It provides a holistic framework that readers can apply immediately while also fostering deeper self- awareness and long-term emotional growth.

INTRODUCTION
LAYING THE FOUNDATION FOR TRANSFORMATION

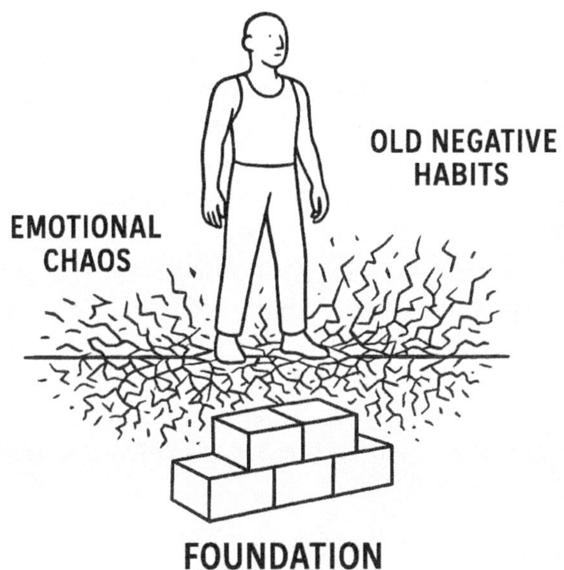

Let's be honest. You are here because the way you react to the world, the things you say, or the thoughts you carry are hurting you. You might feel a constant knot of tension in your shoulders. Maybe you carry a low hum of worry every day. Perhaps you snap at the people you love most, only to regret the words immediately after. That cycle is exhausting. It keeps you isolated and prevents you from living the genuinely connected life you want.

You might believe that negativity, short-fused anger, or habitual rudeness are simply character traits. They are not. They are deeply ingrained habits. They are predictable behavioral patterns rooted in your psychology and biology.

This guide provides a systematic, evidence-based plan to dismantle those patterns. We are not aiming for fake, forced optimism. We are working toward genuine, measurable, and lasting change. This is the complete operating manual for rebuilding your emotional life.

The Hidden Cost of Living Hostile

The way we talk to ourselves and others carries a high price tag. Chronic negativity and a habit of hostility actively diminish your quality of life. They create a wall between you and healthy social connections. When people engage in hostile habits, they often experience isolation and persistent psychological distress.

But the cost extends far beyond feeling bad. Research confirms that constantly suppressing or exhibiting chronic anger affects your physical health. People who habitually restrain or display intense anger face significant measurable risks. These risks include reduced social support, lower relationship quality, and a heightened susceptibility to conditions like chronic pain and coronary heart disease. Your hostility is not just a social friction point. It is a serious physiological issue that demands structured intervention.

The problem is often rooted in inflexible thinking. These are thought patterns that just don't bend, leading you to misinterpret others or catastrophize minor setbacks. These rigid habits become fuel for self-criticism and destructive behaviors. It is crucial to recognize this truth: the problem is a functional impairment, not a moral failure. The path forward involves both adjusting the mental software and improving the physical integrity of your brain's regulatory system.

The Science of Why You Feel Stuck

To fix these habits, we must first look at your brain. Our brains are not built for constant modern happiness. They are built for ancient survival. This means the brain has an inherent tendency toward caution and threat detection. It is called the negativity bias.

This bias means your brain is specifically wired to notice, learn from, and use negative information much more readily than positive information. This is an affective asymmetry. It served an important function long ago, helping your ancestors avoid danger. But today, this neurobiological default often fosters anxiety, perseverative thought, and depressive behaviors. Because of this hardwired tendency, developing a genuinely positive outlook requires conscious, structured effort. You must deliberately work to reverse this natural, ancient wiring.

Chronic stress and long periods of negativity compound this problem. This chronic state leads to negative neuroplasticity. We can actually observe this as a weakening of beneficial neural connections. It includes synaptic loss and neuronal atrophy within key regions like the medial prefrontal cortex (mPFC) and the hippocampus. The prefrontal cortex (PFC) is the key structure for regulating emotions. When these structures are damaged by chronic stress, your ability to regulate feelings becomes functionally impaired. You literally lose control over your impulses and moods.

Changing long-standing negative habits, therefore, requires two actions: adjusting your thought patterns through cognitive restructuring, and repairing the underlying neural structures through positive neuroplasticity.

A major reason you feel stuck is a psychological state known as learned helplessness.This is a conditioned loss of effort. It happens when you feel you have no control over repetitive stressors or failures, leading to deep hopelessness. Chemically, this feeling corresponds to a dampening of striatal dopamine synthesis.

Dopamine is the primary neurotransmitter for motivation and reward. When motivation diminishes, you experience burnout and inertia. Chronic exposure to psychosocial stress causes this dopamine dampening, effectively putting your brain's reward circuits offline.It is not a failure of willpower. It is a reversible brain state.

The Scientific Case for Immediate Action

The great promise of modern neuroscience is neuroplasticity. Your brain changes constantly based on your experiences and your mental habits. This means you have the power to actively overwrite negative emotional programming. This is why both pharmacological treatments and psychotherapies like Cognitive Behavioral Therapy (CBT) work.

They decrease the hyperactivity of the limbic structures, the parts that scream "danger", while increasing the regulatory power of the cortical structures, the parts that say, "Stop and think".

The immediate solution to feeling stuck is conscious behavioral action. When you perceive that your action produces a result, dopamine levels rise almost instantly. This rise restores the brain's reward circuit and affirms your belief in personal agency. This feeling of agency can return quickly. This foundational principle is the core of Action-Oriented Therapy: using concrete, purposeful actions to improve your well-being and overcome challenges. This entire guide is built on this principle. We use practical action to systematically restore motivation, confidence, and self-worth.

This comprehensive guide organizes your transformation into five interconnected, action-oriented systems. We start with internal repair and move toward effective, respectful external interaction. This sequence builds a solid psychological and neurological foundation for all future changes.

Book 1: Rewire Your Brain: Action Steps to Boost Positivity

The first book is about internal reconstruction. It focuses on dismantling negative self-talk and actively building new, positive neural pathways. We use the tested tools of CBT to target internal thoughts and beliefs. The goal is to identify and test the common cognitive errors: the irrational ways your mind twists reality. We move from fixed despair to objective, testable data. We then use Rick Hanson's HEAL method to systematically "take in the good," enriching positive experiences to promote joy, confidence, and inner peace. This practice creates measurable increases in happiness and self-compassion.

Book 2: Take Back Control: Techniques to Calm Anger Now

The second book focuses on immediate, physiological intervention. Before you can change an angry thought, you must calm the angry body. We restore calm using science-based bodily techniques that directly reduce physiological arousal. The 4-7-8 breathing protocol is a prime example.

This technique actively stimulates the respiratory vagus nerve, which counteracts the fight-or-flight stress response. We will teach you how to measure your calm using Heart Rate Variability (HRV), a physiological index of how well your body regulates itself. This book shifts anger management from a subjective feeling to an objective, self-monitored skill. It trains you to interrupt damaging rumination and replace the hostile attribution bias with rational thought .

Book 3: Connect Clearly: Actionable Models for Kind Speech

The third book addresses your external interactions. The aim is to replace damaging, judgmental language with clear, assertive, and empathetic dialogue. Rudeness is often miscommunication, where your intent is lost in your delivery. We introduce the foundational framework of Nonviolent Communication (NVC). NVC trains you to express your observations, feelings, and underlying universal human needs without resorting to judgment or blame.

This approach builds connection rather than conflict. We also introduce the DESC script for structured assertiveness, helping you ask for what you want directly and honestly while respecting the rights of others. Assertiveness reduces stress and boosts self-esteem.

Book 4: Build Inner Strength: Daily Habits for Practicing Gratitude

The fourth book focuses on deepening your emotional resilience. Gratitude is not just being polite. It is a specific, evidence-based psychological intervention. It serves as a therapeutic tool for addressing symptoms of anxiety and depression. Meta-analysis shows gratitude interventions lead to measurable improvements in mental health and positive mood. We explore how gratitude practices physiologically counter core stress hormones.

The practice reduces cortisol levels, which helps detoxify your stress system. It builds lasting internal resources by leveraging the clinical benefits of gratitude, including better sleep and increased resilience during hard times. We show you how structured journaling and appreciation letters build durable neural changes in the brain's social pathways.

Book 5: Define Your Space: Practical Actions to Spread Respect

The final book focuses on self-worth, boundary setting, and maintaining balanced, healthy social relationships. Respect is fundamentally about reciprocity. Social Exchange Theory confirms that relationships thrive when rewards outweigh costs and balance is maintained. This book helps you define your value and spread respect by demanding and giving fair regard.

We define boundaries as essential self-care practices that protect your mental health and prevent burnout . Using the communication tools from Book 3, you learn to set clear limits with conviction and care, ensuring your needs are met. This book provides the practical actions necessary to live your core values, which is the highest form of self-respect.

How to Use This Action Guide

This guide provides clinically validated methods in an accessible, direct format. The structure moves you from recognizing internal distortions to setting necessary relational limits. The efficacy of these methods relies entirely on consistent, deliberate practice.

Treat each book as a laboratory. You will test assumptions about your thoughts and behaviors. You must be willing to engage in the specific actions: writing in your journal, practicing the breathing techniques, and scripting difficult conversations. The sustained effort of applying these tools will physically shape your brain and redefine your interactions with the world.

Change begins with belief in agency. This guide proves that your actions matter, and they will produce results.

Deepening the Scientific Foundation: The Mind-Body Connection in Change

The success of this five-part system relies on fully understanding the continuous feedback loop between your mind and your body. Negative emotions are not confined to subjective experience. They are chemical and physiological states that require physiological intervention.

Emotional regulation depends on a continuous balance. This balance exists between the reasoning power of the prefrontal cortex (PFC) and the rapid, fear-based responses of the limbic system, specifically the amygdala.

When you are chronically stressed or angry, the limbic system is hyperactive. It overrides your PFC's ability to think clearly or rationally. This is why trying to be rational when you are furious just does not work. Your ancient brain takes over, prioritizing impulse over reasoned response.

This explains why the techniques in *Calm Anger* are foundational. The breathing exercises provide a direct, non-cognitive pathway to downregulate the stress response. By engaging the respiratory vagus nerve, you force your body out of sympathetic activation, the fight-or-flight state, and into parasympathetic activation, the rest-and-digest state. This physical calm is the necessary precondition that restores PFC function.

When you slow your heart rate and increase your heart rate variability (HRV), your body signals to your brain that the immediate threat is over. This physical peace creates the neural space required for the cognitive work in *Boost Positivity* and the structured communication in *Kind Speech* to be effective.

The gratitude practice from the fourth book, *Build Inner Strength*, actively reinforces this physiological calming chemically. Gratitude acts as a natural stress detox, measurably reducing levels of cortisol, the primary stress hormone. Chronic elevation of cortisol is known to contribute to the negative neuroplasticity seen in anxiety and depression. By consistently lowering cortisol through daily practices, you are chemically supporting your body's move toward emotional equilibrium. A chemically calm brain is ready for positive growth.

The Mechanism of Neurocognitive Repair

The methods in this book actively target and correct the rigid information processing patterns that define chronic negativity.

1. **Breaking Cognitive Rigidity:** Negativity and depressive affect are characterized by fixed, predictable biases in memory, attention, and interpretation. The core CBT tools, like the Triple Column Technique, directly disrupt this rigidity. By forcing you to actively seek evidence that refutes a negative, automatic thought, you practice cognitive flexibility. This simple exercise strengthens your executive function, which is often weakened by persistent hostility and negativity .

2. **Sensitizing to the Good:** The Positive Neuroplasticity work, using the HEAL method, deliberately sensitizes your brain to "the good". Because sensitization is a general dynamic in the brain, repeated, intentional focus on positive feelings gradually makes your brain faster at registering and retaining beneficial experiences. This process actively reverses the negativity bias from the inside out.

3. **Restoring Behavioral Control:** Reactive anger is often associated with poor executive function, specifically deficits in behavioral inhibition . The pause created by the 4-7-8 breathing technique is a direct act of behavioral inhibition. This pause, the space between a stimulus and your impulsive reaction, re-engages your PFC. When you combine this physical control with cognitive strategies like structured problem-solving (Book 2), you develop alternative, functional strategies for responding to conflict . Empirical studies have demonstrated that these structured programs significantly increase problem-solving skills and decrease anger levels. This is not just learning to suppress anger; it is learning competence.

The third and fifth books provide the mechanism for applying your internal changes to the outside world.

Kind Speech provides the language of connection. Nonviolent Communication (NVC) is the core tool here. It shifts dialogue away from blame and judgment, replacing them with expressions of universal human needs, such as safety, connection, or understanding. By focusing on these shared human needs, the conversation transforms from a hostile confrontation into a collaborative search for solutions. The use of NVC measurably increases empathy and reduces interpersonal tension.

This structured communication is the mechanism for *Spread Respect*, the focus of the final book. Respect must be reciprocal. Social Exchange Theory helps you audit your relationships, ensuring the emotional costs and rewards are equitable. Self-respect is the foundation for this exchange.

Setting clear boundaries, a core action in Book 5, is the practical declaration of self-respect. Boundaries are the limits you establish to protect your mental health, energy, and time. Setting clear limits actively reduces the risk of burnout and prevents chronic energy depletion . When you communicate these boundaries assertively, using the skills learned in *Kind Speech*, you clearly define your value in the social exchange.

The most profound outcome of this entire guide is achieving personal integrity. Integrity means your external behavior consistently aligns with your core internal values. When your actions match your principles, you achieve an unshakable self-respect that commands the respect of others. This internal consistency is the final, durable shift: you move from reacting to the world to living intentionally, defined by resilience and mutually respectful connections.

This complete, five-part system ensures that your change is sustained and fundamental.

System	Goal	Neurocognitive Mechanism
Book 1: Boost Positivity	Rebuild flexible thought.	**Restores PFC function,** reverses negativity bias.
Book 2: Calm Anger	Restore physiological control.	**Engages Vagus Nerve,** increases HRV, and inhibits impulse.
Book 3: Kind Speech	Create clear, respectful dialogue.	**Trains mPFC / dlPFC** for cognitive empathy and social processing.
Book 4: Gratitude	Build chemical resilience.	**Reduces Cortisol,** strengthens reward circuits (compassion / caudate nucleus) .
Book 5: Spread Respect	Enforce personal value.	**Establishes Integrity,** reducing stress caused by relational inequity.

This is your integrated action plan. It is time to start the work.

BOOK ONE
REWIRE YOUR BRAIN: ACTION STEPS TO BOOST POSITIVITY

INTRODUCTION
STEP OUT OF THE SHADOWS:
RECOGNIZING YOUR NEGATIVITY BIAS

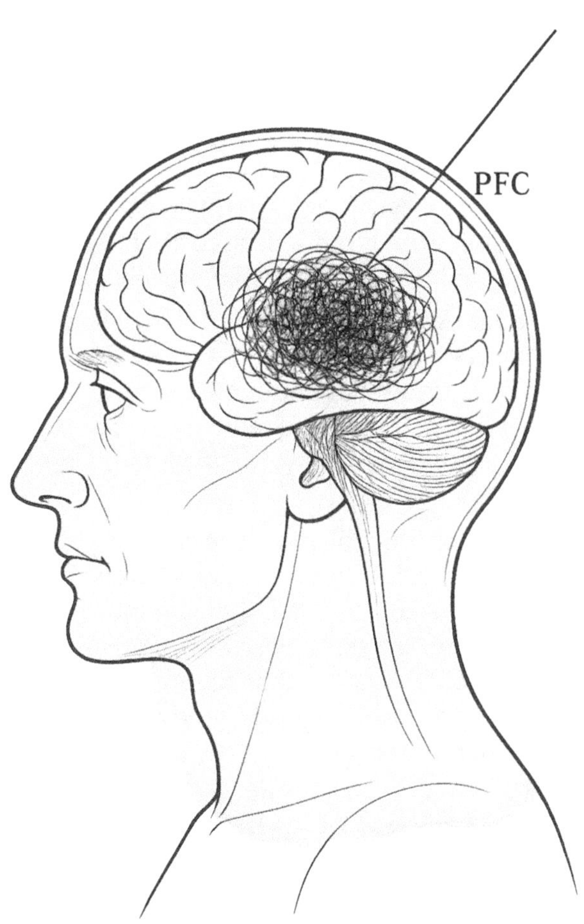

Let's talk about why you feel stuck in a loop of negative thinking. You've probably tried to "just be positive" before. Maybe you even told yourself to stop worrying. It did not work. This failure to simply choose happiness can make you feel weak or defeated. It can make you feel like negativity is a fixed part of who you are, a flaw in your character.

The truth is, your difficulty achieving a genuinely positive outlook is not a personal or moral failure. It is a predictable functional challenge. Your brain is not broken. It is simply wired according to an ancient set of priorities that no longer serve you.

This first chapter must change your basic understanding of your mind. You must realize that the problem is not *you*. The problem is the operating system running inside your head. Once you see the habit of negativity as a faulty program, you can begin the necessary work of rewriting the code.

The Biological Reality: Your Brain Clings to the Bad

The core mechanism driving constant pessimism is called the negativity bias. This is not a philosophical concept. It is a measurable biological default. Across various psychological situations and tasks, the adult brain exhibits an asymmetry: it has a propensity to attend to, learn from, and use negative information far more than positive information.

Think of your brain like a historian. If ten things happened today, nine good, one bad, your brain will spend more time reviewing the bad one. It learns more from it. It prioritizes the memory of it. This is why insults stick longer than compliments, and why criticism overrides success. Your brain is built with Velcro for the negative and Teflon for the positive.

For ancient humans, this bias was essential. Missing a positive opportunity, like a potential food source, was rarely fatal. But missing a threat, a poisonous snake, a predator, meant instant death. The negativity bias, therefore, served a critical, adaptive function, acting as an instant threat detection system that favored survival above all else. The brain that was overly cautious, worrying about every sound in the grass, lived long enough to reproduce.

In modern life, this mechanism is destructive. We live in environments where threats are chronic: financial stress, relational tension, work pressure, rather than acute, immediate physical dangers. Your brain, unable to distinguish between a deadline and a lion, activates the same hyper-alert, negative system. This sustained activation locks you into a state of anxiety and pessimism. It forces you to view your environment through a rigid, negative filter.

212

The Physical Toll of Chronic Stress

The belief that the world is dangerous and that you are inadequate to face it carries a high physical cost. Chronic psychological stress, fueled by the negativity bias, leads to measurable physical damage in your brain. This damage is known as negative neuroplasticity.

Studies show that chronic stress and depressive-like behaviors are associated with impairments in neuroplasticity. This includes observable neuronal atrophy and synaptic loss within key regions like the medial prefrontal cortex (mPFC) and the hippocampus.

Here is what that means in practical terms:

1. **Impaired Regulation:** Your emotional control center is the prefrontal cortex (PFC). The PFC is the wise leader of your brain, responsible for reason, planning, and regulating deep feelings. When stress damages the PFC, your ability to exert control, to stop, think, and choose a rational response, is functionally impaired.

2. **Hyperactive Alarm System:** Simultaneously, chronic stress causes the limbic system, particularly the amygdala, to become hyperactive. The amygdala is your brain's alarm bell. When the PFC is weakened and the amygdala is over-sensitized, the balance shifts. Impulse and fear override reason, leading to the rigid, inflexible thought patterns that characterize anxiety and depression.

You feel stuck in negativity because the physical structures necessary for flexible, positive thinking are temporarily weakened by stress. The goal of this entire book is to repair those structures and restore the PFC's rightful position as the regulator of your emotional life.

The Trap: Spotting Your Thinking Distortions

The negativity bias finds its expression in specific, predictable patterns of irrational thought called cognitive distortions, or cognitive errors. These are unhealthy thinking habits that fuel nearly all common mental health problems, including mood disorders and anxiety. They are not random errors. They are systematic ways your mind twists reality to fit your underlying negative assumptions.

The first step toward change is recognizing the structure of these traps. You must learn to separate the *thought* from the *fact*.

Common Thinking Errors:

Thinking Error	What it is	Example of the Distortion
All-or-Nothing Thinking	Seeing things in only extreme, absolute categories. There is no middle ground.	"I made one mistake on that report, so the whole project is a total failure."
Catastrophizing	Automatically predicting the worst possible outcome, believing the fear is fact.	"My partner is ten minutes late. They must have been in a terrible accident."
Mental Filter	Focusing only on the negative details of a situation while ignoring all positive ones.	You receive four positive reviews and one average review, but you only think about the average one.
Should Statements	Using rigid, moralistic rules about how you and others should behave.	"I *should* never feel tired," or "He *should* know better than to ask that."
Jumping to Conclusions	Interpreting events negatively without any definitive evidence. This includes mind-reading and fortunetelling.	"My boss didn't smile at me today, so I know she hates my work and is going to fire me."

When you believe these distortions, you fuel the negative cycles in your brain. For instance, when you engage in **Catastrophizing**, you are giving immediate, uncritical attention to a negative possibility. Because your brain is wired for threats, it treats that catastrophic thought as an immediate truth, intensifying the stress response and further weakening your emotional regulation.

The cycle sustains itself because these distorted thoughts become the fuel for chronic, negative mood states. Breaking this cycle demands a systematic approach. You cannot simply wish these habits away. You must scientifically test them and replace them with reality-based, balanced alternatives.

Why "Just Thinking Positive" Fails

Many self-help approaches ask you to simply replace a negative thought with a positive affirmation. This method often fails because it ignores the neurobiological default. When you try to force positivity, the fragile positive thought immediately meets the negativity bias, which is the stronger, better-wired system. Your brain rejects the affirmation as fake or inauthentic because it is not based on actual, experienced, felt evidence. The negative system wins, and you feel worse.

The path to lasting change must leverage **positive neuroplasticity**. This concept confirms that just as negative habits can weaken neural connections, repeated beneficial mental habits can build new, positive structures. Your mind has the capacity to actively change your brain over time.

This work is about deliberate, structured effort to override the default setting. It is about creating sensitization for the good. If your brain is built with Velcro for the negative, we must teach it to grow Velcro for the positive. This requires turning momentary positive experiences into lasting neural changes.

Your Action Plan for Rewiring Your Brain

This book provides a systematic action plan to perform this repair and override your brain's negative default. We move through specific, measurable steps, using clinically validated techniques from CBT and modern neuroscience.

1. **Observation (Chapter 2):** You will use the Triple Column Technique to stop blindly accepting your thoughts as truth. You will learn to isolate the *momentary* negative thought and correctly diagnose the specific cognitive distortion that powers it. This recognition externalizes the problem. It allows you to address the bias as a faulty program separate from your core self-worth.

2. **Testing (Chapter 3):** You will treat your worst thoughts as scientific hypotheses, not as fixed facts. You will run behavioral experiments to gather real-world data that confirms or disconfirms your extreme thinking. This empirical approach shifts your internal narrative from fixed despair to observable data, strengthening the regulatory function of your PFC.

3. **Absorption (Chapter 4):** You will actively work against the negativity bias by training your brain to "take in the good." We will use the HEAL method to enrich and absorb beneficial experiences, hardwiring them into your neural structure. This creates resilience and boosts inner strength.

4. **Activation (Chapter 5):** We tackle the feeling of learned helplessness by emphasizing purposeful, structured action. By setting small, measurable goals and focusing on the process, you will restore striatal dopamine function and affirm your belief in personal agency, fighting back against inertia and burnout.

5. **Focus (Chapter 6):** You will use mindfulness and specific cognitive exercises, like Loving-Kindness Meditation, to train your attention away from the inner critic and toward self-compassion and acceptance.This practice actively strengthens your emotional resilience and provides internal peace.

The overall goal is simple: to make calmness, positivity, and flexible thinking your new, accessible default response. This change is not achieved by reading alone. It is achieved by doing. Every chapter provides a measurable action step designed to produce a measurable change in your mood, thoughts, and physiological state. Your new life begins with the decision to take back control of your own mental operating system.

CHAPTER 1

IDENTIFY THE TRAP:
SPOTTING YOUR THINKING DISTORTIONS

If the first chapter convinced you that your brain is simply running on outdated survival software, this chapter gives you the precise tool to debug that code. You cannot fight an invisible enemy. You have to make the destructive thoughts visible, label them correctly, and neutralize them with reason.

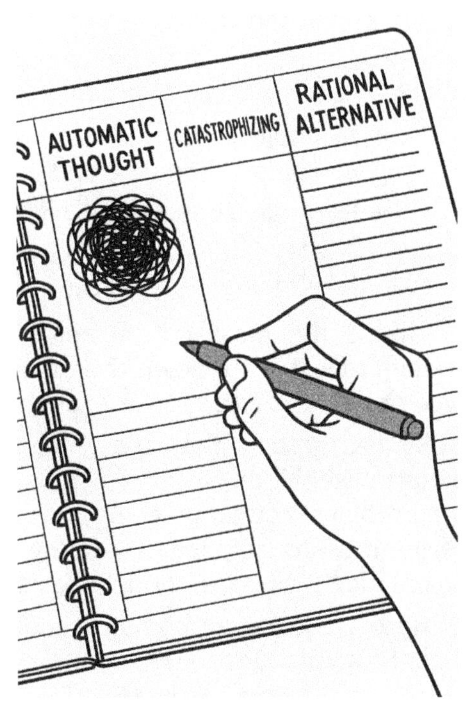

Most people treat their automatic thoughts, the internal dialogue that runs constantly, as absolute truth. If your brain says, "You messed that up, you always fail," you accept it as a statement of fact. This acceptance is the trap. These thoughts are not facts. They are predictable, repetitive, and often highly irrational errors in processing information, known as cognitive distortions.

Identifying these specific, faulty patterns is the absolute cornerstone of Cognitive Behavioral Therapy (CBT). Until you learn to recognize the structure of your internal critic, you remain its servant.

The Triple Column Technique: A Scientific Audit

The most effective, accessible tool for dissecting these destructive thoughts is the Triple Column Technique (TCT). This method, developed by CBT psychologist David Burns, provides a systematic way to challenge and correct your most damaging thoughts. It moves the process from vague feeling to structured, empirical analysis.

To use the TCT, you physically create three columns on a sheet of paper or in a document. The purpose of this structure is to force your mind to slow down and process the thought rationally, rather than emotionally.

Column 1: The Automatic Negative Thought

The first step requires you to document the specific, automatic negative thought (ANT) that just crossed your mind, often triggered by an event, a conversation, or a setback. Capture the thought exactly as it occurred, without editing it for politeness or reason.

The goal here is total honesty. This is what your internal critic is saying.

- **Example Thought:** "I will never get my finances stabilized. I am completely hopeless and will end up alone."

- **Example Thought:** "My suggestion was rejected. That means I have no good ideas and people think I am stupid."

Column 2: The Cognitive Distortion (The Diagnosis)

This is the most critical column for long-term success. It is not enough to just write down the thought. You must correctly *diagnose* the type of thinking error you are committing.

By recognizing that the thought follows a predictable, irrational pattern, like **All-or-Nothing Thinking** or **Fortunetelling**, you externalize the problem. You stop seeing it as a reflection of your worth and start seeing it as an instance of a faulty program running in your brain. This recognition makes the thought easier to dismiss as invalid.

Here are the most common and damaging cognitive distortions that fuel negativity:

1. **All-or-Nothing Thinking (or Black and White Thinking):** This distortion forces you to see everything in absolute, extreme categories. If a performance is not perfect, it is a total failure. If a person is not always kind, they are entirely bad. There is no middle ground, no gray area, and no room for human error or nuance.

   - *Why it is damaging:* It leads to intense self-criticism and prevents you from acknowledging incremental progress or partial success. It fuels feelings of hopelessness because perfection is an impossible standard.

   - *Example Diagnosis:* The thought, "I made one mistake on that report, so the whole project is a total failure," is **All-or-Nothing Thinking**.

2. **Catastrophizing (or Fortunetelling):** This is the automatic prediction of the worst possible outcome. It involves treating the most frightening possibility as if it were a certain, imminent fact. It gives immediate, uncritical attention to a negative possibility.

    o   *Why it is damaging*: It triggers the brain's ancient threat detection system. Your nervous system reacts as if the catastrophe were already happening, leading to sustained anxiety and preventing you from problem-solving logically.

    o   *Example Diagnosis*: The thought, "My manager asked to speak with me later. I know they hate my work and I am going to be fired immediately," is **Catastrophizing** and **Fortunetelling**.

3. **Mind Reading:** This error is the assumption that you know what others are thinking without any factual evidence. You project your own anxieties and negative interpretations onto others.

    o   *Why it is damaging*: It leads to unnecessary interpersonal conflict and self-sabotage. You react to your *assumption* of what they think, not to their actual words or intentions.

4. **Mental Filter:** This distortion involves focusing exclusively on the single negative detail in a situation while ignoring all positive elements. It is the definition of the negativity bias in action.

    o   *Why it is damaging*: It maintains the negative cycle by starving your brain of the positive data it needs to build resilience. If you receive ten compliments and one criticism, the **Mental Filter** ensures you only remember the criticism.

5. **Disqualifying the Positive:** This is an active rejection of good experiences. A positive event is automatically dismissed as a fluke, dumb luck, or something that "doesn't count."

    o   *Why it is damaging*: It prevents the necessary work of positive neuroplasticity. When you reject the good, you actively block your brain from learning from positive experience and changing its wiring.

6. **Should Statements:** These are rigid, critical rules you impose on yourself and others about how behavior *must* be. They often use words like *should, ought,* or *must*. When these rules are broken (as they inevitably are, because they are unrealistic), the result is intense guilt, frustration, and resentment.

o *Why it is damaging:* They eliminate flexibility and compassion. They set an impossible, moralistic standard that prevents you from accepting reality as it is.

7. **Labeling:** This involves attaching a fixed, negative label to yourself or others based on a single action or mistake. Instead of saying, "I made a mistake," you say, "I am a total failure."

   o *Why it is damaging:* Labels are self-fulfilling prophecies. They are global and absolute, defining your entire worth based on one imperfect moment.

By systematically identifying these errors, you gain distance from the thought. You realize: *This thought is not a truth. It is just an instance of the "All-or-Nothing" pattern.* This distance is where your emotional control starts to return.

Column 3: The Rational Alternative (The Correction)

The final step is to construct a balanced, factual, and rational alternative thought. This correction must not be a fake affirmation. It must be based on a cold, honest assessment of the evidence you have (or lack) in the real world.

This is the cognitive restructuring in action: replacing a stress-producing distortion with a balanced thought that does not produce anxiety.

To construct the Rational Alternative, you must ask yourself three key questions:

1. **What is the evidence that supports this thought, and what evidence refutes it?** Reviewing both sides forces a balanced, non-biased view.

   o *Focus:* Look for actual facts, past successes, or instances where the negative belief did not come true.

2. **Are there alternative explanations for this event?** Generate explanations other than the original, negative, and self-blaming one.

   o *Focus:* Could the manager have looked serious because they were focused on an urgent email? Could the friend have forgotten to invite you because they were genuinely busy?

3. **What are the realistic implications if the thought is true?** This question helps to determine the actual consequences, revealing that the outcome is rarely as catastrophic as initially feared.

- o   *Focus:* If the thought is true, if your idea *was* bad, what is the worst realistic outcome? You propose a new idea next week. You do not lose your job or your self-worth.

Practical Application: Using the TCT

Consistent application of the TCT disrupts the fundamental emotional pathways that fuel negativity. You must commit to using this as a daily habit, especially after high-stress or emotionally charged events.

Structured Practice Example

Column 1: Automatic Negative Thought (ANT)	Column 2: Cognitive Distortion	Column 3: Rational Alternative (Based on Evidence)
"My suggestion was rejected at the meeting. I have no good ideas. People think I am stupid."	**Labeling, Mental Filter, All-or-Nothing Thinking**	"It is true my idea was rejected. My coworker pointed out we lack the resources to implement it, which is an external factor, not a personal flaw. I often get complimented on my ability to think outside the box, and a few people even said they liked the concept. One rejection does not make me 'stupid' or mean I 'always' fail. I am capable and creative, and I will try a different approach next week."
"I missed my workout this morning. I am a lazy, undisciplined person and my health routine is ruined."	**Labeling, All-or-Nothing Thinking**	"I missed one workout, but I have gone five days this week. I am not 'lazy'; I am a person who sometimes misses a commitment. This routine is not 'ruined.' I will go this afternoon or start fresh tomorrow. I am disciplined most of the time."

Column 1: Automatic Negative Thought (ANT)	Column 2: Cognitive Distortion	Column 3: Rational Alternative (Based on Evidence)
"My partner hasn't replied to my text in two hours. They are deliberately ignoring me because they are secretly angry at me."	**Mind Reading, Catastrophizing**	"I do not know why they have not replied yet. They are likely in a meeting or driving. I felt anxious because I needed a connection, but I have no evidence they are angry. I will wait ten more minutes before I call. This is probably just a scheduling conflict."

Why Diagnosis Matters More Than Debate

The intermediate step, identifying the type of cognitive error, is the most crucial element for success. This is where the magic of CBT happens.

When you look at your thought and say, "Ah, that is just **Catastrophizing**," you immediately strip the thought of its power. You realize you are not facing an immediate threat; you are only facing a thought pattern. This recognition is why this technique is powerful for long-term change: it teaches you to catch yourself in the act of being irrational.

By recognizing the *pattern*, you are more likely to catch yourself and shift perspective. You stop paying uncritical attention to your inner critic and start treating it like a broken record player that keeps playing the same, old, inaccurate song.

Action Plan: Your Daily Cognitive Audit

To successfully rewire your brain, you must commit to a daily cognitive audit using the TCT.

Daily TCT Commitment:

1. **Capture the Worst Moments:** Carry a small notebook or use a notes app. Immediately after you feel a sudden surge of negative emotion, anger, anxiety, sadness, intense frustration, stop and capture the thought that generated the feeling in Column 1. Do this at least three times per day for the next week.

2. **Diagnose the Error:** Use the list of cognitive distortions to label the thought in Column 2. Try to find the single most accurate label, such as **Catastrophizing** or **All-or-Nothing Thinking**.

3. **Find the Facts:** Use the three guiding questions (Evidence, Alternatives, Implications) to build a rational, reality-based response in Column 3. The goal is to create a thought that is factual and therefore does not generate stress.

The sustained practice of this structured analysis actively weakens the rigid neural pathways associated with negativity. It restores your prefrontal cortex as the governing structure, allowing reason to regulate emotion. You are teaching your brain to prioritize reality over fear. This conscious, consistent effort is the first step in actively overriding the negativity bias and paving the way for positive, lasting change.

CHAPTER 2

RUN BEHAVIORAL TESTS: CHALLENGE YOUR WORST THOUGHTS

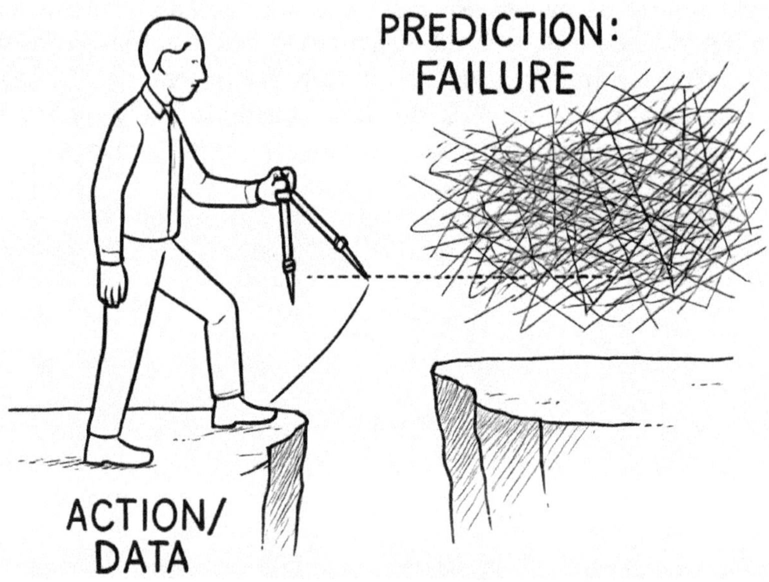

In the last chapter, you learned to stop accepting your thoughts as truth. You used the Triple Column Technique (TCT) to identify the specific errors: the **Catastrophizing**, the **Mind Reading**, the **All-or-Nothing Thinking** that fuels your negative emotional life. That was powerful intellectual work. You gained distance from the thought.

But distance is not destiny.

The next step is the crucial pivot. You must move from merely arguing with your thoughts internally to actively **testing** them in the real world. You have identified your faulty beliefs. Now you must treat them like a scientist treats a theory: **Thoughts are hypotheses, not facts.**

Your brain's negativity bias is a powerful, well-wired system. It will always win an internal debate against reason alone. To truly dislodge a core negative belief, you need undeniable, real-world data. You need to actively prove the old program wrong, and you do that through structured action called Behavioral Experiments (BEs).

The Flaw in Internal Argument

Why does simply debating with yourself often fail?

Imagine you firmly believe, "If I speak up in a meeting, everyone will think I am stupid." You can sit at your desk and argue: *That is a cognitive distortion. I have spoken up before. It is irrational to think I am stupid.* You might feel momentarily better. But the core belief is still active. The next time the situation arises, your body reacts with the same visceral fear, and the catastrophic thought returns with full power.

This happens because the belief is wired into your limbic system, your emotional core, and it has been reinforced thousands of times over years. Your PFC, the rational part of your brain, cannot simply override a deep, emotionally charged neural connection through logic alone. It needs empirical support.

Behavioral experiments are systematically designed tasks intended to generate that empirical evidence. They encourage you to gather data to confirm or disconfirm your extreme negative thinking. They are the most direct way to generate new, corrective experiences that your brain can accept as hard facts. This shift from internal argument to external, measurable action is what fundamentally changes your neural wiring.

Defining Behavioral Experiments

A Behavioral Experiment (BE) is a planned, purposeful action designed to test a specific, maladaptive belief about yourself, others, or the world.

Here is the essential distinction you must understand:

- **Pure Behavioral Exposure** aims to reduce emotional distress by allowing a conditioned fear response to extinguish. You repeatedly face a scary thing until you feel less anxious about it.

- **Behavioral Experiments** are explicitly designed to test the *accuracy* of a negative belief. The goal is cognitive change, the disconfirmation of the erroneous negative belief, using a real-world setting to collect data.

The power is in the design. You are not just doing a scary thing. You are designing a scientific task with a hypothesis, a methodology, and a plan for data analysis. The aim is to gather evidence that directly refutes the rigid, negative thought you identified in the TCT process.

Every effective Behavioral Experiment follows a structured, three-phase process. You must document these steps clearly.

Phase A: Articulate the Belief and Predict the Outcome (Hypothesis)

Before you act, you must write down the exact negative thought you are testing. Be specific. Global, vague thoughts ("I am a failure") are hard to test. Specific predictions are measurable.

1. **Identify the Core Belief (The Thought):** Go back to your TCT audit. Pick one distortion that consistently holds you back, such as **Catastrophizing** or **Mind Reading**.

2. **Formulate the Hypothesis (The Prediction):** State clearly, "If I do X, then Y will happen." Y must be the catastrophic outcome you fear.

Core Negative Belief	Hypothesis (Specific Prediction)
I am romantically undesirable, and people find me repulsive.	**Prediction:** If I ask someone I find attractive for a date, they will react with immediate disgust and disdain.
If I submit imperfect work, I will be immediately fired and humiliated.	**Prediction:** If I tell my supervisor I need one extra day on a deadline, they will angrily accuse me of laziness and threaten my job.

The clearer your prediction, the easier it is to measure the result. Assign a percentage of conviction to the prediction (e.g., "I am 85% certain they will be disgusted"). This provides a pre-experiment benchmark to measure the power of the disconfirmation later.

Phase B: Design the Test and Gather the Data (The Action)

Design a task that specifically targets the hypothesis in a safe, controlled way. The experiment must be achievable and directly challenge the belief.

1. **Design the Action:** What specific, measurable action will you take? *Example: If testing the fear of rejection, the action is asking one person out.*

2. **Define the Data:** What objective data will you collect? This is vital. You are not collecting *feelings*. You are collecting *facts*. *Example Data: The exact words the person used, their visible reaction, and the time the interaction took.*

3. **Plan for Safety/Mitigation:** What can you do if the outcome is negative? *Example: If they reject you, your mitigation plan is to immediately thank them for their time and walk away, upholding your self-respect.*

The action must be taken. This is non-negotiable. Even small, seemingly insignificant actions, like deliberately maintaining eye contact with three strangers for three seconds each, can be powerful tests against beliefs about social anxiety. You are actively gathering evidence to disprove the narrative of fear.

Phase C: Analyze the Result and Restructure the Belief (The Learning)

Once the experiment is complete, you must rigorously analyze the data you collected. This is where you use structured thinking to prevent the negativity bias from hijacking the result.

1. **Compare Data to Prediction:** Did the actual outcome match the catastrophic prediction? Be objective.

2. **Identify Disconfirmation:** Even if the result was negative (e.g., they said no to the date), did the *consequence* match the predicted *catastrophe* (disgust, humiliation)? A simple "no" disconfirms the predicted "disgust and disdain."

3. **Formulate the New Belief:** Based on the evidence, write a new, balanced, factual belief that replaces the old, distorted one.

Key Evaluation Questions for Scrutiny

During the analysis phase (Phase C), you use three key CBT questions to scrutinize the Automatic Negative Thought (ANT) against the real-world data. These questions force the brain out of the all-or-nothing trap and into nuanced, rational thinking.

1. What is the Evidence that Supports this Thought, and What Evidence Refutes it?

This is the central check for reality.

- **The Negative Thought (Hypothesis):** "I tried to delegate a task, and my coworker sighed. I am clearly an incompetent leader."

- **Evidence *For* the Thought:** The coworker sighed.

- **Evidence *Against* the Thought (Data):** The coworker immediately completed the task. They said, "Sure, I can do that." The sigh might have been related to the complexity of the task or an unrelated external stress (e.g., the heat in the room, their morning traffic). My manager gave me high marks for delegation last quarter.

Reviewing both sides forces you to hold a balanced perspective, acknowledging that the negative piece of data (the sigh) does not negate all the other evidence (the compliance, the competence history, the external factors). You use the facts to dilute the power of the feeling.

2. Are There Alternative Explanations for this Event?

The hostile attribution bias, closely linked to negativity, makes you assume negative, malicious intentions in ambiguous situations. This question forces you to broaden your perspective and stop jumping to conclusions (mind reading).

- **The Negative Thought (Hypothesis):** "My friend hasn't returned my text message. They are avoiding me because they are secretly angry at me."

- **Alternative Explanations (Data Review):** 1) They are in a meeting. 2) They left their phone charging. 3) They are driving. 4) They simply forgot. 5) They are dealing with a personal issue that has nothing to do with me.

By generating three to five realistic, neutral alternatives, you drain the emotional intensity from the original thought. The belief "They are angry at me" is no longer the only, or even the most likely, option. This move restores objectivity.

3. What are the Realistic Implications if the Thought is True?

This question directly attacks **Catastrophizing**. You assume, for the sake of argument, that the catastrophic thought is 100% true. Then you assess the *realistic* consequences.

- **The Negative Thought (Hypothesis):** "If I get a formal written warning from my job for being late, my career is completely ruined, and I will be homeless."

- **Realistic Implications:** If I get a written warning, I will be stressed. My career is not ruined; one warning is a chance to correct behavior. I am not at risk of immediate job loss or homelessness. The warning is a concrete signal to adjust my morning routine. I will feel embarrassed, but I will survive and fix the problem.

This process helps you determine the actual, manageable consequences, often revealing that the outcome, while uncomfortable, is not the terminal disaster you initially feared. You shift the focus from *fear* to *problem-solving*.

The Problem: David believes that when he attends a social event, everyone secretly judges his clothes, his job, and his quiet demeanor. He avoids making eye contact because he feels their critical gaze.

Phase A: Hypothesis and Conviction	Phase B: Designing the Test (The Action)	Phase C: Analysis and New Belief
Core Belief: Everyone at the party is critically judging me.	**Action:** David will attend a networking event for 30 minutes. His specific task is to make eye contact with five different people and ask them one neutral question (e.g., "How do you know the host?").	**Data Collected:** David made eye contact with 5 people. 3 returned the eye contact and smiled. 2 were focused on their own conversations and didn't notice him. 0 people pointed or laughed. The average interaction time was 45 seconds.
Prediction: If I look at people, they will recoil or openly stare back with contempt. **Conviction:** 90%	**Data to Collect:** Number of people who recoil / stare. Number of people who return a neutral / positive expression.	**Disconfirmation:** The prediction of contempt and recoiling was 100% disconfirmed. The actual data shows that people are either indifferent or slightly positive. The feeling of being watched was an internal projection (Mind Reading), not a factual occurrence.
	Mitigation: If he feels overwhelmed, David can retreat to the designated quiet corner for 5 minutes.	**New Belief:** "People at social events are primarily focused on their own conversations, not on judging my clothes. When I approach neutrally, I receive neutral or polite responses. My fear is a habit, not a fact."

The success of this experiment is *not* that David made five new friends. The success is that he disconfirmed the catastrophic nature of his prediction using empirical evidence. The data (three smiles, two people not noticing) directly refutes the thought "they stare with contempt." This correction is grounded in reality, making the new belief stronger than the old fear.

Application Case Study 2: Testing Performance Anxiety (All-or-Nothing Thinking)

The Problem: Sarah believes that because she needs help on a small part of a complex work project, she must be completely incompetent and will never succeed in her career.

Phase A: Hypothesis and Conviction	Phase B: Designing the Test (The Action)	Phase C: Analysis and New Belief
Core Belief: Needing help on a project equals total incompetence.	**Action:** Sarah will write an email to her most helpful teammate requesting specific assistance on one small component (a formula error in a spreadsheet). She must ask clearly and concisely.	**Data Collected:** The teammate replied 12 minutes later with the correct formula and added, "Thanks for asking, that formula is tricky." The supervisor was CC'd and did not reply at all. No one mentioned incompetence or laziness.
Prediction: If I ask for help, my teammate will call me incompetent, and my supervisor will lose all respect for me. **Conviction:** 75%	**Data to Collect:** Exact words of the teammate's response. Supervisor's visible reaction (if any). Time delay in response.	**Disconfirmation:** The prediction of being called incompetent and losing respect was completely disconfirmed. The actual data shows that asking for help was a normalized, non-catastrophic exchange that resulted in a solution. The negative outcome (total incompetence) did not occur.

	Mitigation: If the teammate responds negatively, Sarah will remind herself that one rude response does not define her entire career or the entire team.	**New Belief:** "Asking for specific help on a small, tricky component of a project is normal, competent behavior that leads to effective problem-solving. My competence is defined by the full project delivery, not one formula error."

The most important takeaway here is the cognitive shift. Sarah moves from the catastrophic belief ("I am incompetent") to the factual statement ("This formula is tricky"). She used action to prove that imperfection is not failure, disarming the **All-or-Nothing Thinking** that paralyzed her.

The Neuroplastic Power of Disconfirmation

You must understand why this action-oriented process is so effective at rewriting your brain's negative default.

Every time you successfully disconfirm a negative belief with real-world data, you weaken the neural connection that holds that belief. The initial connection (e.g., *speaking up = danger*) is a rigid pathway that has been reinforced over time. When you perform a Behavioral Experiment and the catastrophic outcome does not occur, your brain registers a cognitive error. The prefrontal cortex (PFC), your regulator, uses this objective data to challenge the validity of the old fear-based pathway.

- **Weakening the Old:** The old neural circuit linking the trigger (speaking up) to the catastrophic result (humiliation) weakens. The signal along that rigid path becomes less reliable.

- **Strengthening the New:** A new pathway is strengthened: the one linking the trigger (speaking up) to the factual, non-catastrophic result (solution, indifference, or a neutral response).

This is the power of empirical action. You are not just talking yourself out of a feeling. You are structurally changing the way your brain processes information, restoring the PFC's ability to exert reasoned, top-down control over the fear-processing limbic system. This is how you escape rigidity and cement genuine, lasting positive change.

You now possess the tools to audit your inner dialogue and challenge your fear-based beliefs. The TCT helped you label the enemy. The Behavioral Experiment forces you to defeat it with reality.

The entire foundation of emotional mastery rests on this empirical process. You must be willing to act, to risk a manageable failure, in service of gathering the objective data that will free you from the internal prison of negativity. The goal is to make the rational, balanced thought your most reliable, well-wired default response.

Your sustained, deliberate effort in applying these tools will shape your brain and make true, resilient positivity possible. The next step is learning how to actively capture and enrich the positive experiences that result from this new, confident action.

CHAPTER 3
FEEL THE GOOD: PRACTICING THE HEAL METHOD

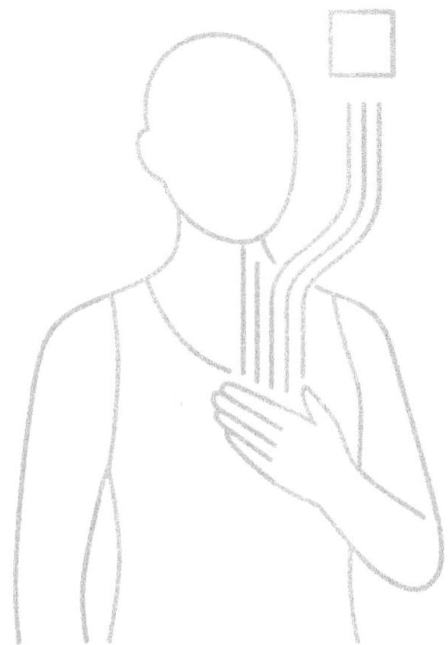

You have successfully learned to stop the bad. You used the Triple Column Technique (TCT) to identify the negative thought patterns, and you used Behavioral Experiments (BEs) to prove those fears wrong with real-world data. You now know that your catastrophic thinking is often irrational.

But simply removing the bad leaves an empty space. If you do not actively replace the old negative wiring with new, robust positive wiring, the old default system will eventually creep back in. Remember, your brain is still wired for the negativity bias; it clings to the bad and lets the good slide right off. We must fix this fundamental asymmetry.

This chapter introduces the science of *positive neuroplasticity*. It gives you a direct, actionable method to sensitize your brain to positive experiences and convert fleeting good moments into lasting emotional resources. This process is how you finally grow the "Velcro" for the positive feelings you want to keep.

The Problem: Teflon for the Good

Most people experience small, good moments every day: the comfort of a warm drink, a moment of connection with a friend, a small success at work, or a few minutes of quiet peace. We often notice these moments for a second, maybe two, and then our minds immediately jump back to a pressing problem, a worry, or a recent failure.

When this happens, you lose the opportunity to train your brain. For an experience to transition from short-term memory to long-term emotional storage, for it to become part of your emotional resource bank, it needs sustained attention. Because the negativity bias is so powerful, the brief positive moments are quickly filtered out and discarded, while the brain focuses intensely on perceived threats or losses.

Psychologist Rick Hanson's HEAL method is a practical, accessible, and evidence-based approach designed specifically to counteract this problem. It uses the power of your own mind to deliberately shape your brain over time through repeated positive mental habits. The goal is simple: turn states of mind into lasting, beneficial *traits*.

Early studies assessing this intervention found that people who used this method reported statistically significant self-reported improvements in happiness, resilience, savoring, and self-compassion. These results were often sustained for months, providing strong evidence that this technique fosters real, lasting neural change that builds emotional well-being.

The HEAL Protocol: Four Steps to Hardwire Happiness

The HEAL protocol involves four specific, actionable steps. You must dedicate a small amount of intentional time each day to move a positive experience through this sequence.

Step 1: Have a Good Experience (H)

The first step is simply noticing or creating a beneficial experience in daily life. This is not about finding a profound, life-altering moment. It is about registering small, everyday events that generate a feeling of contentment, connection, safety, or satisfaction.

Action Focus:

- **Look for the Small Wins:** Did you finish a difficult task? Did you manage to hold your tongue when you were provoked? Did a colleague genuinely thank you for your help?

- **Notice Sensory Comfort:** Focus on the simple experience of physical comfort: the feeling of warm water on your hands, the taste of a good meal, the sun on your skin, or the ease of soft clothing.
- **Acknowledge Inner Strength:** Recognize a momentary feeling of internal competence, moral clarity, or self-respect. If you successfully maintained a boundary from Book 5, that is a good experience to capture.

This step is an act of deliberate, positive selective attention. If you know you are going to record and enrich a positive moment, your brain naturally starts to scan your environment for those good things throughout the day, actively overriding the mental filter that usually focuses only on the negative.

Step 2: Enrich It (E)

This is the most crucial part of the process. Once you have a good experience, you must intensify and extend the positive thoughts and feelings associated with it. You are actively feeding the good experience to your brain's long-term memory system.

Action Focus:

- **Intensify the Feeling:** If the feeling is contentment, make it stronger. If it is pride, let yourself fully own that feeling of competence. Do not intellectualize it; *feel* it.
- **Focus on Sensory Details:** What are the sights, sounds, smells, and physical sensations connected to the experience? If you are enjoying a good conversation, notice the quality of the light, the tone of the other person's voice, and the relaxed feeling in your chest.
- **Extend the Time:** You must actively focus on the experience and its associated feeling for 10 to 30 seconds. This is the neurological consolidation time. Brief flashes of positive emotion are not enough; the sustained focus ensures the experience is registered as durable data by your neural structures.

The goal of this step is to move the positive experience from a fleeting event to a robust, rich, and detailed memory that is ready to be hardwired. This conscious dwelling prevents the Teflon effect.

Step 3: Absorb It (A)

In this phase, you intentionally allow the positive feeling to sink into your entire physical being. You move the experience from a thought in your head to a sensation in your body.

Action Focus:

- **Involve the Body:** Visualize the positive feeling; the warmth, the satisfaction, the peace, sinking deep into your core. Imagine it soaking into your chest, your heart, and your limbs.

- **Feel the Weight:** Notice where you feel the positive shift physically. Is there a softening in your jaw? A relaxation in your shoulders? A gentle warmth in your chest? Allow this physical sensation to build a lasting sense of contentment and self-compassion.

- **Let It Become You:** The goal is to merge the positive experience with your perception of self-worth and inner resources. It is not just "I saw a nice sunset." It is, "I am a person who is capable of feeling this deep sense of peace."

This step directly counteracts the negative neuroplasticity that chronic stress creates. By intensely and repeatedly focusing on positive feelings, you are strengthening the neural connections in your medial prefrontal cortex (mPFC), helping to repair the damage caused by chronic anxiety and self-judgment. You are actively restoring the physical integrity of your emotional regulatory system.

Step 4: Link It (L) - The Overriding Mechanism

This optional but powerful step moves the HEAL method into corrective therapy. The Linking step uses the newly absorbed positive strength to actively desensitize an older, milder negative experience or feeling.

This technique uses the new positive wiring to override the old negative wiring.

Action Focus:

- **Access the Negative:** Briefly recall a persistent, mild negative feeling, perhaps a small, lingering self-criticism or a minor anxiety about a future event. Do not choose an overwhelming trauma. Keep it small and manageable.

- **Bring the Positive to Bear:** Now, bring the rich, absorbed positive feeling (from Step 3) back to the forefront. Let the strong, positive sensation surround and integrate with the negative feeling.

- **Maintain Asymmetry:** The critical rule is that the positive feeling must always remain **"bigger and more powerful"** than the negative experience. If the negative feeling starts to overwhelm the positive one, immediately drop the negative focus and return to enriching the positive feeling (Step 2) until it is fully stable again.

This linkage gradually desensitizes your brain to the negative pattern, proving that the old feeling is not the only reality. You are teaching your neural pathways that the positive experience can successfully buffer, contain, and override the stress of the negative one. This is how you change a negative memory from one that drains your energy to one that is neutral or contained.

The Neuroplastic Power of Deliberate Savoring

The effectiveness of the HEAL method lies in its deliberate, sustained focus, which we call savoring. Savoring is the intentional act of prolonging and amplifying positive emotion. When you savor an experience for 20 seconds, you are activating and reinforcing the neural circuits associated with that positive emotion.

This process creates a functional change in your brain's structure:

1. **Strengthening the Regulator:** You are actively increasing the function of the PFC (your rational regulator) by giving it the job of focusing and sustaining attention on a positive stimulus. This top-down control strengthens its ability to manage impulse and fear.

2. **Sensitizing the Reward System:** By repeatedly enriching and absorbing positive feelings like contentment and self-compassion, you are sensitizing your brain's reward circuits. You are making your brain more responsive to happiness and less reliant on external threats to grab its attention.

This training moves you toward a state of *metaplasticity*, an activity-dependent, persistent change in the neural state that shapes the direction, duration, and magnitude of future synaptic change. In simple terms, you are not just making yourself happy today. You are making yourself more capable of happiness tomorrow.

To successfully integrate positive neuroplasticity, you must commit to a daily practice. This should be done multiple times per day for short, intense bursts, not one long, abstract session.

1. **Set Your Intention:** Decide you will HEAL three small experiences today, one during your morning routine, one during the workday, and one in the evening.

2. **Execute the Steps:** When a positive moment occurs:
   - **H (Have it):** Notice it immediately.
   - **E (Enrich it):** Focus on the physical feeling and the sensory details for at least 15 seconds. Make it intense.
   - **A (Absorb it):** Visualize the feeling sinking deep into your body and becoming part of your inner strength.

3. **Use Linking Strategically:** Use the Linking step only when you have a strong, contained positive feeling and you are targeting a very mild, manageable negative thought or memory. Always prioritize strengthening the positive feeling first.

By applying the HEAL method, you stop relying on luck or circumstance for your mood. You seize control of the information that enters your brain, ensuring that every small success, comfort, or moment of peace is absorbed and converted into durable, resilient inner strength. You are no longer just surviving your life. You are actively building your mind.

CHAPTER 4

BUILD YOUR AGENCY:
USE ACTION TO CREATE HOPE

You have done the foundational work. You have identified the cognitive traps using the TCT, and you have started testing those false beliefs against reality using Behavioral Experiments. You are now intellectually aware of your negativity bias.

But knowledge alone does not guarantee freedom.

Most people reach this point and stop. They understand the patterns but still cannot seem to *act*. They recognize the illogical nature of their fear, yet they remain immobilized by inertia, procrastination, and a profound sense of "stuckness."

This is the central issue we address now: the collapse of motivation. If you feel immobilized, if you constantly struggle to start tasks or feel an overwhelming sense of futility, you are experiencing a state called **learned helplessness**. It is a condition of conditioned loss of effort that is rooted in your neurochemistry, not your character.

This chapter is the instruction manual for overriding that feeling. The scientific solution is simple and profound: **Action restores hope.** We use deliberate, purposeful action to chemically restore your brain's motivation and reward circuit, fundamentally reversing learned helplessness. You will learn to use structured action as your primary psychological intervention.

The Neuroscience of Inertia: When Dopamine Drops

We must first look beneath the feeling of low motivation. The sense of inertia, burnout, and hopelessness you feel is directly linked to chronic exposure to psychosocial stress or adversity.

When you face repeated stressors, such as financial instability, relational conflict, and constant self-criticism, without perceiving any control over them, the brain registers a profound lack of agency. This perception of futility has a measurable chemical result: **dampened striatal dopamine synthesis**.

1. **The Reward Circuit Goes Offline:** Dopamine is the critical neurotransmitter associated with motivation, pleasure, and reward. It is the "wanting" signal that pushes you to seek goals and solve problems. The striatum is the key area for motivation and reward.

2. **Stress Silences Motivation:** Long-term exposure to stress or adversity causes the brain to make less dopamine in the striatum. When the brain's reward circuits go offline, motivation and interest diminish. This is exactly what burnout feels like. You do not lack willpower; you lack the necessary neurochemical drive to start.

3. **Learned Helplessness Takes Hold:** This state describes the conditioned loss of effort. Even when an opportunity for success or escape presents itself, the brain remains still, stuck in learned inertia because it believes that effort will not produce a result.

The paralysis you feel is a reversible brain state. It is a chemical pattern that has taken hold due to overwhelming stress, not a permanent failure of your inner drive.

The Reversal: Action Restores Agency

The solution to learned helplessness is behavioral activation. You must engage in consistent, purposeful action that produces a real, observable result.

The mechanism for recovery is rapid and direct. When you take an action and perceive that your output yields a result, a successful step toward a goal, dopamine levels in the ventral tegmental area (VTA) rise almost immediately. This chemical affirmation reinforces your belief in personal agency: *What I do matters.* This immediate feedback loop restores the brain's reward circuit and affirms that effort is worthwhile.

This principle is the foundation of **Action-Oriented Therapy**. This approach is evidence-based and emphasizes taking concrete, specific actions to improve well-being and overcome challenges.

- **Move Beyond Talk:** Action-oriented therapy goes beyond traditional talk therapy. It focuses on identifying negative patterns and beliefs, then immediately encourages the client to take *specific actions* that lead to positive change.

- **The Empowerment Loop:** Taking purposeful action, whether small or large, creates an immediate sense of empowerment and confidence in your ability to shape your life. For individuals prone to procrastination or feeling immobilized, this practical, solution-focused method is highly effective.

The change you are seeking is generated when you move from intellectual contemplation to physical, measurable action. You are not waiting to feel motivated before you act. You are acting *to generate* motivation.

The Toolkit: Structured Goal Setting for Momentum

To ensure your action successfully generates the necessary dopamine response, it must be structured and measurable. Vague goals like "be better" or "be happier" are useless. They do not provide the brain with the clear signal needed to register success.

The standard for setting goals that generate momentum is the **SMART** framework. These goals are designed to be practical, solution-focused, and, crucially, measurable to affirm agency.

1. Specific: Define Exactly What You Will Do

The action must be precisely defined. Avoid ambiguity. The brain needs a clear finish line to celebrate the successful effort.

- *Vague:* "I will work on my finances."

- *Specific:* "I will spend 30 minutes on Tuesday evening creating a budget spreadsheet and logging my expenditures from the last two weeks."

2. Measurable: Quantify the Effort and Result

The action must have a number attached to it, time, duration, quantity, or frequency. This allows the brain to register objective success, which triggers the dopamine reward.

- *Vague:* "I will start writing my paper."
- *Measurable:* "I will write one full page (approximately 300 words) of my paper today before 5:00 PM."

3. Attainable: Start Small to Guarantee Success

This is the most critical step for reversing learned helplessness. Your initial actions must be intentionally small and easily achievable. You are not aiming for your life's greatest achievement; you are aiming for a guaranteed win.

The problem with feeling stuck is that the brain believes failure is guaranteed. You must override this belief with repeated, undeniable success.

- If your core goal is to clean your entire apartment, your attainable action is to spend **ten minutes cleaning only the kitchen counter**.
- If your core goal is to start running, your attainable action is to **put on your running shoes and walk outside for five minutes**.

These small, purposeful actions immediately trigger dopamine release and restore agency. They affirm that your effort can, in fact, produce a result, no matter how small. This restores motivation and builds the momentum required for larger tasks later.

4. Relevant: Align Action with Core Values

The action must align with a deeper, core reason for change, the personal values that guide your decisions (as we will explore in Book 5). When action is relevant to your self-respect or health, the reward is greater.

- *Action:* "I will spend 45 minutes organizing my chaotic desk."
- *Relevance:* "I am doing this because order promotes mental clarity, and mental clarity aligns with my core value of competence and focus."

5. Time-based: Set a Clear Deadline

Set a definitive start and finish time for the task. This creates a structure and reduces the cognitive load associated with decision-making. Knowing when the effort stops makes starting easier.

- *Action*: "I will review my emails and flag the three most urgent ones."
- *Time-based*: "I will complete this review by 9:30 AM today."

The Momentum Engine: Targeting the Positive Affect System

The benefits of structured action extend beyond simply completing tasks. Action is a powerful tool for generating positive emotion and fundamentally changing how you feel.

Targeting the positive affect system through structured action generates substantial improvements in positive emotions and overall well-being. Research shows that multicomponent psychological interventions focused on positive affect are highly beneficial. They generate improvements in positive emotions and well-being, while simultaneously reducing negative affect and symptoms of anxiety or depression.

How Action Boosts Affect:

1. **Sense of Accomplishment**: Completing a task, even a small one, is an objective success. This feeling of competence directly counters the feelings of inadequacy and hopelessness that fuel learned helplessness.

2. **Interruption of Rumination**: When you are engaged in active, structured problem-solving, you are physically unable to dwell on negative rumination. Rumination, the repetitive focus on a stressful event, physiologically sustains your body's stress response, predicting slower heart rate recovery and heightened anxiety. Action forces your brain to shift its focus from replaying the past to constructively engaging with the present.

3. **Physical Release**: Action is often physical. Even organizing a desk or taking a five-minute walk releases tension and redirects energy that might otherwise be stored as stress or irritability.

By integrating action into your recovery, you are providing your brain with the corrective experience it needs to rebuild its reward system. This process is solution-focused, practical, and highly effective for individuals who previously felt paralyzed by procrastination or sadness.

Action Plan: Generating Hope Through Small Wins

Your task now is to design and execute three small, high-leverage actions this week. These actions must be designed to guarantee a success, no matter how minor, to rebuild your dopamine feedback loop.

Step 1: Identify an Inertia Point

Where do you consistently feel stuck? Is it initiating work? Starting a conversation? Cleaning a specific area? Choose one small area where the feeling of helplessness is strong.

- *Example Inertia Point:* I keep putting off responding to one specific, annoying email.

Step 2: Apply the SMART Framework

Turn the inertia point into a guaranteed win.

SMART Element	Application	Result
Specific	Write the draft email reply outlining the next steps.	A completed draft.
Measurable	I will spend **15 minutes max** on this task.	Time boxed effort.
Attainable	I will only draft it; I do not have to send it yet.	Low pressure, high completion chance.
Relevant	This action aligns with my value of **professional competence** and **clarity**.	Increased self-respect.
Time-based	I will start at 4:00 PM today.	Clear start time.

Step 3: Track the Neurochemical Result

After you complete the 15-minute action, pause and engage in immediate self-reflection:

1. **Assess Agency:** On a scale of 1 to 10 (10 being high), how strongly do you believe your effort produced a tangible result? (The number should be high.)
2. **Note Physical Shift:** Where did you feel the shift in your body? Was the knot in your stomach a little looser? Did your mind feel quieter?
3. **Acknowledge Dopamine:** State the success clearly: "I successfully started and completed the draft email within the time limit. My effort worked. I restored agency."

This deliberate acknowledgment of the small win is what cements the positive neuroplastic change. It proves to your brain that the cycle of inertia is broken, and that you are in charge again.

The Integration of Action: Cementing All Five Skills

The move to action is not just a chapter in a book; it is the engine that drives the entire five-part system.

- **Action and Positivity (Book 1):** Successful action provides the real-world, positive data needed to fuel your Behavioral Experiments and the HEAL method. When you achieve a small win, you have a concrete, positive experience to enrich and absorb.

- **Action and Anger (Book 2):** Problem-solving skills, which are action-oriented, are essential for effective anger management. Structured action provides an alternative strategy for responding to conflicts, moving you away from impulsive reaction toward thoughtful, planned response.

- **Action and Regulation:** Most importantly, consistent action strengthens your prefrontal cortex (PFC). Every time you choose to pursue a SMART goal instead of passively succumbing to inertia, you are exercising the PFC's regulatory capacity. This sustained effort structurally repairs the neurological damage caused by chronic stress, reinforcing all the other skills you are building, from emotional regulation to assertive communication.

Action, therefore, is not a bonus skill. It is the necessary bridge between a stuck, negative life and one defined by hope, clarity, and competence. You cannot wait for the feeling. You must commit to the steps. Your brain will follow.

CHAPTER 5
TRAIN YOUR FOCUS:
REDIRECTING ATTENTION TO THE POSITIVE

You are now engaged in a two-part process of transformation. First, you are dismantling the old structure of negativity by testing your distortions and forcing action. Second, you are actively building the new structure by converting fleeting positive experiences into lasting neural traits using the HEAL method.

The next critical step is training your attention itself. Your attention is the steering wheel of your consciousness, and where it goes, your energy, and your neuroplastic changes, follow. Since your brain is built to prioritize negative input, you must deliberately train your focus to seek, register, and dwell on positive data. This is not passive wishing; it is an active cognitive skill that strengthens your emotional resilience and self-worth.

We will focus on two key, evidence-based practices that redirect your inner focus: **Mindfulness** for detachment and **Loving-Kindness Meditation (LKM)** for cultivating self-compassion. This combination interrupts the inner critic and replaces self-judgment with acceptance.

The Problem of the Inner Critic

The inner critic is the voice that interprets a mistake as a moral failing, that defaults to judgment, and that disqualifies positive experiences. This voice is powerful because it is reinforced by the rigidity of your cognitive distortions (like **Labeling** and **All-or-Nothing Thinking**) and the innate power of the negativity bias. The inner critic is the primary source of self-judgment, which creates stress and actively impedes the repair work you are doing in your prefrontal cortex (PFC).

If you cannot silence the critic, you cannot achieve lasting inner peace. The solution is not to fight the voice, which often makes it louder. The solution is to change your *relationship* with the voice, recognizing it as a collection of thoughts, not as your identity.

Tool 1: Mindfulness for Detachment

Mindfulness is a state of conscious awareness where you intentionally focus on the present moment, acknowledging thoughts, feelings, and bodily sensations without judgment. It is a tool for detachment.

When a negative thought arises ("I am lazy," "I should have done better"), your typical response is to immediately fuse with that thought: you believe it and react emotionally. Mindfulness creates a necessary space between you and the thought.

Action Focus: Non-Judgmental Observation

1. **Stop and Notice:** When the negative thought appears, physically stop what you are doing. Do not react.

2. **Label the Thought:** Without judgment, simply label the thought as a *mental event*. Say, "I am having the thought that I am lazy," or "That is a familiar voice of **Labeling**." This act of labeling separates the thought from reality.

3. **Allow the Thought to Pass:** Imagine the thought as a cloud passing in the sky or a car driving past you. Do not invite it in for tea. Simply observe it and allow it to continue on its path.

This practice is essential because it is activity-dependent. Repeatedly observing negative thoughts without reacting to them weakens the automatic neural response. You are literally training your brain to stop prioritizing the emotional signal sent by the inner critic. Mindfulness allows you to detach from the thoughts, viewing them as temporary mental events rather than absolute, fixed truths.

Once you have detached from the negative thought, you need a positive replacement. This is where **self-compassion** comes in.

Self-compassion is the intentional direction of warmth, kindness, and understanding toward yourself, especially during moments of perceived failure or suffering. It is treating yourself with the same support and kindness you would offer a cherished friend. This practice is crucial for overriding the inner critic and building resilience.

Clinically, self-compassion is proven to work. Studies show that structured exercises focused on self-compassion successfully reduce self-judgment and substantially enhance self-worth and emotional well-being. This is not just a kind feeling; it is a direct cognitive intervention that promotes long-term change.

The most effective, evidence-based method for cultivating this inner warmth is **Loving-Kindness Meditation (LKM)**.

Loving-Kindness Meditation (LKM) Protocol

LKM is a structured thought exercise that uses the repetition of specific phrases to generate and direct feelings of warmth and acceptance, first toward yourself, then toward others.

Action Focus: Directing Kindness Inward

1. **Find Calm (Breathing):** Start by taking a few slow, diaphragmatic breaths (the calming techniques from Book 2, such as 4-7-8 breathing, are perfect here). This downregulates your stress level and slows your thoughts, creating the mental space for the LKM to work.

2. **Target the Self:** Begin by silently repeating a set of self-compassionate phrases. Use an open posture, hands resting gently on your lap, or one hand on your chest, to reinforce the physical sense of warmth.

   o Example Phrases:

     ▪ "May I accept myself as I am right now."

     ▪ "May I be safe and protected from harm."

     ▪ "May I be peaceful and at ease."

     ▪ "May I be kind to myself at this moment."

3. **Visualize Acceptance:** As you repeat these phrases, visualize the feeling of warmth, acceptance, and self-worth sinking into your body. Feel the warmth filling the spaces where tension or self-

criticism usually resides. The goal is to generate and sustain the positive emotional response for several minutes.

Why LKM Works Neurochemically:

LKM does more than just make you feel warm. By directing compassion inward, you are engaging and strengthening key neural circuits. Compassion, the desire to alleviate suffering (whether your own or others'), is associated with activity in brain regions linked to the reward system, specifically the right caudate nucleus.

Individuals who display lower levels of compassion often show reduced neural activity or gray matter volume in these reward areas. By repeatedly practicing LKM, you are strengthening these reward circuits, making self-compassion intrinsically motivating and reinforcing. You are building resilience against the inner critic by chemically rewarding the choice of acceptance over judgment.

Training Your Focus: The Practice of Positive Sensitization

Beyond formal meditation, you must actively train your attention throughout the day to prioritize positive data, a process called positive sensitization. Since the brain operates on a mechanism of sensitization, repeated activation makes neural circuits more responsive. If you repeatedly focus on negativity, the circuit for worry gets faster. If you focus on the good, the circuit for joy gets faster.

This practice works directly with the HEAL method from Chapter 4. It ensures that you are not just having a good experience but are actively increasing the speed and efficiency with which your brain registers and holds onto it.

Action Focus: Intentional Positive Scanning

1. **Micro-Acknowledge Successes:** Make a practice of stopping for 5 seconds when you complete any task, even a small one. Instead of immediately moving to the next thing, acknowledge: "I finished that. I am competent." This stops the negative momentum and provides a concrete piece of positive data.

2. **Seek Out Neutral/Positive Data:** When walking through a store, driving, or sitting in a park, consciously train your focus to look for things that are neutral or pleasant, rather than things that generate irritation or stress. Notice the color of the sky, the sound of the traffic flowing smoothly, or the simple fact that your basic needs (safety, warmth, food) are currently met. This is a deliberate counter-measure against the negativity bias filter.

3. **Anchor with the Body:** Whenever you register a positive feeling, quickly connect it to a physical sensation, as you learned in the HEAL method (Chapter 4). Notice the relaxation in your muscles or the warmth in your hands. This physical anchoring makes the positive experience more robust and easier for the brain to absorb, further reducing self-judgment.

Through consistent practice, these structured thought exercises actively rewire your brain to respond to challenges with self-acceptance rather than criticism. This systematic redirection of attention creates a neural default toward resilience and self-worth.

The Integration of Regulation

Mindfulness and LKM are not isolated practices. They are crucial supports for the entire five-book system.

- **Supporting Cognitive Restructuring (Chapter 2, 3):** Mindfulness creates the necessary space to observe your Automatic Negative Thoughts (ANTs) without reaction, making it easier to step back and apply the TCT. You need to be detached from a thought to successfully question its evidence.

- **Supporting Physiological Calm (Book 2):** Diaphragmatic breathing, the foundation of LKM, supports the downregulation of stress, which is the cornerstone of managing anger. This physiological calm makes it possible to maintain cognitive and emotional control in difficult moments.

- **Building Agency (Chapter 5):** When you approach a task with self-compassion instead of self-judgment, you are less likely to fall into the paralyzing trap of **All-or-Nothing Thinking**. You accept that effort is enough and that imperfection is expected. This compassionate approach lowers the pressure and makes it easier to initiate the action needed to restore dopamine and break learned helplessness.

Your sustained commitment to training your focus is the final, essential step in this book. You are seizing control of your inner narrative. You are replacing the inner critic with a wise, compassionate ally. This internal peace is the most powerful resource you can possess, ensuring that the positive changes you have made are durable and self-sustaining.

Commit to integrating these attention-training tools into your daily routine.

Part A: Mindfulness & Detachment

1. **Daily Audit:** For the next three days, when you feel acute frustration or self-judgment, immediately pause. Write down the negative thought, and then simply observe it for 60 seconds without judgment.

2. **Label the Source:** If the thought is a critique, label it as "The Critic." If it is a prediction, label it as "**Fortunetelling**." This is the core act of detachment.

Part B: Loving-Kindness Meditation (LKM)

1. **Commitment:** Practice LKM for five uninterrupted minutes every morning before starting your day.

2. **Script:** Start with the self-compassion phrases: "May I accept myself as I am. May I be safe. May I be peaceful. May I be kind to myself."

3. **Physical Anchor:** Focus on where you feel the warmth and peace in your body. Allow the positive sensation to linger after the exercise is finished, anchoring the feeling of self-worth into your physical being.

By actively training your focus toward compassion and positive sensitization, you are giving your brain the consistent input it needs to make positivity your new default. You are teaching your mind that you are worthy of kindness, acceptance, and peace. This foundation of self-respect makes every other skill in this guide possible.

CONCLUSION
CEMENTING POSITIVE CHANGE: YOUR NEW NEURAL DEFAULT

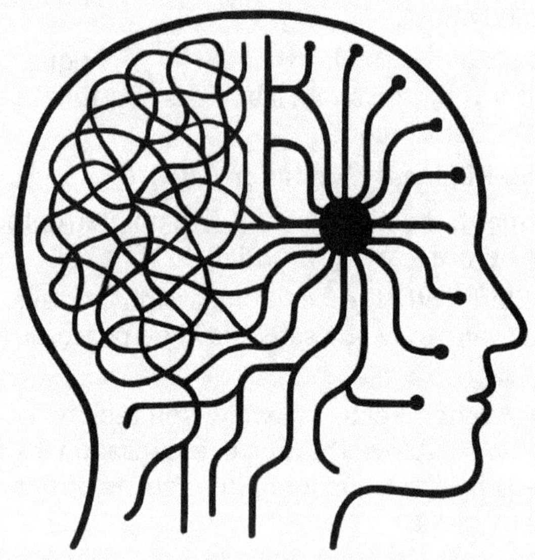

You've now gone through a complete cycle of inner repair. This book, Rewire Your Brain, guided you through a hands-on, practical look at your inner world. You started by realizing your brain tends to default to negative thoughts. Now, you've actively installed new, positive ways of thinking. This final chapter focuses on making that change strong and lasting, so flexible thinking, self-kindness, and control become your brain's new, resilient norm.

Let's quickly revisit the three key steps you took: Analyze, Activate, and Absorb. When you keep using these steps, they tap into neuroplasticity, your brain's way of changing its structure, letting you hold onto emotional balance and confidence for the long haul.

Reviewing the Process: Analyze, Activate, Absorb

What makes this change powerful is how systematic it is. You didn't just try to "think happy thoughts." Instead, you followed a proven method to repair your thinking and brain patterns.

1. Analyze: Breaking Down Rigid Thinking

You began by carefully spotting mistakes in your thinking with the Triple Column Technique (TCT). This was key to moving past rigid thinking, the trap of only seeing events through your immediate feeling, which lies at the heart of negative emotions.

The Action: You treated your thoughts like guesses, not facts. By naming a thought "Catastrophizing" or "Mind Reading," you stepped outside the problem. You understood it was a faulty program running, not a true reflection of your value.

The Brain Effect: This sharp analysis strengthened your brain's thinking center (the Prefrontal Cortex or PFC). You taught the PFC to take charge and calm emotional reactions from the limbic system. This restored your brain's top-down control over emotions.

Next, you did a vital step: testing your fears in real life with Behavioral Experiments (BEs). You found your worst predictions rarely came true. This weakened the old fear pathways in your brain.

2. Activate: Taking Back Control and Building Momentum

Moving into action, covered in Chapter 5, aimed straight at the paralyzing feeling of helplessness that feeds burnout.

The Action: You set small, SMART goals, things you could easily succeed at, like ten minutes of tidying, a page of writing, or one clear conversation. This kicked you out of stuckness.

The Brain Chemistry: Success sparked a quick dopamine boost in the striatum. Dopamine fuels motivation and reward. This showed your effort counts, restoring your belief in personal power and lighting up your brain's reward system. Taking action also breaks the cycle of rumination, the harmful looping over past stress, helping you live in the present again.

3. Absorb: Building Resilience and Self-Worth

Finally, you trained your brain to turn good moments into lasting strength. You flipped the brain's negativity bias.

The Action: Using the HEAL method, you made sure to **Have, Enrich, and Absorb** positive experiences for 10 to 30 seconds. This savoring moved good feelings from brief moments to long-lasting brain connections, a kind of positive rewiring.

The Brain Effect: This practice reinforced brain areas that control emotions and resilience, fighting damage from chronic stress. By focusing on positives, you helped your brain get better at noticing and holding onto peace and self-worth. You also practiced Loving-Kindness Meditation (LKM), proven to lower self-judgment and boost self-compassion by activating the brain's reward circuits.

Lasting Change: From Temporary State to Permanent Trait

The goal is to turn positive feelings into a solid part of who you are, not just a passing mood. This happens through metaplasticity: a process where your brain's state changes dependently on your activities, affecting all future learning and wiring.

You've made the positive path the easiest one for your brain to follow by consistently challenging thoughts with TCT, taking action regularly, and absorbing peace with HEAL. Resilience isn't about dodging problems; it's about bouncing back quickly after setbacks.

When challenges come:

- You spot distorted thinking quickly because TCT is strong.
- You regain calm faster since your PFC controls emotions better thanks to action.
- You find positive support swiftly because HEAL built a foundation of safety and worth.

Looking Ahead: What Comes Next

The stability you built here is the foundation for everything else. The mental clarity and regained power you gained are key for upcoming work on relationships:

- Without a calm PFC (Book 1), managing strong impulses like anger (Book 2) is tough.
- Without clear thinking and control (Book 1), asking for what you need kindly (Book 3) is harder.
- Without noticing good things (HEAL), you can't fully benefit from gratitude and connection (Book 4).
- Without self-kindness (LKM), setting healthy boundaries (Book 5) becomes tricky.

The work is inward and deeply personal. Now, with a rewired brain, you're ready to face perhaps the biggest challenge to your well-being and relationships: uncontrolled anger. The next book will guide you from volatile reactions to real control over your feelings and actions.

Your new neural habit is set. You are no longer defined by old patterns.

REFLECTION QUESTIONS

1. Name three common distorted thoughts you spotted in your journals this month. What facts or balanced thoughts helped prove them wrong?

2. When did you feel stuck by helplessness this week? What small SMART action did you take? What immediate change did you notice emotionally or chemically?

3. How did you use HEAL to savor a good experience today? Which body sensation did you link to that feeling, and how long did you hold it?

4. When was your inner critic loudest? How did you use LKM or mindfulness to step back from judgment and be kinder to yourself?

5. Thinking about your Behavioral Experiments, what strong evidence did you find that a core fear (rejection, failure, humiliation) was an inaccurate prediction?

BOOK TWO

TAKE BACK CONTROL: TECHNIQUES TO CALM ANGER NOW

INTRODUCTION
ANGER IS INFORMATION:
UNDERSTANDING THE CYCLE OF RAGE

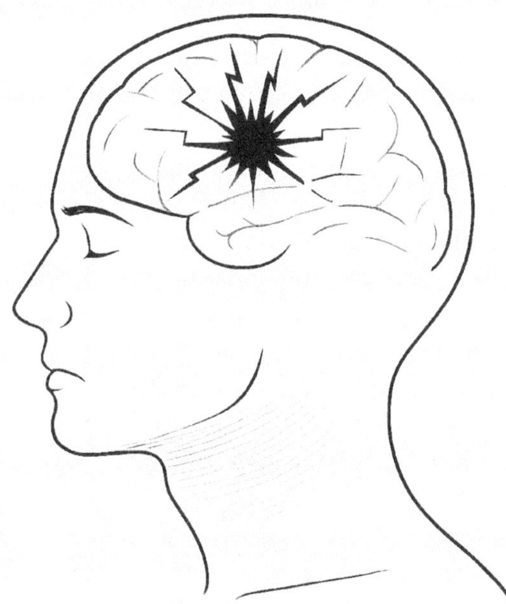

You have successfully stabilized your internal narrative in Book 1. You understand that negativity is a faulty program you can overwrite. But when anger hits, that sudden, hot surge in your chest, the tightness in your jaw, the rapid, judgmental thoughts, all that cognitive work can instantly dissolve. Anger is visceral. It bypasses reason. It makes you feel out of control, not because you lack discipline, but because your body has initiated a complex, ancient physiological response that overrides the rational brain.

If you struggle with anger, you know the cost firsthand. It pushes away the people you value, damages your credibility, and leaves you feeling exhausted and ashamed. Trying to manage it by simply suppressing it is a dead end. Suppression leads to its own set of damaging outcomes, including reduced relationship quality and increased risk for conditions like coronary heart disease and chronic pain. Your body pays a price for that internalized hostility.

This book is dedicated to mastering that physical and emotional surge. We stop seeing anger as a moral failure and start treating it as **information**, a powerful, often distorted signal that an underlying need is unmet or a perceived threat is present. The key to lasting change is understanding that the most effective interventions occur *before* anger reaches the boiling point, when you can still access the skills you learned in Book 1.

The Biology of the Blow-Up: From Signal to Surge

Anger is not purely emotional. It is a full-body, neurochemical event: the activation of your sympathetic nervous system, also known as the fight-or-flight response.

When your brain perceives a threat, whether it is a genuine physical danger or a verbal slight at work, your amygdala, the brain's alarm bell, initiates a cascade of chemical events:

1. **Chemical Release:** Stress hormones like cortisol and adrenaline flood your system. Your heart rate accelerates, breathing becomes shallow and rapid, and blood is diverted from your digestive organs and rational brain (the PFC) toward your large muscle groups, preparing you to fight or run.

2. **Cognitive Shutdown:** Because blood is diverted, the prefrontal cortex (PFC), the region responsible for reason, logic, and emotional regulation, loses resources. In short, the rational part of your brain goes momentarily offline. This is why you say and do things in the heat of the moment that you immediately regret, you literally cannot access your best judgment.

3. **Physical Warning Signs:** This physiological arousal creates immediate, measurable physical changes. You might feel a rapid heart rate, muscle tension (especially in the jaw, neck, and shoulders), flushed skin, or a sudden burst of energy. Learning to connect these physical sensations to the emotion is the first, most crucial action step. They are your early warning system, signaling that you must intervene *now*, before the rational brain is fully compromised.

Differentiating Aggression: Reactive vs. Proactive

To effectively calm anger, you must first understand the type of aggression you are struggling with. Social cognition research differentiates between two primary types:

1. **Reactive Aggression:** This is characterized by affective outbursts. It is typically impulsive, driven by a perceived immediate threat, insult, or provocation. Reactive aggression is strongly linked to the cognitive distortion of **misattributing blame to others** and the tendency to **assume the worst** in ambiguous situations. This is the rage that happens when you think someone "did that just to spite me."

2. **Proactive Aggression:** This aggression is more planned, deliberate, and goal-directed. It is often used to achieve a desired outcome, such as bullying for status or manipulating a partner to get your way. This type is linked to self-centered and disagreeable cognitive patterns.

This book primarily focuses on mastering **Reactive Aggression**, as it is the emotional outburst that most often ruins relationships and feels most out of control. The key to mitigating reactive rage is intervening early, focusing on body regulation, and correcting the two primary cognitive distortions that fuel it: blaming others and assuming the worst.

Why Suppression Fails and What to Do Instead

Many people try to manage anger through **suppression**, pushing it down and trying to ignore it. The problem is that suppression is an ineffective, and often damaging, coping mechanism.

Research confirms that while suppression might prevent an immediate external outburst, it is not a significant predictor of overall health or reduced stress. In fact, maladaptive anger inhibition (habitual suppression) is linked to reduced relationship quality and increased physical distress. When you suppress anger, you keep your body in a high-stress state without releasing the energy. The physiological arousal persists, increasing your long-term risk for psychopathology.

The solution is not suppression. It is **regulation** and **expression**.

- **Regulation:** Using physical and cognitive tools to lower the intensity of the feeling (Book 2).

- **Assertive Expression:** Learning to communicate the underlying feeling and need in a clear, respectful way (Book 3).

The next chapters provide a structured path for this regulation, moving from immediate physical techniques to complex cognitive restructuring.

This book moves sequentially, starting with the body, because if the body is calm, the mind can follow, and progresses to the sustained cognitive work necessary for long-term emotional mastery.

1. **Reset Your Body (Chapter 2):** This crucial first step focuses on immediate, physiological intervention. We will teach you the power of controlled breathing, specifically the **4-7-8 breathing protocol**, to directly stimulate the vagus nerve and counteract the fight-or-flight response. You will gain control over your internal state within minutes.

2. **Stop the Cycle (Chapter 3):** We address **anger rumination**, the repetitive, persistent focus on the stressful event that keeps your stress hormones elevated. You will learn actionable interruption techniques to break this destructive cognitive and physiological cycle.

3. **Check Your Story (Chapter 4):** We dismantle the **Hostile Attribution Bias**, the tendency to assume others' actions are malicious. We use cognitive reappraisal techniques to challenge your internal narrative, replacing blame with rational, constructive interpretations.

4. **Think First (Chapter 5):** You will move beyond mere reaction by learning structured **Problem-Solving Skills** to address the actual root cause of your anger. This moves you from feeling like a helpless victim of circumstance to feeling like a competent, solution-oriented agent.

5. **Measure Your Calm (Chapter 6):** We introduce the use of **Heart Rate Variability (HRV)** as an objective index of your progress in emotion regulation. By understanding this measurable, physiological data, you transform anger management from subjective guesswork into a trackable, scientific skill.

The consistent application of these physical and cognitive tools will build emotional resilience, ensuring that calm and thoughtfulness become your new default response to provocation.

The Foundation of Breath: Physical Control Precedes Mental Control

Before we dive into the specific techniques, you must accept one fundamental principle: you cannot reason your way out of a physiological state.

When your heart is racing and your breathing is shallow, your body is convinced you are in danger. No amount of rational thought will override that deeply wired alarm system. Therefore, the first step in anger management must be physiological. You must first use your body to signal safety to your brain.

Your breath is your immediate, non-negotiable tool for intervention. Deep, slow breathing directly reduces physiological arousal and calms the nervous system. This calming effect is mediated by the respiratory vagus nerve. Stimulating this nerve actively counteracts the stress response. The beauty of this intervention is its immediacy and accessibility. You can do it anywhere, instantly, to regain control when the initial physical warnings of anger begin to surface.

The consistency of this practice will be the anchor for every other skill in this book. You need a reliable, rapid tool to achieve that baseline of calm, that low-stress state where your prefrontal cortex can finally resume its job of regulating your emotions and thoughts.

Integrating with Book 1: The Full Circuit

This book is the action-focused counterpart to your cognitive work in Book 1. The skills are deeply interconnected:

- **PFC Restoration:** The cognitive work in *Rewire Your Brain* (Book 1) repaired and strengthened your Prefrontal Cortex (PFC). The physiological regulation skills you learn here in *Calm Anger* (Book 2) are necessary to keep the PFC online and operational when you need it most.

- **Action for Agency:** The commitment to structured action (Chapter 5, Book 1) is reinforced here. The deliberate act of executing a breathing technique or using a problem-solving script is a proactive action that generates a sense of control, which directly counteracts the feelings of helplessness that fuel reactive aggression.

- **Replacing Distortions:** The ability to identify cognitive distortions (Chapter 2, Book 1) is necessary for successfully dismantling the hostile attribution bias (Chapter 4, Book 2). You apply your analytical skill to the specific distortions that arise during conflict.

By systematically addressing the physiological, cognitive, and behavioral aspects of anger, you are building a genuinely resilient and controlled response system. You are taking back control over your most volatile emotional state.

CHAPTER 1

STOP THE BURN:
RESET YOUR BODY THROUGH BREATHING

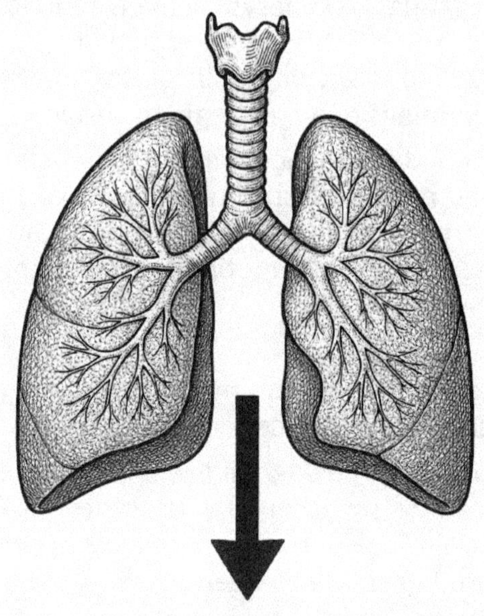

If there was one key takeaway from Book 1, it's that when your body is in panic mode, your emotions have the upper hand. Your logical thinking shuts down as soon as the internal alarm rings. Anger is the strongest of these alarms. When adrenaline and cortisol flood your system, your Prefrontal Cortex, the part of your brain responsible for reason, loses its grip.

Because of this, the first and most effective step in managing anger isn't to debate the angry thought but to calm your body. You must soothe your body's physical reaction before changing your mind's response.

This chapter introduces a powerful tool: controlled breathing. You'll learn a method that activates your body's calming system, overrides the fight-or-flight response, and restores balance in just minutes. This is backed by modern neuroscience, not just theory.

When anger builds, you notice a racing heart, your face warms, muscles tense, you are experiencing your sympathetic nervous system in overdrive. This is the fight-or-flight mode kicking in. At this point:

- Your heart rate spikes to quickly deliver oxygen to your muscles, readying you for action.

- Your breath becomes shallow and fast, usually held high in your chest, which signals your brain that danger is present.

- Your vagus nerve (the main calming nerve running from brain to body) disengages, removing the natural brake on this alarm state.

Trying to reason with yourself or others in this heightened state is like negotiating with a brain running low on resources. The key is to consciously reactivate the vagus nerve to send a message of safety to your body.

How Controlled Exhalation Works

Breath is unique because, while usually automatic, you can control it consciously. Changing your breath lets you switch your body from panic back to calm.

The secret is in the exhale. A slow, deep exhale stimulates the vagus nerve. This signals your heart and brain that the threat is gone, reducing your physiological stress level in real time. The effect can be tracked by Heart Rate Variability (HRV), which represents the natural variations between heartbeats. When stressed, HRV drops; during calm, it rises. Deep breathing increases HRV, showing your nervous system is stabilizing.

The 4-7-8 Breathing Technique

One of the best methods for quickly calming yourself is the 4-7-8 breathing technique. Rooted in ancient yogic practices called pranayama, it's simple yet powerful for resetting your nervous system. Regular practice sharpens your body's ability to switch modes fast.

Here's how to do it:

1. Preparation: Sit comfortably with an upright posture. Begin by exhaling fully through your mouth, making a soft "whoosh" sound. This clears your lungs and starts the relaxation.

2. Inhale: Close your mouth and breathe in quietly through your nose for a slow count of 4 seconds, filling your belly, not just your chest.

3. Hold: Hold your breath for 7 seconds to allow oxygen to circulate thoroughly.

4. Exhale: Breathe out with a steady "whoosh" sound through your mouth for 8 seconds. This long exhale is what activates your calming system.

5. Repeat: Do this cycle at least 4 times, focusing exclusively on your breath and count to divert attention from angry or anxious thoughts.

Why 4-7-8 Helps

This technique offers both immediate and lasting benefits:

- It reduces anxiety by drawing your focus away from worries and onto breath regulation.
- It supports heart health by improving HRV and lowering blood pressure, especially in younger adults.
- It promotes better sleep by soothing the nervous system and slowing a racing heart.

Using this tool when anger first sparks gives you a physical way to regain control before thoughts take over.

Building Breathwork into Your Anger Awareness

Don't wait until anger overwhelms you to try this, use it as a preventative measure. Start by noticing your body's earliest signs of anger, which indicate sympathetic activation:

Warning Sign	Where It Shows Up	What It Feels Like
Tightening / Clenching	Jaw, fists, shoulders	Tense muscles ready to react
Flushing / Heat	Face, neck, ears	Warmth from rising blood
Shallow Breathing	Chest, stomach	Rapid, shallow breaths
Internal Pressure	Head, chest	Feeling like you might explode

If you spot any of these sensations, immediately start the 4-7-8 breathing cycle. Treat the signal like a fire alarm; don't wait to confirm danger. Stop, breathe, and reset with the controlled exhale.

This approach does two things: it buys you time for your logical brain to come back online and it interrupts the spiral of negative thoughts by shifting focus to breath.

Taking Calm as Your Baseline

Mastering anger control starts by stopping the physical burn early. The 4-7-8 protocol is your go-to tool for instantly engaging your body's own calming system.

This is the foundation for all the strategies the rest of this book will cover. You need this baseline of calm to use later cognitive and communication skills effectively. Make a habit of practicing even when calm, so this calming reflex strengthens. When anger flares, stop the burn. Just breathe. You're reclaiming control of both your body and mind.

CHAPTER 2
DEFUSE THE BOMB:
INTERRUPTING ANGER RUMINATION

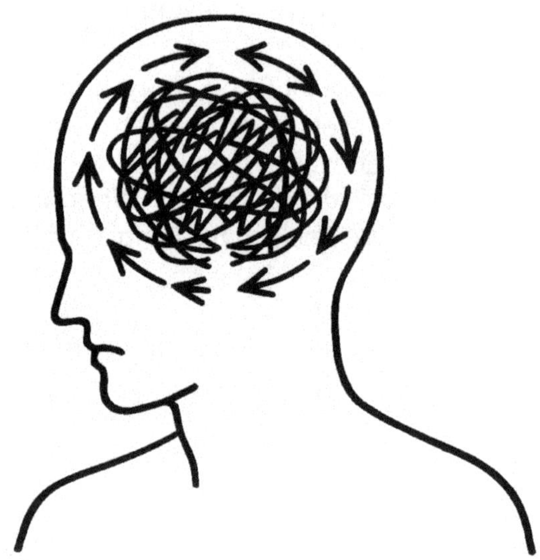

You have established physiological control. When anger's heat begins to rise, you now have the 4-7-8 breathing protocol to force your body out of sympathetic overdrive and restore resources to your rational brain. This ability to *stop the burn* is vital.

But anger often does not stop when the immediate event is over. You may have walked away from the argument or hung up the phone, yet the conversation continues to run on a toxic loop in your mind. You replay the scene, thinking of things you *should* have said, rehearsing future confrontations, or dwelling on the injustice of the situation.

This toxic cycle is called **anger rumination**. It is one of the most damaging psychological habits you can adopt, and it is a major factor in sustaining chronic hostility and stress. This chapter focuses on interrupting that toxic loop, protecting your health, and ensuring that conflict ends when the event ends.

Rumination is defined as the repetitive, persistent focus on the thoughts and feelings related to a stressful or provocative event. It is the mental equivalent of picking at a wound: it prevents healing and ensures the body remains in a heightened state of stress long term.

Research confirms that anger rumination is profoundly detrimental, sustaining negative affective, cognitive, and, critically, **physiological** responses long after the initial stressor has passed.

Here is the measurable damage that rumination causes:

1. **Slower Physiological Recovery:** Studies focusing on stress exposure (such as public speaking tasks) found that rumination predicted a **slower recovery of heart rate** following the stressor. This physiological lag means that instead of returning to an emotional baseline (the rest-and-digest state) minutes after the conflict, your body remains stuck in the high-alert, fight-or-flight state for hours or even days.

2. **Heightened Negative Appraisals:** People who habitually ruminate often generate more negative appraisals of the stressful task *after* it has ended. The thought process convinces you the event was more stressful, threatening, and damaging than it actually was. This creates a cognitive feedback loop where the rumination justifies itself by making the situation seem worse.

3. **Increased Risk for Psychopathology:** Consistent rumination and high levels of perceived stress are significant predictors of heightened anxiety, heightened depression, and decreased overall physical health and well-being. By prolonging the stress response, rumination increases your risk for chronic psychological and physical ailments.

Rumination is a chemical and cognitive commitment to suffering. You cannot afford to let the replay button run unchecked. The only way to mitigate this damage is through actionable interruption.

The Strategy: Cognitive and Behavioral Interruption

When rumination begins, your task is to immediately deploy a structured **diversionary tactic**. This tactic must be powerful enough to physically and mentally shift your focus away from the toxic loop. The interruption must be a planned action, not a passive hope.

We deploy two types of interruption: cognitive and behavioral.

Tool 1: Cognitive Interruption (Thought Replacement)

The moment you catch the loop starting, when you hear the words *should have* or *how dare they*, you must force a mental shift away from the retrospective blame and towards a productive, rational focus.

Action Focus: The Stop-and-Switch

1. **Stop Signal:** Use an immediate, internal signal to halt the loop. This can be a silent, firm word like "Stop," or a visual metaphor, such as imagining a red traffic light or hitting the "pause" button on a remote control. This action acknowledges the thought without fusing with it, echoing the detachment skills you learned in Book 1.

2. **Thought Replacement (Reappraisal):** Once the thought is paused, you must immediately replace it with a predetermined, constructive focus. This uses the principle of **Cognitive Reappraisal**, which is the process of altering the internal narrative to reduce the emotional intensity of a situation.

Instead of letting your mind run wildly, you give it a structured, non-emotional job. This job must be focused on factual reality or problem-solving.

Toxic Rumination Example	Constructive Replacement Focus
"They were deliberately rude just to undermine me. I need to plan a devastating counter-attack."	**Focus on Facts:** "What is the single, non-emotional fact I know about that interaction? *Fact: They stated they would not complete the task until tomorrow.*"
"I should have been faster and more clever. I look like a total idiot."	**Focus on Process:** "What small, specific step can I take right now to solve the remaining problem? *Step: I need to draft three potential solutions for the next meeting.*"
"I am so angry that my heart is racing. This is unbearable."	**Focus on the Breath:** "My job right now is to execute the 4-7-8 protocol until my heart rate slows. I am safe and focused on the count."

By forcing a switch to a factual or self-regulating task, you bypass the emotional circuitry that was driving the rumination. You are using your executive function (PFC) to discipline the limbic system, diverting attention away from the conflict and toward self-control.

Tool 2: Behavioral Interruption (Physical Redirect)

When the rumination is intense and purely cognitive strategies are failing, you must use a **physical redirect**. This involves actively changing your physical state or location to break the loop.

Action Focus: Change the Channel

1. **Physical Activity:** Engaging in physical activity is essential because exercise releases tension and boosts mood-enhancing endorphins, providing a healthy redirect for stored nervous energy. This is not about aggressive exercise; it is about disruption.

   o *Examples:* Go for a ten-minute fast walk, do a set of push-ups, or simply stand up and stretch vigorously. The physical change breaks the mental pattern.

2. **Sensory Grounding:** Engage your five senses to ground yourself firmly in the present moment, pulling your attention away from the internal replay.

   o *Examples:* Touch an object with a distinct texture (a cold glass of water, a rough stone). Focus intensely on the texture, temperature, and weight. Or, intensely observe five specific, small objects in your immediate environment, noting their color and detail.

3. **Scheduled Worry Time:** If the thought persists, make a contract with yourself. You are not suppressing the thought entirely, but postponing it. Tell yourself, "I will not think about this now. I will allocate 15 minutes at 7:00 PM for scheduled worry time." Then, you must commit to that promise. When 7:00 PM arrives, you can review the issue with your TCT and problem-solving skills (Book 1, Chapter 5), but only for the allotted time. This restores control over the thoughts.

The immediate goal is to physically or mentally shift focus to stop the damaging physiological cycle. When the physical body is still, the mind can continue to spin. You must break that stillness.

The Role of Thought Replacement in Neuroplasticity

Successfully interrupting rumination has a direct neuroplastic impact that reinforces the work you did in Book 1.

Every time you choose to stop the toxic loop and deliberately engage a constructive thought (Thought Replacement), you are strengthening the neural pathway associated with self-control and rational engagement.

- **Weakening the Loop:** The old ruminative circuit, where the trigger leads inevitably to repetitive negative thought and sustained stress, weakens through lack of use. The signal along that path becomes less reliable.

- **Strengthening the Regulator:** The new circuit, which links the trigger to the interruption signal and the subsequent constructive focus, is strengthened. This process actively reinforces your PFC's ability to exert reasoned, top-down control over emotional impulses.

Consistency is key. The more you interrupt the pattern, the easier it becomes, until eventually, your brain's default will be to engage a constructive solution rather than fall into the destructive replay.

The Relationship Between Rumination and Cognitive Distortions

Rumination often feeds directly off the cognitive distortions you learned to identify in Book 1. The repetitive loop is rarely based on objective facts; it is usually a continuous restatement of an irrational distortion.

Cognitive Distortion	How It Fuels Rumination	Interruption Strategy
Hostile Attribution	"He didn't include me in the email because he wants me to fail. This is malicious." (Replay focuses on *their* perceived evil intent.)	**Reality Testing (Book 1):** Focus on alternative explanations (e.g., forgetfulness, time pressure).
Should Statements	"I *should* have been perfect. I *shouldn't* have gotten emotional. This is unacceptable." (Replay focuses on impossible standards.)	**Self-Compassion (Book 1):** Replace "should" with "It is acceptable that I am imperfect. I will accept reality and try again."

Cognitive Distortion	How It Fuels Rumination	Interruption Strategy
Catastrophizing	"Because the argument was so intense, the relationship is now certainly ruined forever." (Replay focuses on the predicted terminal consequence.)	**Implications Check (Book 3):** Focus on the realistic consequence: The relationship is stressed, but repair is possible with a planned conversation.

By recognizing the underlying distortion, you can dismiss the entire ruminative chain as invalid. If the core thought is irrational (**Hostile Attribution**), the ensuing 30 minutes of self-torture are also irrational and not worth your time or physiological resources.

Action Plan: Interrupting the Replay

Your commitment is to turn immediate interruption into a reliable habit this week.

Step 1: Identify Your Toxic Script

Listen to your inner voice during rumination. Write down the one or two most common phrases your mind repeats. (e.g., "They will never respect me," or "This whole thing is my fault.")

Step 2: Commit to Immediate Cognitive Interruption

The moment you hear the toxic script begin, immediately deploy the **Stop-and-Switch** technique.

- **Signal:** Say "Stop" silently and firmly.
- **Switch:** Immediately engage in a predetermined, constructive cognitive task. (Example: Force yourself to plan the next two lines of the *Kind Speech* script you will use for repair, or spend 60 seconds listing three good things that happened earlier today.)

Step 3: Use Behavioral Redirect (When Necessary)

If the cognitive switch fails (the loop restarts within 30 seconds), immediately initiate a physical redirect.

- **Action:** Leave the room and perform five minutes of vigorous physical activity (walking, cleaning, stretching).
- **Grounding:** Focus intensely on a sensory detail (the cold of water, the rough texture of a wall) to anchor your mind firmly in the non-ruminating present.

By committing to this action-oriented interruption, you are actively protecting your psychological and physiological health. You are teaching your brain that conflict has a beginning and an end, and that sustained stress is no longer your default response. You are defusing the bomb, and the silence that follows is the sound of your resilience growing.

CHAPTER 3
CHECK YOUR STORY:
DEFEATING THE HOSTILE ATTRIBUTION BIAS

You have learned to calm the raging body using controlled breathing and to interrupt the destructive cycle of rumination. These are essential skills. But the ability to manage anger in the moment means nothing if you continue to operate from a core belief that the world, and the people in it, are actively trying to harm you.

Most reactive anger, the impulsive rage that causes you to lash out or shut down, is not triggered by genuine danger. It is triggered by a **misinterpretation**. You see an ambiguous action and instantly assign the worst possible, most malicious intent to it.

This cognitive distortion is known as the **Hostile Attribution Bias (HAB)**. If someone bumps you in a hallway, your automatic thought is, "They did that on purpose to disrespect me." If a coworker doesn't reply to an email, the story you tell yourself is, "They are deliberately ignoring me to undermine my work." This bias is the fuse that lights the explosive surge of reactive anger.

This chapter teaches you how to systematically check your story against reality. You must dismantle this bias by treating your assumptions about others' intentions as what they are: fearful, irrational predictions that require rigorous, evidence-based testing.

The Anatomy of Hostility: When Perception Becomes Threat

The Hostile Attribution Bias is one of the foundational cognitive distortions fueling reactive aggression. Research on aggression clearly shows that impulsive, affective outbursts are strongly predicted by the tendency to **misattribute blame to others** and to **assume the worst** in ambiguous social situations.

When HAB is active, your mental filter is set to detect malice. Your brain, having just restored some calm using the breathing techniques from Chapter 2, is immediately hijacked by this thought pattern, sending you right back into sympathetic overdrive. The thought creates the threat, and the body reacts accordingly.

The HAB Cycle:

1. **Ambiguous Action:** A coworker offers blunt feedback on your report, stating, "This conclusion is confusing."

2. **Hostile Interpretation (HAB):** Your brain instantly generates the story: "They think I am incompetent. They are trying to embarrass me in front of the team."

3. **Emotional Reaction:** You feel intense anger, humiliation, and a defensive need to fight back or withdraw aggressively.

4. **Reactive Behavior:** You snap back, become rude, or aggressively shut down the conversation.

This cycle is destructive because it is not based on facts. The facts were: "The conclusion is confusing." Your reaction was based entirely on your *interpretation* of the coworker's internal intent, an interpretation you cannot prove. By altering this internal narrative, you can dramatically reduce the emotional intensity of the situation, allowing you to return to an emotional baseline and respond thoughtfully instead of impulsively.

The Core Intervention: Cognitive Reappraisal

The antidote to HAB is **Cognitive Reappraisal**. This is the fundamental process of altering the internal narrative or interpretation of a situation to reduce its emotional intensity. It is the process of checking your story.

Cognitive Reappraisal is a direct action that uses the repaired regulatory power of your PFC (from Book 1) to challenge the emotional interpretation. It involves three quick, structured steps:

1. **Identify the Distorted Thought:** State the HAB assumption clearly. (*"They did that to make me look bad."*)

2. **Challenge the Accuracy:** Systematically question the evidence for that assumption. (*"What facts do I have that prove malicious intent?"*)

3. **Replace with a Constructive Interpretation:** Formulate a balanced, rational alternative. (*"They were likely under stress and spoke too quickly, or they were focused on the task, not my feelings."*)

By consistently altering your internal narrative, you reduce the immediate emotional surge. This allows the person, the thoughtful, problem-solving self, to re-engage, instead of the impulsive, reactive self. The goal is to establish mental space between the ambiguous action and your emotional response.

Action Tool 1: Reality Testing the Intent

The first tool against HAB is **Reality Testing**. You must adopt a scientific, skeptical attitude toward your own mind reading. You cannot afford to react to assumptions. You must react only to verified facts.

Reality Testing requires actively seeking clear, objective evidence to support your negative interpretation. In almost every case, this testing reveals that the extreme assumption is inaccurate or, at the very least, cannot be proven.

The Three Questions of Reality Testing:

When you feel the surge of reactive anger, and you suspect HAB is active, immediately run the scenario through these questions, using the analytical skills you mastered in Book 1 (TCT).

1. What is the Evidence for Malicious Intent?

HAB rests on the assumption that the other person *intended* to cause harm or disrespect you. You must isolate this core assumption and demand proof.

- *Scenario:* A colleague sends an email that severely criticizes your budget proposal, calling it "unrealistic and poorly sourced." Your immediate hostile thought is: "They are trying to destroy my reputation."

- *Reality Test*: List the objective, verifiable facts that *prove* malice.
  - *Evidence For Malice*: The language was harsh ("unrealistic and poorly sourced"). They did not offer solutions.
  - *Evidence Against Malice*: The criticism was directed at the *budget*, not your character. The colleague has a reputation for being direct and focused on accuracy. They copied the supervisor, which is standard procedure, not a secret attack. The criticism is fact-based (if the sources were weak).
- *Conclusion*: You find that the evidence for **malicious intent** is weak, while the evidence for **objective criticism** (driven by the coworker's need for accuracy) is strong. The attack was on the *work*, not the *person*.

2. What is the Objective, Neutral Fact?

You must separate the emotional story from the non-negotiable fact. This act of separation immediately reduces the emotional volatility.

- *Hostile Story*: "My partner is refusing to help me because they think their time is more valuable than mine."
- *Objective Fact*: "My partner has not yet helped with the dishes."
- *Hostile Story*: "That driver aggressively cut me off to prove a point."
- *Objective Fact*: "That driver changed lanes quickly in front of me."

By grounding yourself in the neutral fact, you eliminate the emotional heat generated by the assumed hostility. You can now approach the situation (e.g., the dishes or the driving) as a problem to solve, not a personal attack to avenge.

3. What Would a Neutral Observer See?

When you are flooded with anger, your vision is tunnel-like and self-centered. You must force a perspective shift. Imagine a camera recording the event, or ask yourself, "If a kind, neutral stranger watched this interaction, what would they conclude about the other person's intent?"

- *Scenario*: You saw a friend fail to wave back at you across a crowded room. Your thought: "They deliberately snubbed me."
- *Neutral Observer Test*: A neutral observer would note: 1) The room was loud and crowded. 2) The friend was mid-conversation, looking at the person they were speaking to. 3) The friend smiled at someone else nearby.

- *Conclusion:* The observer would conclude the friend *did not see you*, or their attention was preoccupied. The story of the "deliberate snub" is a cognitive projection, not a fact.

Consistent use of Reality Testing forces your thoughts out of the emotional limb (the amygdala) and into the rational limb (the PFC), strengthening your capacity for control.

Action Tool 2: Generating Alternative Explanations

The second, non-negotiable step against HAB is the deliberate creation of alternative explanations. HAB relies on binary thinking: either the person is *good* or they are *malicious*. This is a form of All-or-Nothing Thinking, which you learned to fight in Book 1.

You must force your brain to generate multiple, neutral, non-hostile reasons for the ambiguous action. By generating alternatives other than the original, negative, blaming explanation, you broaden your perspective and reduce aggressive behavior.

The Three-Option Rule:

When reacting to an ambiguous action, you must immediately generate three plausible, non-hostile alternative explanations before you are allowed to respond or ruminate.

Ambiguous Action	Initial Hostile Story (HAB)	Three Neutral Alternatives
A colleague submits a task late without warning.	"They are lazy and incompetent, trying to make the rest of us work harder."	1. They are facing a difficult, immediate family emergency.
		2. They misread the deadline or were given conflicting information.
		3. They are struggling with a complex part of the task but are too ashamed to ask for help.
You ask a question, and your supervisor replies with a sigh and	"They are annoyed at me and think my question was	1. They are extremely stressed from an urgent email they just received.

Ambiguous Action	Initial Hostile Story (HAB)	Three Neutral Alternatives
a short, irritable answer.	stupid."	2. They did not sleep well last night due to external stress.
		3. They were focused on another project and the interruption broke their concentration.
Your close friend cancels your plan at the last minute with a vague excuse.	"They don't value our friendship and are avoiding me."	1. They feel exhausted and need legitimate solitary downtime (prosocial self-care).
		2. They genuinely forgot another appointment that cropped up.
		3. They are financially strapped and feel embarrassed to admit it.

The simple act of generating these neutral options immediately lowers the emotional temperature. It introduces ambiguity, and ambiguity is the enemy of the hostile attribution bias. If three other explanations are plausible, the hostile story loses its status as *fact* and is downgraded to *speculation*.

The Cognitive Skill of Empathy Training

The long-term solution to defeating HAB is training the cognitive skill of **empathy**. Empathy is the ability to understand and share the feelings of others. It requires cognitive flexibility, which is the ability to attend closely to another person's mental state and generate creative, internally generated responses.

Training empathy directly targets the rigid, black-and-white thinking of HAB. It forces you to consider the contextual and social factors that influence another person's emotional reaction, making it less likely that you will attribute simplified, malicious intentions to them.

Action Focus: Perspective Rehearsal

When someone provokes you, before you respond:

1. **Assume the Best Stressor:** Instead of assuming malice, assume they are reacting to an outside stressor. What is the most plausible, non-hostile reason for their behavior? (*"They are cutting me off because they are running late for an emergency."*)

2. **Generate Their Internal State:** Based on that assumed stressor, try to interpret their internal experience. Are they feeling panic? Fear? Shame? (*"They are likely feeling frantic and out of control, not angry at me."*)

By practicing this perspective rehearsal, you strengthen the neural pathways associated with sophisticated social behavior (the mPFC and dlPFC). This reduces aggressive behavior by providing you with alternative, constructive strategies for responding to perceived threats or conflicts. You replace the automatic, hostile narrative with a nuanced, compassionate hypothesis.

Making Rationality the Default

The work in this chapter, checking your story, reality testing, and practicing empathy, is how you ensure that the skills from Book 1 remain operational when conflict arises. You cannot regulate an emotion that your mind keeps generating through hostile stories.

By moving away from external blame and toward a rigorous internal audit, you stop letting the ambiguous actions of others dictate your emotional state. You seize control of your interpretation, which is the ultimate act of agency in anger management. You are making rationality the default response, preparing yourself for the final, necessary step: structured problem-solving to address the root cause of the conflict, which is the focus of the next chapter.

CHAPTER 4

THINK FIRST: USING PROBLEM-SOLVING SKILLS UNDER STRESS

You have accomplished the immediate work of emotional regulation. You know how to stop the physical surge of rage using controlled breathing, and you know how to stop the toxic internal replay using interruption tactics. Crucially, you learned to check your story, refusing to let the Hostile Attribution Bias trick you into assuming malice.

Now, we face the biggest challenge: what do you do with the regulated calm?

Anger often serves as a distorted signal that a problem exists and you feel powerless to solve it. You get angry because, at a fundamental level, you feel **blocked** and **incompetent** to address the stressor. If you regulate your emotion but fail to address the underlying conflict or unmet need, the frustration simply builds again, eventually overwhelming your hard-won calm. You cannot sustain peace if the conditions that provoke you remain constant.

Effective anger management programs recognize this truth: they do not just focus on suppression or emotional control. They emphasize developing practical, constructive skills to address the very stressors that cause the anger. This chapter teaches you to use **structured problem-solving** as the ultimate, constructive alternative to impulsive aggression. You will learn to move from volatile reaction to thoughtful, planned competence.

The Scientific Case for Competence

Reactive aggression is often associated with failure in **executive function**: specifically, deficits in behavioral inhibition. Aggressive, impulsive behavior is the result of failing to stop, think, and choose a rational response. When you lack a clear plan or skill set to handle a conflict, the easiest and fastest response is often the impulsive, angry one.

Problem-solving skills training directly counteracts this executive function deficit. It provides a structured, learned path that forces you to engage the rational Prefrontal Cortex (PFC), directly replacing impulsive reaction with planned action.

The results are measurable. Structured anger management programs that incorporate problem-solving skills training have been empirically shown to produce significant, positive change.

- **Decreased Anger, Increased Skill:** Studies reveal that participants who undergo this structured training experience a significant decrease in anger levels and, simultaneously, a significant increase in problem-solving skills and communication skills.
- **Competence Over Feeling:** The scores of the experimental groups on problem-solving skills significantly increased after the training program, while the control groups showed no such improvement. This highlights a crucial truth: changing anger is about changing competence, not just changing feelings. You replace the feeling of helplessness with the functional skill of solution-finding.

When you feel capable of solving a problem, the internal alarm that signals "threat" or "helplessness" stops ringing. You move from the passive stance of a victim reacting to circumstance to the active stance of an agent choosing a solution. This is the ultimate act of agency in emotional control.

The 5-Step Structured Problem-Solving Model

To ensure your problem-solving is constructive and not hijacked by residual emotion, you must follow a systematic, step-by-step process. This framework forces clarity, prevents emotional shortcuts, and directs your energy toward resolution.

Step 1: Define the Problem Factually and Specifically

The most common failure in problem-solving is starting with an emotional definition. You cannot solve a feeling. You must define a concrete, actionable problem.

- **Emotional Definition (Unsolvable):** "The problem is that my manager is disrespectful and arrogant." (This is a judgment, not a problem.)

- **Factual Definition (Solvable):** "The problem is that my manager assigns me tasks through text messages after 8:00 PM, infringing on my personal time and causing stress." (This is a specific, measurable behavior.)

You must use the skills from Book 1 (TCT) to strip the emotion away and reduce the issue to its objective, neutral facts. If the problem is still vague, like "I feel overwhelmed", you must ask yourself: *What specific circumstance, conversation, or task is causing the overwhelmed feeling?* The problem definition must be **Specific** and **Measurable** (the "SM" in the SMART goal framework).

Action Commitment (Step 1):

- **Avoid "Why":** Avoid asking, "Why am I angry?" This encourages rumination and blame.

- **Focus on "What":** Ask, "What specific behavior, event, or lack of resource is creating this difficulty?"

- **Identify the Gap:** Define the discrepancy between the current reality and your desired outcome.

This clarity ensures your problem-solving efforts target the root cause, not the emotional symptom.

Step 2: Generate Solutions Without Judgment (Brainstorming)

Once the problem is defined factually, the next step is to generate a wide range of potential solutions. Critically, during this brainstorming phase, you must adopt a rule of **zero judgment**.

The natural impulse, especially when feeling insecure or angry, is to immediately shoot down ideas: "That's stupid," "That won't work," or "I could never do that." This judgment is the voice of the inner critic (Book 1) and the fear of failure (Learned Helplessness). It prematurely shuts down creativity.

Action Commitment (Step 2):

- **Quantity Over Quality:** Set a target to generate at least five to ten distinct potential solutions, no matter how unrealistic they may seem initially. Write down every idea.
- **Include Extremes:** Include both highly aggressive solutions (e.g., "Quit my job immediately") and highly passive solutions (e.g., "Do nothing and hope it goes away"). This helps to anchor the range of possibilities and makes the rational middle ground easier to see later.
- **Focus on Self-Action:** Ensure at least half the solutions focus on actions *you* can take to change your behavior or environment, rather than relying on others to change theirs.

This generative phase is crucial because it immediately combats the learned helplessness state by proving to your brain that **you have options**. The abundance of options restores the dopamine flow associated with agency, reinforcing the motivation to act.

Step 3: Evaluate Consequences (Cost-Benefit Analysis)

Now, you apply cold, hard reason. You take the list of ten solutions and subject each one to a realistic, impartial cost-benefit analysis. This step prevents you from impulsively choosing the most emotionally satisfying but ultimately destructive solution (e.g., lashing out).

Action Commitment (Step 3):

For each potential solution, ask two sets of questions:

1. **Short-Term Impact (Costs):** What are the immediate negative consequences of this action? (Will it cause more conflict? Will it cost money? Will it create more work?)
2. **Long-Term Impact (Rewards):** What are the ultimate positive outcomes of this action, and how well does it align with my core values (e.g., integrity, peace, health)? (Will this solve the problem permanently? Will I feel respected? Will it prevent future anger?)

This evaluation forces a time perspective. Reactive anger is focused only on the immediate release of tension (a short-term reward). Problem-solving forces you to prioritize long-term, sustainable rewards, which is a hallmark of strong executive function and emotional maturity.

Step 4: Choose the Best Action and Plan Implementation

Based on your evaluation in Step 3, select the solution that maximizes long-term positive rewards while minimizing realistic short-term costs. Once chosen, the action must be defined clearly within the SMART framework to ensure completion.

Action Commitment (Step 4):

- **The Choice:** Select the most effective, constructive, and **Attainable** solution. (Example: "I will use the DESC script to assert a time boundary with my manager.")
- **Implementation Plan (SMART):** Define the step:
  - *Action:* I will send the boundary-setting email.
  - *Time-based:* I will write the draft by 10:00 AM tomorrow and send it at 2:00 PM.
  - *Measurable:* The success is sending the email, regardless of the immediate response. (You separate the action from the outcome.)

By focusing on the process, the *sending* of the email, rather than the outcome, the *manager's feeling*, you retain control and ensure a guaranteed win, which is essential for reinforcing agency.

Step 5: Implement and Review (Adaptation)

The final step is to execute the plan and then review its effectiveness honestly. You must measure the result against your initial goal, not against a standard of perfection.

- *Review Question 1:* Did the action solve the problem as defined in Step 1?
- *Review Question 2:* What were the unexpected costs or rewards?
- *Review Question 3:* If it did not fully solve the problem, what is the next small, measurable action I can take (return to Step 2)?

This final review closes the loop, transforming any necessary failure into a data point for learning, rather than a reason for aggressive self-blame. This adaptive approach replaces the rigidity of the inner critic with the flexibility of a scientist.

The Role of Emotional Regulation in Problem-Solving

You cannot execute this 5-step model while feeling intense anger. The cognitive resources required for Step 3 (Evaluation) and Step 2 (Non-judgmental Brainstorming) are simply unavailable when the amygdala is running the show.

This is where the integration with Chapter 2 becomes non-negotiable.

Action Sequence Under Stress:

1. **Trigger Event Occurs (e.g., The manager texts after 8 PM).**
2. **Physical Cue Arises (The Burn):** You feel the heart rate spike, the jaw clench, the heat rise.
3. **Immediate Interruption (Chapter 2):** Stop everything. Execute the 4-7-8 breathing protocol until the heart rate slows and the physical tension decreases. You must achieve a baseline state of calm.
4. **Cognitive Audit (Chapter 4):** While calm, quickly check your story. Is this **Hostile Attribution Bias**? What are three non-malicious reasons for the text? (Example: "They are disorganized, not malicious.")
5. **Problem-Solving Initiation (Chapter 5):** Only once the initial emotional heat is gone, you can safely engage Step 1: "What is the factual problem that needs solving?"

By integrating the physiological calm (breath) and the cognitive audit (checking the story) *before* engaging problem-solving, you ensure that the solution is constructive, not reactive. This structured response system is the hallmark of resilient emotional health. It provides a highly effective alternative strategy for responding to perceived threats or conflicts, which is proven to reduce aggressive behavior.

Problem-Solving for Aggression and Executive Function

Problem-solving directly addresses the neurocognitive deficits associated with reactive aggression. Aggressive, impulsive behavior is often linked to poor **behavioral inhibition** and frontal lobe dysfunction.

When you feel provoked, your impulse is to yell, slam a door, or send an angry text. This is an inhibition failure. The 5-step problem-solving process is a deliberate, highly structured inhibition drill.

- **Inhibition:** By forcing yourself to pause (Step 1) and generate multiple, non-judgmental options (Step 2), you inhibit the immediate aggressive impulse.

- **Executive Control:** By forcing a rational cost-benefit analysis (Step 3), you engage your PFC in a high-level cognitive task, pulling resources away from the emotional limbic system.

This intentional engagement of the PFC, choosing the hard, rational path over the easy, emotional one, strengthens your neural ability to maintain control in all future conflicts. You are replacing the aggression circuit with a competence circuit.

The Default of Competence

You have learned that controlling anger is not about superhuman willpower. It is about having a superior set of skills and a reliable sequence of actions. You can calm your body, interrupt the destructive replay, and prevent hostile interpretations.

This chapter completes the practical toolkit by giving you the final skill: structured competence. By consistently applying the 5-step problem-solving model under stress, you transform the feeling of helplessness into one of genuine empowerment and control. You are ensuring that when conflict inevitably arises, your default response is not rage, but thoughtful action. This resilience, the ability to act constructively when provoked, is the ultimate sign that you have taken back control. The next chapter will provide you with the objective data to prove that this internal shift is happening.

CHAPTER 5
MEASURE YOUR CALM:
USING HRV TO TRACK REGULATION PROGRESS

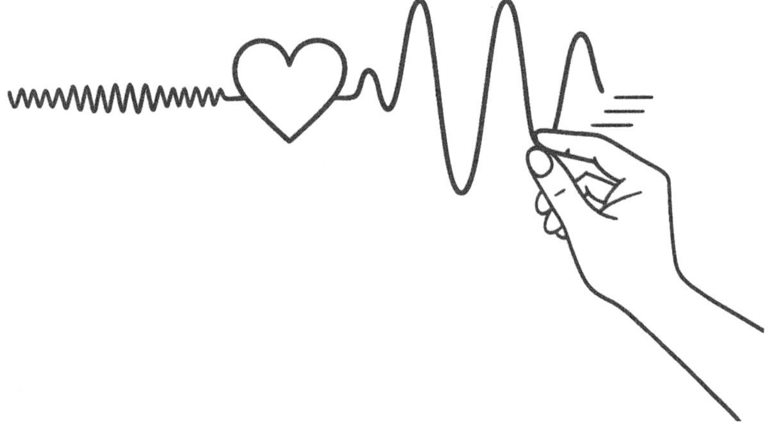

You have successfully built an action-oriented system for handling anger. You have physical tools (controlled breathing) to stop the immediate physiological surge, cognitive tools (reappraisal) to prevent the surge from restarting, and behavioral tools (problem-solving) to address the root cause of the frustration.

The critical question now is: How do you know if it is working?

Emotional change often feels subjective. You might feel calmer today, only to worry tomorrow that the old anger will return. To build lasting confidence in your resilience, you need objective, measurable proof that your internal systems are strengthening. You need a way to move anger management from subjective effort to trackable, scientific skill.

This proof exists in your own body: **Heart Rate Variability (HRV)**. HRV is a precise, physiological index of how well your body and brain regulate internal stress. By learning to measure and influence your HRV, you gain an objective metric of your progress in emotional control, ensuring that calm becomes a verifiable, resilient state.

Heart Rate Variability (HRV) is not the measure of your heart rate itself. It is the measure of the healthy, desirable fluctuation in the time interval between successive heartbeats. Your heart rate is not perfectly metronomic; it naturally speeds up slightly when you inhale and slows down slightly when you exhale. This fluctuation is a good thing.

HRV is often referred to as an index of the balance between your two key nervous systems:

1. **Sympathetic Nervous System (The Accelerator):** Activated by stress, fear, or anger. When this system dominates, the heartbeat becomes rigid, uniform, and fast. This results in **low HRV**.

2. **Parasympathetic Nervous System (The Brake):** Activated by relaxation and calm, primarily through the vagus nerve. When this system dominates, the heart rate exhibits greater, healthier fluctuations. This results in **high HRV**.

A higher, healthier HRV indicates stronger vagus nerve function, improved overall health, and, critically, **improved emotion regulation capacity**. When you are highly reactive, stressed, or experiencing chronic anger, your HRV drops low, signaling that your brake pedal (the parasympathetic system) is disengaged. When you successfully calm yourself using the techniques from this book, your HRV should rise immediately. This objective data proves your intervention worked.

HRV Biofeedback: Training Your Internal Brake

HRV biofeedback training uses technology (often a small sensor worn on a finger or chest) to give you real-time visual or auditory feedback on your HRV levels. This allows you to literally see the impact of your breathing and mental focus on your internal state.

The technology measures your current HRV and guides you to breathe at your optimal pace: the rate that maximizes the fluctuation between heartbeats. For most people, this optimal pace is around 6 breaths per minute (a slow inhale and a slower exhale).

How Biofeedback Works:

1. **Real-Time Data:** You watch a monitor that graphically displays your HRV. When you breathe quickly or hold tension, the line is jagged and low.

2. **Guided Practice:** You are guided to slow your breath, focusing particularly on the long, controlled exhale (the key to vagus nerve stimulation, as discussed in Chapter 2).

3. **Visible Success:** As you hit the optimal pace, the graph or sound signal instantly changes, showing a large, smooth wave of fluctuation (high HRV). This provides tangible, immediate proof that your conscious effort is physically changing your internal state.

The measurable results of this training are compelling and support its use as a tool for anger management:

- **Increased Vagal Tone:** Studies show that training using biofeedback leads to higher HRV during anger induction compared to control groups. This means participants who trained with biofeedback were physically more resilient to the physiological spike caused by provocation.

- **Reduced Anger Intensity:** Furthermore, studies combining HRV biofeedback with structured cognitive-behavioral strategies have shown a **significant decrease in both the intensity and frequency of anger episodes**. These improvements were often maintained for six months following the intervention, demonstrating a lasting shift in emotional resilience.

Using HRV biofeedback shifts anger management from a vague promise to a quantifiable, self-monitored skill. It provides the objective validation you need to build confidence in your ability to maintain calm, even when provoked.

Practical Application: Self-Monitoring Without a Machine

Even without dedicated biofeedback equipment, you can use the *principles* of HRV monitoring to improve your self-awareness and track your regulation progress. The concept is called **Subjective-Objective Correlation**.

You pair your internal, subjective feeling of stress with an objective, measurable physical response you can track.

Action Tool 1: The Three-Minute Baseline Check

You must learn to check your physiological state before and after an intervention.

1. **Baseline Measurement:** When you are calm (such as first thing in the morning or after a 4-7-8 session), count your resting heart rate by placing two fingers on your wrist or neck. Count the

beats in 15 seconds and multiply by four to get beats per minute (BPM). Note the quality of your breathing: slow, deep, or shallow? This is your *calm baseline.*

2. **Anger Induction Check:** The moment you feel the physical warning signs of anger, the "burn" described in Chapter 2, immediately pause. Before you act, take a rapid 15-second count of your heart rate and check your breath quality. This confirms that your body is in sympathetic overdrive.

3. **Intervention and Re-Check:** Immediately execute four cycles of the 4-7-8 breathing protocol. After the fourth cycle, re-check your heart rate and breath quality.

The Goal: You should see a measurable drop in BPM (Objective) and a noticeable shift in breath quality (Subjective). The objective evidence (lower BPM) confirms that your intervention (4-7-8) successfully stimulated the vagus nerve and counteracted the fight-or-flight response. This physical, measurable success reinforces your belief in the technique.

Action Tool 2: Tracking the Vagal Brake

You can track your increasing resilience by monitoring two key physiological indicators that rely on the vagus nerve:

1. **Recovery Time (The Bounce-Back):** How long does it take for your heart rate and breathing to return to your *calm baseline* after a stressful event or argument? When you start this practice, recovery might take 20–30 minutes. As your resilience and HRV improve, your recovery time should steadily decrease to 5–10 minutes. Tracking this metric confirms you are successfully interrupting rumination (Chapter 3) and restoring physiological balance faster.

2. **Trigger Tolerance (The Peak Heart Rate):** As your regulatory system strengthens, you should notice that the same old triggers (e.g., traffic, a rude colleague) no longer cause the dramatic spike in heart rate they once did. The anger might register, but the *intensity* (the highest BPM achieved) should be lower. This indicates that your vagal brake is stronger and engages faster.

HRV training is fundamentally about improving your body's ability to maintain dynamic equilibrium, its capacity to adapt and recover from stress. By treating your heart rate and breath as objective data points, you gain confidence that your internal systems are repairing.

Integrating HRV and Cognitive Skills

The measurable calm generated by HRV-focused techniques is the critical bridge between the body and the mind. When your HRV is high, your PFC is operational, making the complex cognitive work from Book 1 and the problem-solving skills from Chapter 5 of Book 2 possible.

- **Enabling Cognitive Reappraisal:** It is impossible to generate the required three neutral, non-hostile alternative explanations (Chapter 4) when your body is pumping adrenaline. You must first use breath to lower the physiological arousal (increase HRV). The subsequent calm *enables* your PFC to access the memory, logic, and cognitive flexibility needed for successful reappraisal.

- **Supporting Problem-Solving:** Structured problem-solving (Chapter 5) requires rational assessment of consequences and creative generation of solutions. This high-level thinking is a PFC function. By ensuring your body is in a regulated state (high HRV) before attempting problem definition, you guarantee that your solutions are constructive, not impulsive.

The combination of biofeedback, even self-monitored biofeedback, with cognitive-behavioral strategies results in the most sustainable decrease in the frequency and intensity of anger episodes. You are not just learning a trick; you are fundamentally changing the operating parameters of your nervous system.

Trusting the Objective Data

The work in this book has been dedicated to empowering you with control. You now possess the tools to stop the physical burn (Chapter 2), stop the mental replay (Chapter 3), and stop the hostile narrative (Chapter 4).

Chapter 6 provides the verification. By understanding and tracking your Heart Rate Variability, even through simple self-monitoring, you transition from hoping for change to proving it. The objective, measurable data of your own heart rate confirms that your deliberate actions are physically building resilience and increasing your capacity for emotional regulation.

This confidence, built on verifiable evidence, ensures that you can trust your calm. You are no longer vulnerable to unpredictable surges of rage. You are ready for the final step: cementing this controlled response as your reliable, default state.

CONCLUSION
BUILDING RESILIENCE:
MAKING CALM YOUR DEFAULT RESPONSE

You have completed the essential work of taking back control. This book, *Take Back Control*, moved you from a state of impulsive reaction, where anger was a physiological hijacking, to a state of measured, thoughtful response. You proved that anger is manageable, not inevitable. It is not an uncontrollable force of nature, but a predictable, reversible set of physical and cognitive responses.

The transition achieved here is profound. You moved from externalizing blame, believing others were responsible for your feelings, to accepting internal control. By focusing on your body, your thoughts, and your competence, you established a new system where calm is not a lucky accident. It is your reliable, default state.

Let us review the integrated sequence of actions you have mastered, confirming how each skill structurally reinforces the others to build genuine emotional resilience.

The effectiveness of this system lies in its unwavering commitment to action, starting with the physical and moving sequentially to the cognitive.

1. The Physiological Override: Restoring the Brake

You recognized that you cannot reason with a body convinced it is in danger. Therefore, the first step in control is physical.

- **The Action:** You mastered the **4-7-8 breathing protocol** and the principle of the controlled exhale. The moment you detect the physiological warning signs of anger, the "burn", you initiate this technique immediately.

- **The Neuroscientific Effect:** The long, controlled exhale actively stimulates the respiratory vagus nerve, which is the main component of your parasympathetic nervous system (the "brake"). This action overrides the fight-or-flight response, lowers physiological arousal, and, critically, restores blood flow and resources to your Prefrontal Cortex (PFC). This intervention is the non-negotiable step that gives your rational mind the time and resources it needs to function.

By consistently applying this tool, you strengthen the physical capacity for emotion regulation. This is visibly confirmed by increased Heart Rate Variability (HRV), which is the objective metric proving your vagal brake is stronger and engages faster.

2. The Cognitive Firewall: Stopping the Leak

With the body regulated, you addressed the mental patterns that previously caused anger to persist and return.

- **The Action (Chapter 3):** You learned to interrupt **anger rumination**, the repetitive, toxic replay of conflict, using structured cognitive and behavioral diversionary tactics. By employing the **Stop-and-Switch** technique, you broke the damaging loop that sustains high-stress hormones long after the event has passed. This protects your health and accelerates your physiological recovery time.

- **The Action (Chapter 4):** You learned to check your story by dismantling the **Hostile Attribution Bias (HAB)**. You used **Reality Testing** and the **Three-Option Rule** to prove that your assumptions of others' malice were often irrational projections, not facts.

- **The Neuroplastic Effect:** This cognitive work directly reduces the triggers that cause your amygdala (alarm bell) to fire, strengthening the control exerted by your PFC. You replace the rigid, blaming thought patterns that fuel reactive aggression with flexible, reality-based hypotheses. This is how you stop letting the ambiguous actions of others dictate your emotional state.

3. The Competence Circuit: Replacing Helplessness with Agency

The final, essential step was moving beyond mere emotional control to functional, constructive engagement with the stressor.

- **The Action:** You committed to the **5-Step Structured Problem-Solving Model**. This framework forces you to define the problem factually, generate non-judgmental options, and select the solution that maximizes long-term gain over short-term impulsive release.

- **The Neuroscientific Effect:** This structured engagement of high-level cognitive function strengthens executive function and **behavioral inhibition**, deficits often associated with aggressive behavior. By consistently choosing the hard, rational path of problem-solving (Chapter 5) over the easy, emotional path of aggression, you strengthen the neural circuit for competence. This measurable shift directly counteracts the feeling of **learned helplessness** by repeatedly affirming that your effort *can* produce positive, measurable results.

The results of this integrated approach are sustained and measurable: Anger management programs focused on problem-solving demonstrate a significant decrease in anger levels and a corresponding increase in problem-solving skills, leading to better overall adjustment when compared to control groups. You are not just learning to feel calmer; you are learning to be **functionally more competent**.

The Commitment to Resilience

Resilience is not the absence of stress or anger. It is the efficiency and speed with which you can execute this intervention sequence when provocation occurs. Your goal is to make this structured response, Calm Body, Check Story, Find Solution, an automatic reflex.

Your continued success relies on two non-negotiable principles:

1. **Objective Verification:** You must continue to monitor your physiological data. Tracking your Heart Rate and Recovery Time (Chapter 6) provides the empirical evidence that your resilience is increasing. When you see your heart rate return to baseline faster after an argument, you gain confidence that your system is repaired, making it easier to trust your new, calm default.

2. **Repetition and Practice:** Neuroplastic change requires repetition. Every time you successfully execute the 4-7-8 breathing protocol, you reinforce the vagal brake. Every time you consciously generate three alternative explanations for a hostile thought, you weaken the Hostile Attribution Bias. The sustained application of these action tools ensures that the positive changes you have wrought in your body and mind become durable traits, not temporary states.

The next challenge lies in how you use this profound internal calm to engage with others. Volatile anger is rooted in poor communication, a failure to express needs clearly and assertively. The foundation of calm you have built here is the absolute prerequisite for the successful communication strategies you will learn in Book 3.

You have taken back control of your internal world. Now, let us learn how to speak with kindness and power.

REFLECTION QUESTIONS

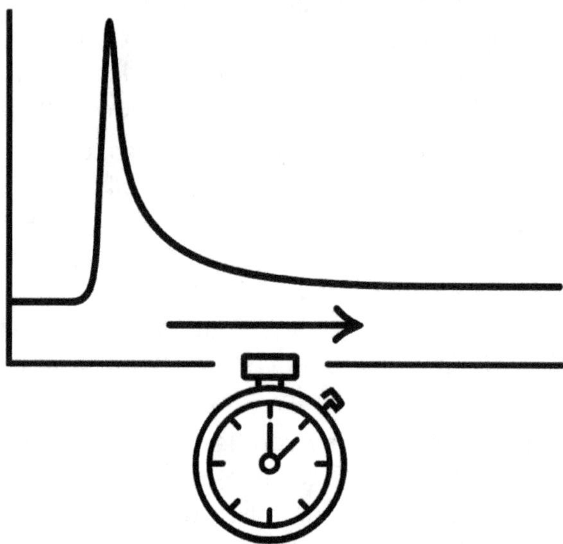

1. Describe the physiological warning signs (e.g., in your jaw, chest, or breathing) you now recognize before anger escalates. How often this week did you successfully initiate the 4-7-8 breathing protocol during this *early* stage?

2. What is the highest Heart Rate (BPM) you measured during a moment of stress this week, and how long did it take for your heart rate and breathing to return to your *calm baseline* after you performed the 4-7-8 breathing technique?

3. Describe a moment this week where you experienced anger rumination. What specific interruption strategy (e.g., physical redirect, **Stop-and-Switch**) did you use to break the cycle, and how quickly did the ruminative loop halt?

4. Identify the most common ambiguous action that triggers your Hostile Attribution Bias (e.g., a delayed email, a blank stare). What were three non-hostile, realistic alternative explanations you generated to neutralize that thought this week?

5. Describe a recent conflict or frustration that you addressed using the **5-Step Problem-Solving Model**. What was the specific, measurable action (Step 4) you chose, and how did executing that action replace the feeling of helplessness with a sense of competence?

BOOK THREE

CONNECT CLEARLY:
ACTIONABLE MODELS FOR KIND SPEECH

INTRODUCTION

THE IMPACT OF WORDS:
WHY HURTFUL SPEECH CAUSES DAMAGE

You have secured your internal life. You can now calm your body when provoked (Book 2) and control your thoughts when challenged (Book 1). That resilience is the highest form of self-respect. Now, we turn outward.

The greatest challenge for a person leaving behind rude or hurtful habits is communication. The words you use, and how you use them, are the primary instruments for building, maintaining, or destroying relationships. A simple argument, poorly phrased, can override months of careful internal work. You can be calm internally, yet your words can still cause immense damage, leading to conflict, isolation, and regret.

Hurtful speech and chronic rudeness represent a fundamental breakdown in **prosocial behavior**, the actions intended to help others and characterized by concern for their feelings and welfare. When you engage in verbal aggression, you erode the very fabric of social connection. Conversely, learning kind, clear, and assertive speech is vital because it is the mechanism by which you forge trust, articulate your needs, and uphold your dignity without resorting to anger.

Hurtful habits are not only destructive to the recipient; they are detrimental to the speaker's well-being. Prosocial behaviors, simple acts of kindness, like holding a door or offering clear support, provide measurable benefits for the person offering the help. Research shows that people who frequently engage in prosocial actions are more likely to experience better moods and, critically, tend to experience negative moods less frequently. Kindness is a natural stress detox.

Hostile communication, however, prevents these benefits and introduces significant relationship costs:

1. **The Intent vs. Perception Gap:** Rudeness is often a function of miscommunication, where the speaker's intent does not match the listener's perception. Every conversation, in effect, involves three dynamics: What was said, what was meant, and what was heard. A direct communicator, for instance, might say exactly what they mean without hedging, aiming for clarity. But this bluntness can be perceived by the listener as harshness or rudeness, especially when social grace is lacking. The speaker's desire for clarity is lost, and the listener receives only the damage.

2. **Defensiveness and Alienation:** Language that relies on moralistic evaluation, judgment, demands, or blame is guaranteed to make the listener defensive. When people feel accused ("You always do that," "You are the problem"), they stop listening and immediately move to protect themselves. This defensiveness prevents the honest addressing of the underlying problem, leading to unresolved conflict and alienation.

3. **Social Exchange Failure:** From the perspective of Social Exchange Theory (SET), all relationships are sustained by balancing rewards against costs. Respect, validation, and kindness are high rewards. Rudeness, judgment, and emotional dumping are high costs. When your communication style consistently imposes high emotional costs on others, the relationship is judged as inequitable and often diminished or ended. Spreading respect, therefore, is about communicating in a way that establishes you as a high-value partner in social exchange.

To move past these damaging patterns, you need a precise, structured language that minimizes friction and ensures your message, your true need, is delivered and received with mutual respect. You need models for clear, compassionate communication.

The Problematic Language of Judgment

Most people grew up speaking a language that encourages labeling, comparing, demanding, and pronouncing moral judgments, rather than being aware of what we are genuinely feeling and needing. This judgmental language is insidious and pervasive. It is why conflict escalates so quickly.

When you say, "You are so lazy for leaving the dishes out," you are not describing a fact; you are attaching a global, negative **label** (a cognitive distortion from Book 1) to a person based on a single behavior. The listener does not hear your frustration about the dirty kitchen. They hear, "I judge your core worth as deficient," and they react accordingly.

This language, the language of comparison, blame, and moralistic evaluation, is what we must replace. The objective is to shift your communication from expressing *judgment* about the other person to expressing your *feelings and needs* related to their actions. This fundamental shift is what builds connection instead of conflict.

The Four-Part Action Plan for Clear Connection

The remaining chapters provide the structured, actionable models needed to master clear, kind speech. This plan moves you from recognizing the damage of hostile language to implementing practical, assertive communication frameworks.

1. **Use the Need-Based Language (Chapter 2):** You will learn and implement the **Four Steps of Nonviolent Communication (NVC),** moving away from judgments and toward articulating observations, feelings, needs, and specific requests. This builds a foundation of mutual trust and connection, preventing conflicts before they start.

2. **Speak with Power (Chapter 3):** You will master **Assertiveness** as a core communication skill, learning to stand up for your rights and express your needs directly and honestly while respecting the rights of others. We introduce the **DESC Script** as a precise, four-step framework for managing difficult conversations and setting clear expectations.

3. **Engage the Other (Chapter 4):** You will train the cognitive skill of **Empathy**, the ability to understand the feelings of others, which

is essential for nuanced social interaction and requires cognitive flexibility in the brain. This skill helps you accurately interpret the contextual factors of a conversation.

4. **Connect with Self and Others (Chapter 5, 6):** You will learn techniques to move past internal judgment toward **Compassion**, and you will master the difficult, final step: **repairing conflict** using kind, accountable dialogue.

The foundation for this work is the internal calm you cultivated in Book 2. You must achieve physiological regulation before attempting these high-stakes conversations. Now, with your body calm and your mind clear, you can take control of your words.

The Scientific Imperative: Why Structured Communication Works

Communication models like Nonviolent Communication (NVC) and the DESC script are not just subjective tools; they are structured frameworks that force the brain to engage its regulatory circuits and improve social cognition.

- **Increased Empathy:** Research shows that NVC training increases empathy and successfully reduces interpersonal tension and conflict. Even brief training can lead to improved empathy months later, demonstrating the lasting cognitive impact of this structured approach. By forcing you to articulate the other person's *feelings* and *needs*, NVC strengthens the neural pathways in your prefrontal cortex linked to social cognition.

- **Reduced Defensiveness:** Assertive models, particularly the DESC script, significantly decrease defensiveness in the listener. This occurs because you are trained to use "I" statements to express your feelings and needs, rather than "You" statements, which trigger blame and defensive reactions. By making the conversation about your internal state, you invite collaboration instead of resistance.

- **Stress Reduction:** Assertiveness itself is a proven coping skill that reduces stress and anger. By standing up for your interests directly and respectfully, you eliminate the buildup of resentment that often fuels chronic frustration. When you respect yourself enough to set boundaries and state your needs, your body registers lower stress levels.

The move toward clear, kind, and assertive speech is an act of self-respect that generates social rewards for everyone involved. It guarantees you the best chance of successful communication because the direct, respectful delivery ensures the message is heard, not lost in an aggressive or passive delivery style.

CHAPTER 1
SAY WHAT YOU MEAN:
THE 4 STEPS OF NONVIOLENT COMMUNICATION

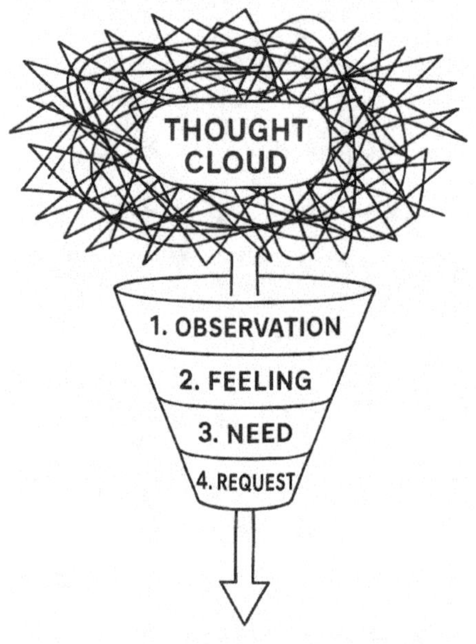

You have mastered the hardest part: achieving internal calm (Book 2). You can regulate the surge, stop the toxic replay, and check your assumptions about malice. You are now internally prepared to engage in high-stakes conversations without letting emotion hijack your response.

However, internal control is only half the battle. When you open your mouth, you face the persistent risk of falling back into the default language of conflict. Most people, even when calm, speak a language rooted in judgment, blame, and demands. This language, as we established, makes the listener defensive, causing the conversation to fail instantly, regardless of your good intentions.

This chapter provides the critical linguistic structure to ensure your words build connection and clarity instead of conflict. You will learn the **Four Steps of Nonviolent Communication (NVC)**, a framework developed by psychologist Marshall Rosenberg. NVC is not about being passive or nice; it is a radically clear and assertive method for expressing yourself and hearing others through the lens of shared human needs, bypassing judgment and reducing friction. This structured language is the foundation for genuine, kind speech.

The Scientific Necessity of Needs-Based Language

NVC is fundamentally based on a scientific hypothesis: all human behavior is an attempt to meet universal human needs (e.g., safety, understanding, connection, autonomy). When needs are met, we feel pleasant emotions (joy, contentment). When needs are unmet, we feel unpleasant emotions (frustration, anger, sadness).

The problem with conventional language is that when our needs are unmet, we express this through blame and judgment: "I am frustrated because *you* are so irresponsible." This statement attacks the other person's character, guaranteeing defensiveness and stopping any productive conversation.

NVC works by training individuals to translate these destructive judgments into factual observations and articulated needs. This structured approach accomplishes three critical goals that promote prosocial behavior:

1. **Reduces Defensiveness:** By using "I" statements and focusing on observable actions rather than inherent character flaws, NVC lowers the listener's immediate emotional reaction. The listener is invited to collaborate rather than resist.

2. **Increases Empathy:** The framework forces both parties to look for the universal human need beneath the surface emotion. By identifying the shared need (e.g., *I need connection, You need respect*), empathy is automatically fostered, which reduces interpersonal tension.

3. **Builds Mutual Trust:** Consistent use of NVC, even in brief training sessions, has been shown to increase empathy and reduce interpersonal tension and conflict. This practice builds a durable foundation of mutual trust and respect in day-to-day communication, preventing minor friction from escalating into major conflicts.

NVC is often referred to as preparation for the biggest conflict of your life, because it trains you to act with trust and respect when you are about to say the insult that could ruin a relationship forever.

NVC requires strict adherence to four sequential steps. These steps move you logically from the objective facts of the situation to a clear, actionable request.

Step 1: Observation (Just the Facts, No Judgment)

The first step requires describing the concrete actions or words seen or heard, without adding any evaluation, judgment, or comparison. This is the hardest step for most people, because conventional language fuses observation and judgment instantly.

- **Problematic Judgment:** "You never listen to me." (This is a generalization and a label.)

- **Neutral Observation:** "I noticed that when I was talking about the meeting just now, you looked down at your phone for thirty seconds." (This is a verifiable, objective fact.)

The goal is to provide a clear, neutral piece of data that the other person cannot easily dispute. If the observation contains judgment, the conversation ends before it begins, because the listener immediately shifts into justifying or defending their character. You must stick to what a neutral camera would record.

Step 2: Feelings (Share Pure Emotion, Not Blame)

The second step is to share the genuine emotional response to the observation. You must use "pure feeling words", words that describe your internal state (e.g., sad, happy, frustrated, confused), rather than "blame words", words that imply the other person caused your state (e.g., rejected, manipulated, ignored).

- **Blame Word (Masked Judgment):** "I feel *ignored* when you look at your phone." (The word "ignored" is a judgment that assigns malicious intent to the other person.)

- **Pure Feeling Word:** "I felt **hurt** and **frustrated** when I saw you looking at your phone." (Hurt and frustrated are genuine internal states.)

Using "I feel" statements is critical here. Assertive communication (which NVC supports) requires you to express your thoughts and feelings directly using "I" statements, which avoids putting the listener on the defensive, ensuring they are more likely to listen. This step builds empathy by opening up your emotional world to the listener.

Step 3: Needs (Express the Universal Human Requirement)

This is the most transformative step. You must articulate the universal human need that lies beneath the feeling. This is the **source** of your emotion. Needs are basic human requirements shared by everyone, such as respect, safety, understanding, connection, or autonomy.

- **Initial Thought:** "I felt hurt."
- **Underlying Need:** "I need to feel **heard** and **valued** when we talk."

Stating the need is crucial for two reasons:

1. **It Builds Empathy:** It shows the listener that your reaction is not arbitrary; it is rooted in a fundamental human requirement that *they also share.* This fosters immediate connection and collaboration.

2. **It Defuses Conflict:** Once the core need is identified, the conversation shifts from debating the phone usage to collaborating on meeting the need for "being valued." This is a problem you can solve together. We are often not taught to think in terms of needs, but mastering this translation is the key to lucidity in interpersonal relationships.

Step 4: Request (Make a Clear, Specific, Actionable Invitation)

The final step is to make a clear, specific, and actionable request that, if granted, will help meet your needs. The request must be phrased as an invitation to collaborate, not as a rigid demand or a consequence.

- **Vague Demand:** "I need you to respect me more." (Too vague; the person does not know what action to take.)
- **Clear Request:** "Would you be willing to put your phone down and confirm you heard the last two sentences when we talk?" (This is a specific, measurable action.)

A request is a request only if the other person is free to say "no" without fear of punishment, guilt, or shame. If you apply coercion or guilt, it is a demand, and a demand is an act of aggression that will destroy trust. You must be prepared to hear "no" and then return to Step 2 to explore the feelings and needs underlying their refusal.

Practical Application: Using NVC in a High-Stakes Scenario

Imagine you are frustrated because your team member, Jordan, consistently arrives five minutes late to key planning meetings, delaying the start time. You feel disrespected and resentful.

The Old Language (Judgmental)	The NVC Framework (Needs-Based)
Judgment / Label: "Jordan, you are so irresponsible and inconsiderate. You need to stop being late all the time. You are wasting everyone's time."	**1. Observation (Neutral Fact):** "Jordan, I have noticed that over the past two weeks, you have arrived five minutes after the scheduled start time for the morning planning meeting."
Masked Feeling / Blame: "I feel completely disrespected by you and your laziness."	**2. Feelings (Pure Emotion):** "When that happens, I feel **frustrated** and a little **anxious**."
Demand / Blaming others: "You need to fix this because it makes me look bad."	**3. Needs (Universal Requirement):** "My need for **efficiency** and **respect for time** is not being met, and I need to feel **confident** in our team's schedule."
Vague Demand: "I expect you to be on time from now on."	**4. Request (Actionable Invitation):** "Would you be willing to commit to arriving by 9:00 AM sharp, or if you can't, let me know by email 30 minutes prior so we can adjust the agenda?"

The difference is structural. The old language targets Jordan's *character*. The NVC language targets your *needs* and a *specific action*. This clarity invites Jordan to partner with you to solve the problem (meeting the need for efficiency), rather than defending their worth against a harsh label.

Training Your Empathy Circuits

The successful application of NVC requires internal work that directly connects with the skills you developed in Book 1 (Focus and Compassion).

To move from Step 2 (Feelings) to Step 3 (Needs), you need **emotional self-reflection**, the ability to accurately identify the specific emotion you are feeling and articulate the underlying need. This emotional self-awareness is essential for healing and growth, and the meta-analytic evidence supports emotional self-reflection for addressing anxiety and depressive symptoms.

Furthermore, NVC strengthens your ability to empathize with the *other* person. After you speak your four steps, you must empathize with their response. Even if they react defensively, you must try to interpret the feeling and need beneath their defensiveness.

- *If Jordan snaps, "I'm not lazy, I was dealing with a crisis!":*
- *Your Empathy Hypothesis:* "It sounds like you are feeling **defensive** and need **understanding** or **acknowledgment** of your difficulty."

This ability to quickly generate a hypothesis about the other person's internal state, what is passing through their mind, relies on **cognitive flexibility** and strengthens the frontal brain activity linked to empathy. This systematic search for the underlying need makes you less likely to attribute malice, reinforcing the work you did to defeat the Hostile Attribution Bias in Book 2.

A New Foundation for Trust

You now have a powerful, actionable model to replace hostile or passive communication. NVC is not a quick fix; it is a fundamental shift in language that takes consistent practice: a lot of unlearning and learning.

By embracing the four steps, Observation, Feelings, Needs, Request, you ensure that all your communications are grounded in facts, driven by genuine human needs, and delivered as an invitation to collaborate. This structured approach builds a durable foundation of mutual trust and respect, ensuring that your words, finally, connect clearly. This is the essential prerequisite for mastering assertiveness and setting boundaries, which is the focus of the next chapter.

CHAPTER 2

ASK FOR WHAT YOU WANT:

USING ASSERTIVENESS AND THE DESC SCRIPT

In the last chapter, you mastered the language of connection using Nonviolent Communication (NVC). You learned to translate hostility and judgment into observations, feelings, and underlying needs. That skill, translating *I feel frustrated* into *My need for efficiency is unmet*, is the essential internal work.

But translation is not enough. You must now learn to deliver that translated message with clarity, conviction, and power. You need the skill of **assertiveness**.

Assertiveness is the crucial bridge between inner calm and external action. It is the ability to stand up for your personal rights, to express your thoughts, feelings, and beliefs in direct, honest, and appropriate ways, while simultaneously respecting the rights and beliefs of others. Without assertiveness, your clear statement of needs (from NVC) can be delivered aggressively (leading to conflict) or passively (leading to your needs being ignored). Both styles are guaranteed to sabotage the health and integrity you are striving to build.

Ineffective (Aggressive / Judgmental)	Effective (DESC - Describe)
"You never help me with the setup; I always have to do it myself."	"Jerry, for the last three presentations, I did all of the technical setup by myself, and it took me almost an hour each time."
"You constantly interrupt me."	"I noticed that when I was speaking in the meeting this afternoon, I was interrupted four times."
"This project is a mess."	"The current project timeline shows we are three days behind schedule."

E: Express Your Feelings or Thoughts

The second step is to express your feelings or thoughts about the described situation. This step requires strict adherence to **"I" statements** to avoid triggering defensiveness in the listener.

- **Connection to NVC (Chapter 2):** This employs the **Feelings** principle of NVC, but with a specific focus on phrasing.

- **Why It Works:** Beginning sentences with "You" instantly puts people on the defensive, leading them to stop listening and start formulating a counter-argument. By shifting the focus to your internal state ("I feel..."), you report an internal fact that the listener cannot dispute: they cannot tell you how *you* feel. You invite understanding, not blame.

- **Action Rule:** Use phrases like, "I felt..." or "I think..." or "I am concerned that..."

Ineffective (Blaming / Defensive)	Effective (DESC - Express)
"You make me frustrated and overwhelmed."	"I felt overwhelmed, exhausted, and frustrated having to handle the setup alone."
"You are so disrespectful."	"I feel devalued when I am interrupted, and I find it hard to maintain my focus."
"You clearly don't care."	"I am concerned that this delay will negatively impact our final deliverable date, and I feel anxious about that."

S: Specify the Change You Want (The Request)

The third step is to clearly and specifically articulate the preferred alternative behavior or outcome you want to see happen. Assertiveness requires clarity. The request must be actionable, measurable, and reasonable.

- **Connection to NVC (Chapter 2):** This links directly to the **Request** step of NVC.

- **Why It Works:** Vague requests ("Be nicer," "Be more helpful") are easily ignored or misinterpreted. A specific request gives the other person a roadmap for success and makes their compliance simple.

- **Action Rule:** Use phrases like, "I would like us to..." or "I request that..."

Ineffective (Vague / Demanding)	Effective (DESC - Specify)
"You need to contribute more time."	"I would like us to work together on the technical setup for the next presentation, dividing the tasks equally."
"Stop being late."	"I request that we agree to start our morning check-ins exactly at 9:00 AM, regardless of who is present."
"I want you to respect my time."	"I would appreciate it if all work-related texts were sent only between 9 AM and 5 PM on weekdays."

C: Consequences (Specify the Outcome)

The final step is to specify the consequence of the desired action. This consequence should emphasize the **positive benefit** of the change for *both* parties. This frames the request as a collaborative opportunity, not a threat.

- **Why It Works:** This is the motivational hook. It addresses the listener's self-interest. You are showing them, "If we do this, *we* both win." This aligns the request with the principles of Social Exchange Theory, maximizing the perceived reward for compliance.

- **Action Rule:** Focus on shared benefits: "This way we can..." or "The result will be..."

Ineffective (Negative Threat / Guilt)	Effective (DESC - Consequences)
"If you don't help, I will just do it wrong, and it will be your fault."	"This way we can complete the setup in less time, giving us both a chance to gather our thoughts and be more prepared before we present."
"If you don't stop texting me, I will eventually burn out and quit."	"Maintaining these time boundaries will protect my focus and ensure that when I am working, I can give you my best quality performance."
"If we don't start on time, I will feel ignored."	"Starting our check-ins on time will increase our overall meeting efficiency and ensure we leave the room feeling aligned and confident."

The Neurocognitive Power of Assertiveness

The success of the DESC script and assertive communication is not a psychological accident; it is based on predictable neurocognitive responses and measurable behavioral outcomes.

1. Reduced Defensiveness (The "I" Statement Effect)

The use of "I" statements in the Express phase is a highly engineered cognitive intervention. Beginning a sentence with "You" (e.g., "You are rude," "You made me feel") is processed by the brain as an immediate personal threat. This triggers the amygdala and the fight-or-flight response, sending the listener into a defensive mode where cognitive resources are diverted to self-protection.

By contrast, an "I" statement ("I felt frustrated," "I am concerned") is an expression of an internal state. It is a non-threatening report on your reality. It is an invitation to empathy, not a call to arms. Assertiveness, therefore, is crucial for successful communication because the direct, respectful delivery ensures the message is heard, not lost in the static of hostility. This skill directly builds on the control you achieved in Book 2, leveraging your calm to keep the listener calm.

2. Increased Agency and Self-Esteem

Assertiveness is a core communication skill that measurably boosts self-esteem and earns the respect of others.

- **Combating Learned Helplessness:** Recall the feelings of helplessness (Book 1, Chapter 5). Learned helplessness is broken by purposeful action that yields results. When you passively avoid conflict, you reinforce the belief that your needs are not important and that your effort (to communicate) will not produce a desired result. When you successfully execute the DESC script, you prove that your effort *can* successfully advocate for your needs, restoring agency and reducing the chronic stress that results from unmet needs.

- **Measurable Efficacy:** Assertiveness training is a proven method for behavioral change. Studies confirm that participants who undergo assertiveness training significantly improve their assertiveness levels. For example, in one study, 23.5% of participants improved their assertiveness category after the training, compared to only 4% who regressed. This structured practice creates real, measurable improvements in competence.

3. Stress and Anger Reduction

Assertiveness reduces chronic anger and stress. By consistently standing up for your interests in a direct and respectful manner, you prevent the slow, toxic buildup of resentment.

Resentment is often repressed anger, the frustration over unmet needs that you were too passive to voice. This unexpressed frustration can lead to stress and internal emotional buildup, which manifests as irritability, anxiety, and eventual aggressive outbursts (reactive aggression). Assertiveness is the healthy emotional release valve. It prevents the passive erosion of self-worth while avoiding the aggressive explosion. This allows you to control anger and improve your overall coping skills.

Action Plan: Scripting Your Assertive Life

The only way to master the DESC script is through practice. When facing a difficult situation, you must commit to writing out the script first.

Step 1: Identify Your Current Passive/Aggressive Point:

Choose one specific interaction this week where you typically default to passivity (e.g., agreeing to a commitment you do not have time for) or aggression (e.g., snapping at a family member over a recurring chore).

Step 2: Draft the DESC Script:

Write out all four parts clearly and concisely, focusing on short, factual sentences (sentences should average 10–20 words).

- *D*: Describe the fact (e.g., "The laundry basket has been sitting in the hall for three days.")
- *E*: Express your feeling (e.g., "I feel overwhelmed and unsupported when I see it there.")
- *S*: Specify the desired action (e.g., "I request that the laundry be moved to the washing machine before 8 PM each evening.")
- *C*: State the positive consequence (e.g., "This way, the chore can be integrated into our routine, and our common areas will feel calmer.")

Step 3: Practice and Deliver:

Practice the script out loud, maintaining a calm, even tone (leveraging your work from Book 2). The calm tone is essential, as it ensures the message, not the delivery, is the focus.1

By embracing the DESC script, you are choosing intentional action over impulsive reaction. You are moving from a communication style dictated by fear to one defined by self-respect and clarity. This is how you ensure your needs are met while upholding the dignity of others, establishing a durable foundation of relational integrity.

CHAPTER 3

WALK IN THEIR SHOES:
TRAINING YOUR EMPATHY CIRCUITS

You know how to stand your ground now. You can calmly state your needs and ask for what you want using the clear structure of the DESC Script. That is essential self-respect. But when you are dealing with other people, a calm voice and a clear script are only half of the solution.

If you fail to accurately understand the mental state of the person listening to you, your perfectly crafted message can fall apart. Imagine asking a stressed coworker for help: If you do not sense they are overwhelmed, your assertive request, while polite, might feel like the final burden that causes them to snap. You failed to read the room.

We must actively develop **empathy**, the ability to accurately understand what is going on inside another person's head and heart. Empathy is not some innate, fixed quality. It is a trainable cognitive skill. It is the cost of admission for effective communication. If you want your kind speech to land correctly, you must learn to walk in their shoes.

The True Definition: Empathy is a Cognitive Act

We often confuse empathy with other, softer feelings. Let us be precise about the skill we are building:

- **Sympathy** is feeling *pity* or *concern for* someone else's distress. You feel bad for them.

- **Empathy** is the ability to understand and, to a degree, experience their emotional state from *their* viewpoint. It involves both affective (feeling what they feel) and cognitive (knowing what they think) components.

- **Compassion** is the desire to actively *alleviate* the suffering of others. This is an action-oriented response we will focus on in the next chapter.

To communicate clearly, you need the **cognitive side of empathy**, what psychologists call perspective-taking. You need to quickly assess the contextual factors, their underlying feelings, and their likely intentions. This skill is required to make your NVC and DESC scripts successful. You must accurately guess their core needs before you specify your request, or the whole conversation misses the mark.

The Neuroscientific Challenge: Overcoming Rigidity

Why does this feel difficult? Because your brain's default setting promotes *rigidity*, not flexibility.

You are wired to prioritize your own safety and perspective first. When someone is irritable, your brain instantly tries to find a meaning that relates to you: *Did I cause this? Are they mad at me?* This is a remnant of the negativity bias, which can quickly spiral into the **Hostile Attribution Bias**, the automatic assumption that their irritability is aimed at causing you disrespect or harm.

Training empathy is the systematic practice of breaking that rigidity. It is the deliberate engagement of your brain's regulatory structures to run a complex, external social program.

The Brain's Empathy Circuits:

Achieving accurate perspective-taking relies heavily on the frontal lobes of your brain, specifically the areas dedicated to **Theory of Mind**, the ability to attribute mental states, intentions, and beliefs to others.

1. **The Medial Prefrontal Cortex (mPFC) and Dorsolateral Prefrontal Cortex (dlPFC):** These structures are essential for high-level social cognition. Their maturation is associated with an increased capacity to decode complex emotions and interpret the situational factors that drive another person's feelings. When you ask, "Why did she say that?" these areas are working to generate multiple, flexible answers.

2. **The Amygdala and vmPFC:** These areas handle the emotional processing. They allow you to register the *intensity* of the other person's emotion without being completely overwhelmed by it yourself.

When you practice empathy, you are strengthening these neural pathways. You are literally making your brain better at decoding complex human behavior. You are making your social intelligence more flexible and less dependent on your own internal fears. This enhanced cognitive flexibility reduces aggressive reactions because you are less likely to fall into simplistic, blaming assumptions.

Action Tool 1: The Contextual Check

The most damaging assumption you can make during a conflict is that the other person's behavior is 100% about *you*. Most of the time, their visible irritation, defensiveness, or short replies are heavily influenced by factors you cannot see. This tool forces you to pause, regulate (Book 2), and look for those external factors.

Action Focus: The "What's Stressing Them?" Drill

The moment someone responds to you with an unexpected negative emotion: snapping, defensiveness, or a vague withdrawal, you must pause before continuing your assertive communication. Run this quick diagnostic internally:

1. **Isolate the Observation and Feeling (NVC Check):** State the fact and their likely feeling. *Example: "My colleague's voice was sharp when she said 'No' (Observation). She is likely feeling frustrated or stressed (Feeling)."*

2. **Generate a Contextual Hypothesis (The Check):** What is the most plausible, *non-hostile* external factor influencing her irritability? You need at least two options.

   - **Hypothesis A (Simple Stress):** *She is trying to finish a high-priority task, and my question broke her concentration, violating her need for focus.*

- ○ **Hypothesis B (External Pressure):** *She just had a difficult phone call from a family member or a tense exchange with her manager.*

3. **Formulate the Empathic Need:** Based on your hypothesis, what is her probable unmet universal need? *Example: If Hypothesis A is true, her need is for **autonomy** and **focus**.*

This exercise strengthens the part of your brain that interprets situational factors. By simulating the external pressures on them, you make it less likely you will attribute their behavior to intentional malice aimed at you. This preserves your internal calm, reinforces the work you did to defeat the Hostile Attribution Bias (Book 2), and allows you to respond with appropriate kindness rather than defensiveness.

Action Tool 2: The Perspective Rehearsal

To cement true empathy, you must actively practice taking the other person's perspective (Perspective Rehearsal). This is often used in social skills training because it forces your brain to generate a full internal narrative that is not your own. You are running a script from their point of view.

Action Focus: Scripting Their Reality

Choose a recent interaction where you felt frustrated or misunderstood, and then script the scenario from the other person's exact viewpoint. You are applying the NVC steps (Observation, Feeling, Need) to *them*, based on what *they* saw you do.

1. **Their Observation:** What specific, factual actions did they see you take? *Example: "I saw him come home late and immediately start watching television on the sofa."*

2. **Their Feeling:** What emotion did that observation likely trigger in them? *Example: "I felt overwhelmed and anxious."*

3. **Their Need:** What universal human need was unmet by your action? *Example: "My need for **partnership** and **predictability** was not met, because I was left with the entire load of evening chores."*

This intentional effort transforms the conflict in your mind. You move from the belief "They are mad at me because I am bad" to the realization "They are anxious because their need for predictability is not met." This shift changes the entire nature of the problem, moving it from a personal attack to a clash of systems, which is something you can solve constructively.

The power of your assertive communication (DESC Script) relies entirely on the accuracy of your empathy training. You cannot successfully complete Step S (Specify) and Step C (Consequences) without first engaging your empathy circuits.

DESC Step	Empathy is Required Because...
D: Describe	You must describe the situation using language that does not trigger their defensiveness. Empathy helps you choose neutral words.
S: Specify the Request	You must ensure your request is *actionable* for them and does not violate a core need of theirs (e.g., their need for autonomy, control, or time). If you empathize that they are overwhelmed (Need: **Ease**), you must revise your request to minimize the burden.
C: Specify the Consequences	The consequence must focus on a **shared benefit** that appeals to *their* interests and needs (Social Exchange Theory, Book 3, Chapter 1). Empathy tells you what they value most: time, peace, or efficiency. You frame the consequence to address that value.

This continuous cross-checking ensures that your assertive message is not just delivered clearly, but strategically. When you demonstrate that you understand and respect the other person's needs, even while standing up for your own, you increase the likelihood of collaboration and compliance. This ability to express yourself effectively while respecting the other person's rights and beliefs is what boosts your self-esteem and, crucially, earns their respect, making them more willing to meet your request.

The Flexible Mind

Empathy is the key skill that transforms blunt honesty into kind, effective communication. It moves your mind away from the rigidity of self-centered fear and into the flexibility required for sophisticated social behavior.

By engaging in Contextual Checks and Perspective Rehearsals, you are strengthening the neural pathways of social cognition. You are learning to read the human world with accuracy, ensuring that your kind speech is not only well-intentioned but profoundly effective. This ability to walk in their shoes is the final prerequisite before we address the deepest internal work: moving past judgment and into compassion and acceptance, the topic of the next essential chapter.

CHAPTER 4

MOVE PAST JUDGMENT:
SHIFTING TO COMPASSION AND ACCEPTANCE

You have built the essential structure for external kindness. You can empathize with the context and needs of others (Chapter 4), and you can communicate your own needs with clarity and respect (Chapter 3). You are now adept at handling the exchange of information.

But communication is only sustainable if it is fueled by a generous internal state. If you approach every conversation with a demanding, critical, or judgmental internal attitude, your external kindness will feel forced and eventually deplete you. The inner critic, that voice you started challenging in Book 1, often survives by pointing its finger at others, constantly evaluating them against an impossible standard of "shoulds" and "oughts."

To move past this demanding state, you must cultivate **compassion** and **acceptance**. This involves applying the same self-kindness you practiced in Book 1, but extending it outward. Compassion is not merely a soft feeling; it is a powerful emotional response that is measurable in the brain's reward circuits. It is the action-oriented desire to alleviate suffering, both your own and that of others. By intentionally replacing judgment with acceptance, you build an internal reservoir of emotional resilience that makes kind speech genuine and effortless.

The Internal Cost of Judgment

Judgment is a rigid thinking habit. It involves imposing moralistic, absolute standards on others, often rooted in your own fears, insecurities, or cultural conditioning. When you judge, you eliminate nuance. You assign fixed, negative labels to complex human behavior (e.g., "They are lazy," "They are incompetent," or "They are malicious").

This habit carries three major costs:

1. **Fueling Cognitive Rigidity:** Judgment is a form of the cognitive distortion **Labeling** (Book 1). By constantly labeling others, you reinforce the rigid, black-and-white thinking that your PFC is trying to overcome. This prevents the flexible, nuanced thinking required for empathy and problem-solving.

2. **Activating Stress:** A demanding, judgmental mind is a mind under constant stress. When others fail to meet your impossible standards, you feel anger and resentment, triggering the physiological surge you worked to control in Book 2.

3. **Blocking Connection:** Judgment eliminates the possibility of connection. When you look at someone through a judgmental lens, you are incapable of seeing their underlying human need (NVC, Chapter 2). This prevents the possibility of collaboration and ensures that conflict is met with defensiveness, not trust.

The shift from judgment to compassion is the ultimate antidote to these costs. You are changing the fundamental lens through which you view yourself and others.

The Scientific Power of Compassion

While empathy is understanding another's feelings, **compassion** is the emotional response that includes a motivation or desire to alleviate that suffering. Compassion is not abstract; it is a robust, rewarding neurological experience.

Research into the neural correlates of compassion reveals a fascinating truth: compassion is reinforced by your brain's own reward system.

- **Reward Circuit Activation:** Studies indicate that compassion is associated with activity in specific brain regions linked to reward, most notably the **right caudate nucleus**. This area is part of the striatum, which is central to motivation and positive reinforcement (the same area where dopamine dampening leads to learned helplessness, Book 1, Chapter 5).

- **Motivation for Prosociality:** People who display lower compassion tend to show reduced neural activity or gray matter volume in these reward areas. This suggests that compassion is an intrinsically motivating state. When you successfully engage in compassionate action or thought, your brain registers a neurochemical reward, reinforcing the behavior.

By actively cultivating compassion, you are building a behavior that is chemically self-sustaining. Compassion is not a sacrifice; it is a highly rewarded state that strengthens your ability to engage in prosocial, kind behavior.

Action Tool 1: Cultivating Self-Compassion with LKM

You must first direct compassion inward. You cannot offer acceptance to others that you deny to yourself. The inner critic's most damaging work is punishing you for perceived failures. You must replace this criticism with kindness.

The most effective, evidence-based technique for cultivating self-compassion is **Loving-Kindness Meditation (LKM)**, which you were introduced to in Book 1, Chapter 6. LKM uses the repetition of specific phrases to generate feelings of warmth and acceptance, providing a structured way to interrupt cycles of self-judgment and criticism.

Action Focus: Extending the Self-Compassion Script

Practice LKM for ten uninterrupted minutes daily.

1. **Find Calm:** Start by engaging deep, slow, diaphragmatic breathing (4-7-8 method, Book 2) to downregulate your stress level and create mental space.

2. **Target the Self:** Begin by silently repeating the self-compassion script, feeling the warmth in your chest.
   - *Script:* "May I accept myself as I am right now. May I be safe and protected. May I be peaceful and at ease. May I be kind to myself."

3. **Extend to Others (The Compassion Bridge):** Once the feeling of warmth is stable and focused on yourself, expand the circle outward, applying the exact same warmth and acceptance to others.

   - *First, a neutral person:* "May this person also be safe and peaceful."

   - *Second, a person in conflict:* Focus on someone you often judge or who frustrates you. Repeat the phrases, focusing on their humanity: "May this person also find acceptance. May they be free from suffering."

The Internal Shift: This practice forces you to confront the rigidity of your judgment. When you direct kindness toward a difficult person, you bypass the labels you assigned them and access the core human being underneath. This trains your brain to choose acceptance over criticism, building profound emotional resilience.

Action Tool 2: The Acceptance Audit

Compassion is applied through the lens of acceptance. Acceptance is the acknowledgment of reality as it is, without the demand that it be different. Judgment is the demand that reality conform to your expectations ("It shouldn't be this way").

The **Acceptance Audit** is a powerful cognitive tool that uses the NVC framework (Chapter 2) to challenge the "shoulds" and shift to reality.

The Three Steps of the Acceptance Audit:

1. **Identify the Judgment (The Should Statement):** Pinpoint the absolute demand you are placing on yourself or others. *Example: "My colleague **should** know how to do this simple task without asking me."* (The judgment is that they are incompetent, and they are violating your standard of expertise.)

2. **Identify the Unmet Need:** Beneath the judgment, what is the *real* need being violated? *Example: Your need is for **ease**, **autonomy** (not to be interrupted), and **competence** (you need confidence in the team's ability).*

3. **Reframe to Acceptance and Action:** State the reality without judgment, and then focus on addressing the need constructively.

Judgmental Thought	Factual Acceptance	Compassionate Action (NVC / DESC)
"He **shouldn't** interrupt me; he's so rude."	*Acceptance:* "The reality is that he interrupted me. He likely needs **clarity** (Empathy Check, Chapter 4) and has poor boundary skills."	*Action:* I will use the DESC script to set an assertive time boundary, meeting my need for **focus** without labeling him as rude.
"I **should** be perfect on this assignment; I'm failing."	*Acceptance:* "The reality is that I am imperfect. I made a mistake, but this is a learning opportunity."	*Action:* I will apply self-compassion (LKM) and initiate a SMART goal (Book 1, Chapter 5) to correct the mistake.

By reframing the judgment as an unmet need that requires a constructive solution, you move your focus from angry, static criticism to dynamic problem-solving. This process actively supports the flexibility of your PFC, allowing you to deal with conflict lucidly and effectively.

The Integration of Acceptance and Clarity

The work in this chapter ensures that the assertive communication models from Chapter 3 are delivered with genuine connection, not cold efficiency.

- **Assertiveness with Care:** When you operate from acceptance, your DESC script naturally becomes more empathetic. You can describe a colleague's late submission factually, express your frustration, and specify a deadline change, all while acknowledging the reality that they may be struggling with external stress (Contextual Empathy Check, Chapter 4). This combination of **firm clarity and compassionate acceptance** is the highest form of professional communication.

- **The Power of Calm:** Acceptance is deeply supported by the physiological regulation you mastered in Book 2. Diaphragmatic breathing helps downregulate overall stress levels, slowing your thoughts and creating the mental space needed to intentionally replace critical inner dialogue with rational, compassionate self-talk.

The intentional practice of acceptance is how you move beyond the rigid self-centeredness of negative habits. You are building an inner strength that allows you to tolerate the inevitable imperfections of yourself and others without collapsing into judgment or reactive anger. This durable shift makes kind speech not just an external act, but a natural outflow of your compassionate internal state. You are ready to apply this acceptance to the ultimate challenge: repairing broken trust.

CHAPTER 5

MEND THE RIFT:
USING KIND DIALOGUE TO REPAIR CONFLICT

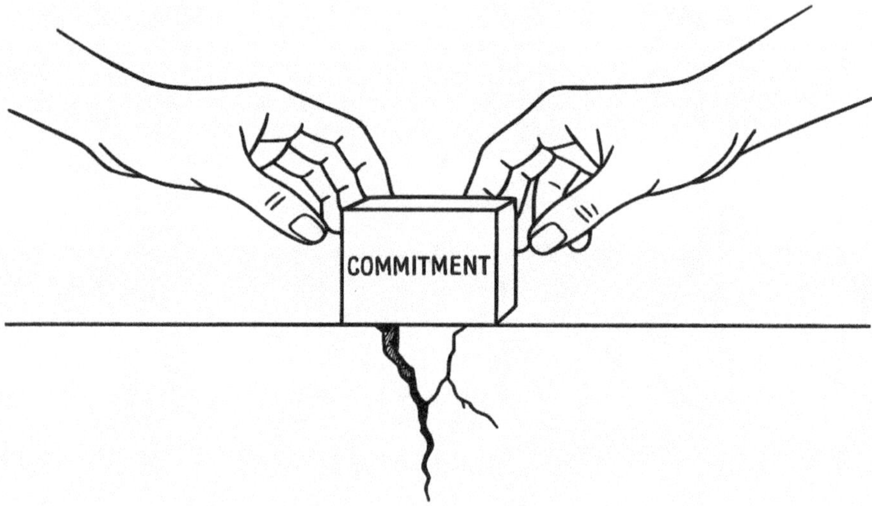

You have put in the work. You have achieved profound internal quiet. You can now calm your body when provoked, you refuse to assume the worst intent in others, and you can state your needs clearly using the DESC Script.

But let us be honest: you are human. You will slip up. You will raise your voice when you are tired. You will say something thoughtless when you are stressed. Hurtful words will escape, trust will be violated, and the emotional security of your relationship will rupture.

The measure of your newfound mastery is not how well you avoid these mistakes. It is how effectively you **repair** them. A rupture is an inevitability. A failure to repair is a choice. If you leave the damage untouched, the conflict festers, driving the relationship back toward the hostility and defensiveness you worked so hard to eliminate.

This chapter provides the structured, kind dialogue necessary for relational repair. It requires genuine accountability, focused listening, and a commitment to rebuilding emotional security. When handled correctly, the repair process transforms conflict from a destructive event into a powerful opportunity to strengthen trust.

The Real Damage: Why "I'm Sorry" Is Not Enough

When you speak hurtful words, the damage is not just emotional. It is neurological. Hurt triggers the same fear response as a physical threat. The brain registers a rupture in the relationship as a violation of safety, activating the amygdala and sending the body into stress mode.

An apology that includes an excuse or a condition ("I'm sorry you felt that way, *but* I was stressed") completely fails to mend the rift. Why? Because it denies the listener's reality. It sends the message that their feelings are less valid than your justification. This destroys the accountability required to restore trust.

The science of effective repair confirms a critical truth: you must take responsibility for the **impact** of your words, independent of your initial intent. You might have *intended* to sound only direct, but if your words were *perceived* as rude and hostile, you are fully accountable for the resulting pain. This act of owning the consequence is what weaves connection back into the interaction and begins the work of rebuilding security.

Action Tool 1: The Accountable Apology

The typical apology focuses on the speaker's feelings ("I feel bad"). The accountable apology focuses exclusively on the listener's violated needs. It uses the language of NVC (Chapter 2) and the structure of assertiveness (Chapter 3) to achieve maximum clarity and accountability.

An effective apology must be structured in three sequential, non-negotiable parts. You must never use the word "but" or any phrase that shifts blame to the listener ("if you hadn't...").

1. Acknowledge the Specific Behavior (D: Describe)

Start by factually describing the specific behavior you regret. This shows the listener that you were paying attention, that you understand exactly what you did wrong, and that you are taking ownership of the action, not just the feeling.

- **Ineffective (Vague):** "I'm sorry I was mean earlier."
- **Accountable (Specific):** "I acknowledge that I raised my voice above a respectful volume, and I used the generalizing phrase, 'You always leave me to do this work.' That specific action was mine." (This is a factual statement of the precise, regretted behavior.)

2. Express Regret for the Resulting Feeling and Need (E: Express & Empathy)

Express genuine regret for the *impact* your action had on the other person, explicitly linking their feeling to their underlying human need. This step engages your empathy circuits (Chapter 4) and validates their vulnerability.

- **Ineffective (Conditional):** "I'm sorry you were sensitive about what I said."

- **Accountable (Empathic):** "I truly regret that my loud voice and generalizing language caused you to feel humiliated and deeply invalidated. I understand that your core need for **respect** and **acknowledgment of your effort** was severely violated by my words."

When you identify and validate the core universal human need (e.g., respect, safety, value), the listener often experiences an immediate emotional release. They feel heard, which is the necessary prerequisite for them to lower their defensive wall.

3. State a Future Commitment (S & C: Specify and Consequences)

End by stating a clear, specific, and measurable commitment to a different behavior next time. This is the crucial step that replaces the past failure with a clear path for future success and earns back trust. Trust is built not on words, but on predictable, positive behavior.

- **Ineffective (Vague Promise):** "I promise I'll try to be better in the future."

- **Accountable (Action-Oriented):** "My commitment is this: Next time I feel frustrated by the workload, I will first initiate the 4-7-8 breathing protocol, and I will then use the DESC script to state my needs factually. I commit to never using generalizing or judgmental language again. This is how I will rebuild our trust, ensuring our communication is constructive."

This structured, accountable apology closes the gap created by the hostility. It transforms the moment of rupture into a process of self-correction, which the listener can observe and trust.

Action Tool 2: De-escalating Post-Conflict Defensiveness

Even after a perfect apology, the other person may remain defensive, emotional, or resistant to letting go of the conflict. This is usually because their core need still feels vulnerable or exposed. If you continue to defend yourself here, you restart the conflict.

To move past this residual defensiveness, you must use empathy and reflective listening as a de-escalation tool. This requires you to silence your own narrative and focus entirely on confirming the other person's internal reality.

Action Focus: Reflecting the Unmet Need

When the other person continues to voice frustration or blame, do not defend your past action. Instead, reflect back their probable feeling and need until they feel entirely heard.

1. **Listen Past the Blame:** Listen past the words of judgment ("You are so selfish!") to the underlying, universal human need (e.g., "They need **fairness** or **support**").

2. **Reflect and Validate:** Use a soft, non-judgmental tone to reflect their internal state back to them. Frame it as a question to confirm your empathy check. *Example: "It sounds like you are still feeling extremely **angry** and **unsupported**, and your core need for **equity** in our workload is completely unmet. Is that what you are telling me?"*

The Scientific Result: When a person hears their deepest need validated without argument, the emotional intensity often dissipates instantly. NVC studies highlight that listening for and validating the need is the most powerful method for getting past defensiveness and opening the door to collaboration. By reflecting their reality, you fulfill the fundamental human need to be understood. Only once this need is met can they shift from emotional reaction to rational problem-solving.

The Integration of Repair: From Hostility to Competence

Repair is the ultimate integration test for all the skills you have learned in the first two books. A successful repair process is sequential and systematic:

1. Preventing the Second Surge (Book 2 Mastery)

   - **Failure Point:** You feel the heat of their continued anger.

   - **Intervention:** Immediately engage the **4-7-8 breathing protocol** to prevent your own emotional re-surge. Use physiological regulation to keep your PFC online so you can listen calmly, without engaging their hostility defensively.

2. Auditing the Damage (Book 1 & 2 Mastery)

   - **Failure Point:** You contributed to the rupture with hostile language.

- **Intervention:** Interrupt any **rumination** (Book 2, Chapter 3). Then, apply the **TCT** and **Reality Testing** (Book 1, Chapter 3 and Book 2, Chapter 4) to your own thoughts: *Did I use Labeling? Was my generalization (always/never) a cognitive distortion?* This audit prepares you for the honest, factual apology (Action Tool 1).

3. Initiating Collaboration (Book 3 Mastery)

- **Failure Point:** You need to transition from apology to a solution.

- **Intervention:** Once the Accountable Apology is delivered and their need is reflected and validated (Action Tool 2), immediately initiate the **5-Step Structured Problem-Solving Model** (Book 2, Chapter 5). The problem is no longer the argument; the problem is the *unmet need* (e.g., the need for equity in chores). The focus shifts from blame to a measurable, constructive action plan.

The ultimate outcome of this sequence is moving both parties away from the volatile, affective outburst (reactive aggression) toward the controlled, planned response. Problem-solving interventions have been shown to increase self-control, providing individuals with alternative, constructive strategies for responding to conflict, which measurably reduces aggressive behavior.

Trust Built Through Accountability

The ability to successfully repair conflict transforms relationships. Every time you successfully navigate a breakdown using structured accountability and empathetic listening, you reinforce the relationship's foundation of mutual trust.

The skills you learned in this book, NVC, the DESC script, and Empathy Training, are designed precisely for this moment: to ensure that when your integrity is tested, you possess the language and the internal control to uphold it. You are proving that your commitment to self-respect and relational health is stronger than your impulse to be right. This mastery of repair is the definitive sign that you have achieved connection through clarity, setting the stage for the next deep internal work: building inner strength through gratitude.

CONCLUSION
COMMUNICATE WITH CONNECTION: YOUR FOUNDATION FOR MUTUAL TRUST

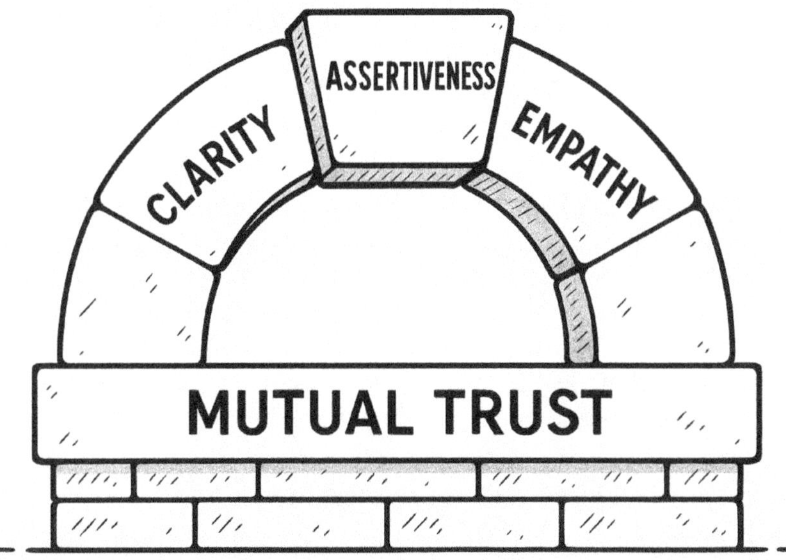

You have completed the essential work of mastering communication. This book, *Connect Clearly*, moved you from reacting with hurtful words and defensive silence to engaging with assertive clarity and compassionate understanding. You have fundamentally restructured the way you speak, listen, and interact.

This transformation, from hostility to clear connection, is the bedrock for all healthy relationships. It is the guarantee that your words will build trust, not erode it. The ultimate measure of this mastery is the durability of the foundation you have established: a foundation built on mutual respect, vulnerability, and the predictable use of structured language.

Let us review the integrated skills you have gained, confirming how the combination of NVC, assertiveness, and empathy ensures that kind speech becomes your resilient and reliable default.

The success of your new communication style is due to its systematic, three-part structure. You learned to use each skill in sequence, leveraging your internal calm (Book 2) to achieve external clarity.

1. The Clarity of Needs-Based Dialogue (NVC)

You began by rejecting the language of judgment and blame that characterized your past hurtful habits.

- **The Action:** You mastered the **Four Steps of Nonviolent Communication (NVC)**, translating vague frustration into **Observation, Feeling, Need, and Request**. You learned that anger or frustration is simply a signal that a universal human need (e.g., for safety, connection, or autonomy) is unmet.

- **The Relational Effect:** By speaking in terms of verifiable facts and genuine human needs, you bypass the listener's defensiveness. This invites collaboration instead of resistance, making the listener more receptive to your message and fostering a stronger foundation of mutual trust. Research shows that NVC training increases empathy and reduces interpersonal tension, proving the effectiveness of this needs-based structure.

2. The Power of Respectful Action (Assertiveness)

Knowing your needs is not enough; you must deliver them with conviction. Assertiveness is the core skill that ensures your needs are met while upholding the dignity of others.

- **The Action:** You mastered the **DESC Script** (Describe, Express, Specify, Consequences) for managing high-stakes conversations. This structured, sequential framework forces you to deliver your requests directly, honestly, and respectfully, avoiding the pitfalls of passive avoidance or aggressive demands.

- **The Psychological Effect:** Assertiveness is a critical coping skill that reduces stress and prevents the toxic buildup of resentment (unexpressed anger) that fuels future hostile outbursts. By standing up for your rights and interests, you confirm to yourself and others that your needs are important. This action reinforces agency, which you learned is vital for countering learned helplessness (Book 1, Chapter 5), and it measurably boosts self-esteem.

3. The Nuance of Perspective-Taking (Empathy and Acceptance)

The structure of your communication is only successful if it is fueled by internal acceptance and genuine understanding of the other person.

- **The Action:** You trained your **Empathy Circuits** by practicing **Contextual Checks** and **Perspective Rehearsal** (Chapter 4). This actively strengthens the frontal lobe areas responsible for "theory of mind", the ability to understand the situational and social factors driving the other person's behavior.

- **The Emotional Effect:** This training makes you less susceptible to the Hostile Attribution Bias (Book 2), ensuring you respond to a person's irritability with nuance and understanding, rather than immediate, defensive hostility. Furthermore, by practicing **Compassion and Acceptance** (Chapter 5), you moved past internal judgment and built a self-sustaining emotional reserve, fueled by the neurochemical rewards of kindness. This internal state makes your external kind speech feel authentic, not forced.

Relational Integrity: The Ultimate Outcome

The consistent application of these structured verbal tools builds a durable foundation of **mutual trust**. This integrity is what defines the long-term success of your new habits.

- **Predictability:** Assertive communication is predictable. People trust you because they know what you mean, they know you will not resort to passive-aggression, and they know you will not explode into reactive rage. This clarity is a high reward in the social exchange (Social Exchange Theory, Book 5), and it stabilizes your relationships.

- **Safety in Conflict:** Crucially, you mastered the dialogue necessary for **Relational Repair** (Chapter 6). By committing to the Accountable Apology, focusing on the specific behavior and the violated need, you proved that your commitment to integrity is stronger than your impulse to be right. This skill transforms conflict from a destructive threat into a strengthening opportunity.

The mastery of kind speech ensures that the hard-won internal calm you secured in Book 1 and Book 2 is protected. Your words will no longer sabotage your peace.

The next challenge, addressed in Book 4, is to deepen the internal well of emotional strength, ensuring that your resilience is not reliant on the behavior of others. We turn now to **gratitude**, a powerful, scientific intervention that further reduces stress hormones, increases physical health, and cements the positive focus you started building. This internal strengthening ensures your kind speech flows from a deep, unwavering source of inner abundance.

REFLECTION QUESTIONS

1. Describe a recent high-stakes conversation. Did you use pure feeling words (e.g., frustrated) or masked judgment words (e.g., ignored)? Use the NVC format to clearly restate your true underlying unmet need.

2. Write down an example where you successfully used the **DESC script** to deliver an assertive boundary. Specifically, how did the **Consequences** phase appeal to the other person's interests (using empathy)?

3. Describe a time this week when someone responded to you with unexpected anger or irritation. What **Contextual Hypothesis** did you generate (Chapter 4) to neutralize the hostile attribution bias, and what unmet need did you guess was driving their behavior?

4. Describe a moment where you felt an impulse to judge a colleague or friend. How did you apply the **Acceptance Audit** (Chapter 5) to move your mind from judgment to focusing on objective reality and constructive action?

5. Reflecting on a recent conflict, how did you use the three steps of the **Accountable Apology** (Chapter 6) to mend the rift? What specific commitment did you make for future behavior to rebuild trust?

BOOK FOUR

BUILD INNER STRENGTH:
DAILY HABITS FOR PRACTICING GRATITUDE

INTRODUCTION
GRATITUDE IS MORE THAN THANKS: DEFINING THE CLINICAL TOOL

You have secured the external world. You have learned to regulate your impulses (Book 2) and to communicate with assertive clarity (Book 3). You can handle conflict. But to ensure these skills are resilient and durable, to make sure you do not regress when the next big stressor hits, you must deepen your inner strength.

This final stage of internal repair is not about fixing a flaw; it is about building a psychological asset: **gratitude**.

For many, gratitude is simply a polite social custom, saying thank you for a gift or a service. In this book, we define gratitude not as a fleeting good feeling, but as a specific, evidence-based **psychological intervention**. This is a commitment to a structured mental habit that actively rewires your brain, reduces your stress hormones, and dramatically increases your emotional resilience.

If you struggle with lingering anxiety, persistent worry, or a feeling that life is constantly unfair, gratitude is your most powerful tool for counteracting those states. The goal is to fundamentally shift the balance of your internal world so that you are reliably nourished by what you have, rather than depleted by what you lack.

The Scientific Deficit: The Bias Against Abundance

To understand the power of gratitude, we must revisit the fundamental bias you first encountered in Book 1: the **negativity bias**.

Your brain is designed to attend to, learn from, and dwell on negative information far more than positive information. This bias serves as an ancient survival mechanism, but in modern life, it ensures that your mind operates like a **Mental Filter** (a cognitive distortion from Book 1): it automatically seeks out perceived threats, inadequacies, and losses while ignoring or minimizing experiences of contentment and abundance.

This focus on lack and threat has three major costs that gratitude directly addresses:

1. **Emotional Depletion:** The constant focus on what is wrong or missing sustains a low-level state of dissatisfaction, which is emotionally draining and contributes to depressive and anxious behaviors.

2. **Toxic Comparison:** When focused on lack, the mind defaults to toxic emotions like envy, jealousy, and resentment. You compare your current state (what you lack) to others, which instantly triggers feelings of inadequacy and self-judgment.

3. **Sustained Stress Chemistry:** The internal feeling of constant threat keeps your stress system on high alert. This prevents the physiological calm (high HRV, low heart rate) you worked so hard to achieve in Book 2 from becoming your default state.

Gratitude is the direct, intentional counter-measure to this chemical and cognitive default. It is a behavioral strategy that forces the mind to prioritize and process positive data, strengthening the "Velcro" for the good that you started building with the HEAL method.

Gratitude as a Clinical Intervention

The benefits of engaging in gratitude practices are not speculative; they are measurable in large-scale clinical meta-analyses. Scientific studies confirm that structured gratitude interventions serve as a powerful therapeutic complement for addressing chronic negative emotional states.

1. Measurable Reductions in Anxiety and Depression

Meta-analytic evidence has quantified the impact of consistent gratitude practice on mental health indicators:

- **Anxiety Symptoms:** Participants who incorporated gratitude interventions experienced a measurable decrease in anxiety symptoms, with a **7.76% lower Generalized Anxiety Disorder (GAD-7) score** than control groups.
- **Depression Symptoms:** The same analysis showed that gratitude interventions led to a significant reduction in depressive symptoms, with a **6.89% lower Patient Health Questionnaire-9 (PHQ-9) score** than control groups.

These statistics confirm that deliberate acts of gratitude are not superficial mood boosters. They are functional psychological actions that reduce the burden of anxiety and depression, increase overall positive mood, and lead to greater feelings of life satisfaction.

2. Enhancing Emotional Resilience

Gratitude practices are strongly correlated with **resilience**, the ability to bounce back quickly from adversity. By consistently focusing on what is present and good, gratitude builds a firewall against toxic emotions. It forces the brain to look for resources rather than focusing only on loss, which is essential for coping with difficult circumstances with a broader perspective and greater awareness.

This consistent effort to appreciate what remains, rather than dwelling on what is missing, leads to a sustained increase in overall optimism and emotional strength. This means that when a conflict inevitably arises (Book 3), you approach it from a place of sufficiency, not emotional neediness.

The Mechanism of Action: Rewiring Your Focus

The core mechanism by which gratitude works is through the alteration of **selective attention.**

If you commit to recording something positive that occurred today (such as through journaling), your brain naturally begins to actively **scan and notice** those good things in your life throughout the day. This anticipatory effect, knowing you will reflect on the good later, actively overrides the mental filter of the negativity bias.

This structured scanning forces your brain to register positive experiences: the moment of kindness received, the success achieved, the physical comfort felt. This intentional, repeated focus on positive data facilitates the necessary neuroplastic change (HEAL method, Book 1), strengthening the neural pathways that promote joy and contentment. The brain literally becomes more sensitized to positive input.

The Two Pillars of Gratitude Practice

To achieve these measurable benefits, gratitude must be practiced in structured ways. This book focuses on the two most effective, evidence-based interventions:

1. **Written Consistency (Gratitude Journaling):** This practice, explored in Chapter 2, provides the daily, low-friction tool necessary to maintain consistency and train your selective attention. Structured journaling is essential for altering daily cognitive habits and tracking physical benefits like improved sleep.

2. **Relational Depth (Appreciation Letters):** This intensive practice, covered in Chapter 4, targets specific social bonds. Research indicates that gratitude letters produce more intense immediate benefits and longer-lasting effects than journaling because they activate stronger social cognition processes, leading to more robust neuroplastic changes in the brain's social pathways.

This dual approach ensures you build both a deep, stable internal resource and strong, positive external relationships.

Integrating Gratitude into Your New Self

The practices in this book are not isolated. They reinforce every skill you have learned so far, ensuring the entire system remains resilient:

- **Supports Calm (Book 2):** Gratitude provides a powerful, natural detox for the stress system. By reducing the primary stress hormone, **cortisol** (Chapter 3), gratitude lowers the baseline physiological arousal in your body. This supports the vagal tone and higher HRV you established in Book 2, making it easier to stay regulated and calm when conflict hits.

- **Fuels Assertiveness (Book 3):** When you approach a difficult conversation from a place of gratitude, acknowledging the resources you have, you are less likely to demand, blame, or regress into hostility. Gratitude is the generous emotional state that makes clear, kind, and assertive communication genuine.

- **Increases Prosocial Action:** Gratitude is a direct predictor of prosocial behavior, the desire to help and share with others (Chapter 6). When you feel grateful for the support you receive, you are chemically and cognitively motivated to repay that kindness, creating a positive, reciprocal loop in your social exchanges.

The commitment to gratitude is the final, essential step in building an inner strength that is independent of circumstance. You are seizing control of your emotional destiny by choosing to focus on abundance. This simple daily habit is the key to maintaining your new outlook and health.

CHAPTER 1

WRITE IT DOWN: STARTING YOUR EVIDENCE-BASED GRATITUDE JOURNAL

In Book 1, you learned how the brain defaults to focusing on negativity, the **negativity bias**, because it is wired for survival. This natural filter causes you to prioritize worries, perceived threats, and losses over moments of contentment. If you do not actively intervene, those brief positive moments slide right off, like water on Teflon.

The commitment to structured **gratitude journaling** is the simplest, most accessible, and most consistent way to permanently fix this problem. It is not just about writing a list of things you are thankful for; it is an evidence-based intervention that forces your brain to redirect its attention. The simple daily act of writing down what is good trains your mind to scan your environment for positive data, fundamentally rewiring your focus.

This chapter is your practical guide to starting and sustaining an evidence-based gratitude journal. We will define the structure, explain why consistency matters, and detail how moving beyond simple lists of objects to genuine relational depth is what creates lasting neuroplastic change.

The Scientific Power of Selective Attention

The success of gratitude journaling lies in its capacity to alter your **selective attention**.

Selective attention is the cognitive process that allows you to focus on specific stimuli while filtering out others. If you are anxious, your selective attention filters for potential threats. If you are in a state of gratitude, your selective attention shifts to filter for experiences of abundance and well-being.

- **The Anticipatory Effect:** When you commit to a gratitude journal, your brain knows, consciously or unconsciously, that it will have to record something positive later in the day. This knowledge forces your brain to begin noticing those good things throughout the day, even before you sit down to write. This systematic "scanning" for positive data actively overrides the **Mental Filter**, the cognitive distortion that previously caused you to ignore all positive elements in a situation (Book 1, Chapter 2).
- **Rewiring the Focus:** By repeatedly engaging this positive selective attention, you create a process of positive sensitization. This process strengthens the neural pathways that promote joy and contentment (HEAL method, Book 1), making your brain faster and more efficient at registering and holding onto beneficial experiences.

The journal is simply the tool that forces this intentional, powerful cognitive shift. Without the written commitment, the positive moments remain fleeting and fail to integrate into your long-term emotional resilience.

Structuring Your Evidence-Based Journal

For the gratitude journal to work as a clinical intervention, it must be structured. Inconsistent or vague entries ("I'm grateful for my family") fail to provide the mind with the rich, detailed focus needed to facilitate real neuroplastic change. The intensity of focus is what moves the experience from a momentary good feeling to a durable psychological trait.

Rule 1: Consistency is the Neuroplastic Key

For maximum impact, the journal should be a consistent practice. Research has found that consistency in practice significantly increases positive affect and overall life satisfaction.

- **Frequency:** While some studies use weekly journaling, a daily commitment provides the greatest advantage for training selective attention and sustaining the necessary focus. The goal is to build a reliable habit.
- **Timing:** Dedicate a specific time each day, such as before bed or immediately upon waking, to writing your entries. This commitment transforms the practice into an automatic routine, reducing the resistance that comes with needing to "find time."

Rule 2: Go for Depth, Not Just Quantity

You must move beyond simple lists of objects (e.g., "Food, Car, House"). Effective journaling requires you to focus on the *why* and the *how* of the event, engaging deeper emotional and cognitive processes.

For each entry, you must answer these three questions:

1. **What:** State the specific event, interaction, or comfort you are grateful for. (Example: "The conversation I had with my colleague, Sarah, this afternoon.")
2. **Why:** Explain the *cause* of the good feeling and how the event was beneficial to you. (Example: "Because she actively listened to my new idea and gave me constructive feedback that improved the pitch.")
3. **How:** Describe the feeling and sensation in detail. This connects the cognitive thought to the physical body, which is essential for emotional absorption (HEAL method, Book 1). (Example: "I felt a deep sense of validation and competence. I felt the physical tension leave my shoulders when she offered her support.")

This sustained focus on the depth of the experience, rather than superficial listing, facilitates the neural change required to hardwire beneficial experiences into your emotional bank.

Rule 3: Target Effort and Intent (Relational Focus)

To maximize the benefits of gratitude, you must often focus on the effort or intent of other people, rather than just material objects. This is a critical step that strengthens social cognition and relational bonds.

- **Focus on Agency:** Instead of simply writing "I am grateful for my comfortable bed," write: "I am grateful that my partner made the effort to tidy the room before I came to bed, demonstrating their care and commitment to my comfort."
- **Focus on Effort:** Instead of, "The coffee was good," write: "I am grateful for the dedication of the barista who crafted that drink perfectly, providing me with a moment of peaceful enjoyment this morning."

By targeting the agency and effort of others, you are reinforcing the values of kindness and prosocial behavior in your social world. You are acknowledging that positive outcomes are often the result of intentional effort, not just luck.

Measurable Health Benefits: Sleep and Stress

The sustained practice of gratitude journaling yields quantifiable benefits that extend far beyond mood, directly impacting your physical wellness. This provides objective proof that your cognitive practice is changing your body.

1. Improved Sleep Quality

Chronic negativity, rumination, and anxiety are notorious for disrupting sleep, often by sustaining high heart rates and active minds (Book 2). Gratitude directly counteracts this.

- **The Mechanism:** By intentionally shifting your focus to positive experiences before bed, you naturally lower the psychological arousal that keeps you awake. This helps to soothe a racing heart and calm frazzled nerves.
- **The Proof:** Studies indicate that people who consistently practice gratitude journaling report **better quality sleep** and often fall asleep in a shorter period of time. This improvement in sleep is a direct, measurable benefit that reinforces the efficacy of the intervention. Better sleep, in turn, strengthens your PFC function, making emotional regulation easier the next day.

2. Cortisol Reduction and Immune Support

Gratitude provides a natural detox for the stress system. The practice actively reduces the levels of **cortisol**, your body's primary stress hormone.

- **The Mechanism:** A state of gratitude activates the parasympathetic nervous system ("rest-and-digest"), shifting resources away from the constant high alert that characterizes chronic stress. This dampening of the stress response directly lowers cortisol levels.

- **The Proof:** Studies connecting gratitude and appreciation found that participants experienced a reduction in cortisol levels and had better cardiac function. This reduction in cortisol is particularly important because high cortisol is often linked to diminished immune function. By lowering cortisol through gratitude, you are actively supporting your immune system and increasing your physiological resilience against chronic ailments.

Gratitude is a behavioral intervention that chemically regulates the negative stress response, building genuine physiological resistance to environmental stress.

Integration with Your Existing Skills

The gratitude journal serves as the practical application lab for all the skills you have learned so far, cementing them into one system:

1. **Reinforcing the HEAL Method (Book 1):** The journaling process is the mandatory second phase of the HEAL method. You use the journal to *Enrich* and *Absorb* the positive experience. By writing the *Why* and *How* of the good feeling, you ensure the positive memory is detailed and robust enough to create lasting neural change.

2. **Counteracting Rumination (Book 2):** The journal forces a shift in your attention's object. Instead of dwelling on past conflicts or future worries (rumination), your mind is constructively focused on the present moment's positive data. This practice, when done consistently, makes it easier for you to interrupt the toxic replay loop when anger strikes.

3. **Fuels Compassion (Book 3):** By focusing on the effort and kind intent of others, the journal strengthens your capacity for compassion. This practice helps you reduce toxic emotions like envy and resentment by forcing a comparative focus on what is good in your life, rather than what is missing in comparison to others.

The commitment to a structured gratitude journal ensures the continuous sensitization of your brain toward positive affect. This simple, evidence-based habit is the engine that drives your inner strength, setting the stage for deeper relational appreciation.

CHAPTER 2

FEEL THE HEALTH BENEFITS:

GRATITUDE'S EFFECT ON STRESS AND SLEEP

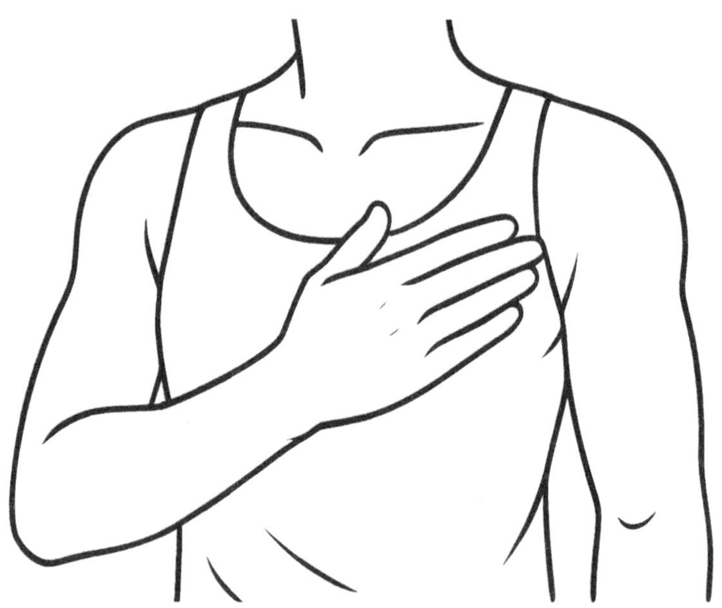

In the previous chapter, you learned how to start your gratitude journal, training your selective attention to consistently register positive data. This cognitive shift, from looking for lack to looking for abundance, is powerful for your mental state.

But the effect of gratitude is not confined to your mind. It is a powerful physiological intervention. The mental habit of appreciation generates measurable, verifiable physical changes in your body, directly addressing the damage caused by chronic stress and anxiety (the initial problem addressed in Book 2).

This chapter provides the scientific evidence for gratitude's physical power. We will explore how consistent gratitude practice detoxifies your stress system by lowering cortisol, strengthens your cardiac function, and, crucially, improves the quality of your sleep. By understanding these deep, physical benefits, you gain confidence that your deliberate effort to cultivate appreciation is a vital part of your long-term health plan.

Gratitude as a Chemical Detox: Lowering Cortisol

Chronic negativity and sustained hostility (the habits this entire guide is working to reverse) keep the body in a state of low-level physiological arousal: a continuous sympathetic overdrive. This state is highly damaging, and it is chemically maintained by the stress hormone **cortisol**.

Cortisol is the primary chemical messenger in your body's fight-or-flight response. While essential for immediate danger, chronic, high levels of cortisol are linked to inflammation, weakened immune function, and the negative neuroplasticity that impairs emotional regulation in the brain (Book 1). You cannot achieve sustainable inner strength if your body is constantly flooded with the chemical signal of stress.

Gratitude acts as a direct, natural detox for this system.

- **The Mechanism of Downregulation:** Committing to a daily gratitude practice forces your mind to dwell on feelings of contentment, safety, and sufficiency. This emotional state activates the **parasympathetic nervous system**, your "rest-and-digest" system, shifting resources away from the constant high alert that characterizes chronic stress. This systemic shift directly dampens the HPA (hypothalamic-pituitary-adrenal) axis, which is the system that produces cortisol.

- **The Measurable Proof:** Studies on gratitude and appreciation have found that participants experienced a measurable **reduction in cortisol levels**. This reduction confirms that the deliberate mental habit of appreciation chemically regulates the negative stress response. By lowering cortisol, you are actively supporting your immune system and increasing your physiological resilience against chronic ailments.

This physiological dampening is why gratitude is correlated with resilience. When your cortisol levels are lower, your body is simply better equipped to handle stress. You are more resilient to emotional setbacks and negative experiences, allowing you to approach challenges with more awareness and a broader perspective, rather than collapsing into emotional reaction.

Strengthening the Heart: Cardiac Function and Resilience

The benefits of gratitude extend directly to your cardiovascular system, reinforcing the internal regulation work you mastered in Book 2 (HRV).

Recall that Heart Rate Variability (HRV) is the measure of the healthy fluctuation between heartbeats, and high HRV is strongly associated with better vagal nerve function and superior emotional regulation. Chronic stress and anger are linked to low, rigid HRV, which places the heart under increased workload.

- **The Cardiac Benefit:** Studies found that participants who engaged in structured appreciation experienced **better cardiac function**. This occurs because the sustained, positive emotional state promoted by gratitude encourages rhythmic, slow breathing and engages the parasympathetic system (the vagal brake), which stabilizes heart function.

- **Increased Resilience to Setbacks:** When you practice gratitude, you are essentially training your body to maintain a state of calm balance. This training helps your heart and nervous system cope better with sudden negative input. Gratitude makes you more resilient to emotional setbacks because your body is not starting from a place of high physiological arousal.

This objective evidence means that the practice of appreciating the good in your life is not a luxury; it is a vital, self-administered intervention for maintaining cardiovascular and emotional health. It ensures that the high HRV and low heart rate you achieved through breathing exercises (Book 2) are maintained throughout your daily life.

The Sleep Solution: Breaking the Cycle of Arousal

One of the most immediate and appreciated benefits of gratitude journaling is its profound impact on sleep quality. If you struggle to fall asleep or maintain sleep, the primary culprit is often high **psychological arousal**, the constant, toxic loop of worry and planning that keeps your mind active at night.

- **The Failure of Suppressing Worry:** Trying to simply *force* yourself to stop worrying rarely works, because the anxious thoughts are often fueled by the negative bias and sustained by physiological tension (low HRV, high cortisol).

- **The Gratitude Intervention:** Gratitude provides a functional replacement for worry. By intentionally shifting your focus to three to five specific things you are genuinely appreciative of before you lie down, you force your mind to engage with positive, calming data. This conscious shift interrupts the toxic cycle of planning and rumination that keeps you awake. It redirects your attention away from threats and toward safety and contentment, which are the necessary internal conditions for sleep.

- **The Measurable Proof:** Studies consistently indicate that people who regularly practice gratitude journaling report **better quality sleep** and often fall asleep in a shorter period of time. By soothing a racing heart and calming the nervous system, gratitude acts as a natural relaxant, allowing your body to transition smoothly into a regenerative state. Better sleep, in turn, strengthens your Prefrontal Cortex (PFC), enhancing your emotional regulation and memory the next day.

Gratitude is thus a direct behavioral remedy for the stress-induced sleep disruption that characterizes high-pressure modern life.

The Mechanism of Deep Focus: From Superficial to Enduring

The power of gratitude to induce these health benefits depends on the intensity and duration of your focus. Simply thinking a quick thank you is a good start, but it does not generate lasting chemical change. You must commit to **savoring** the experience.

This chapter reinforces the principles of the **HEAL Method** (Book 1, Chapter 4), emphasizing the importance of *Enriching* and *Absorbing* the feeling for at least 15 to 30 seconds. When journaling, this means going deep into the *how* and *why* of the feeling:

- **The Cognitive Detail:** Why did the conversation feel good? (Because my colleague validated my idea.)

- **The Emotional Detail:** What specific emotion did that trigger? (Pride, competence, ease.)

- **The Somatic Detail:** Where did I feel it in my body? (Warmth in the chest, relaxation in the jaw.)

This sustained, detailed focus on positive affect is what facilitates the neuroplastic change that lowers your body's stress threshold. It is this depth of engagement that makes gratitude a functional tool for physiological health.

Gratitude as Internal Fortitude

This chapter confirms that the daily habit of gratitude journaling is not a soft suggestion; it is a critical intervention for maintaining your physical and emotional equilibrium. It actively detoxifies the chemical residue of past negativity and hostility.

By consistently integrating journaling, you are lowering your cortisol levels, improving your cardiac resilience, and guaranteeing better sleep. This foundation of internal fortitude ensures that the emotional strength you have built is resilient, reliable, and deeply wired. You are moving from relying on external circumstances for happiness to generating inner strength through your own intentional focus.

The next step is to take this deep internal resource and apply it to your most important relationships. We move now from the solitary act of journaling to the powerful, bonding act of written appreciation.

CHAPTER 3

GO DEEPER: USING WRITTEN APPRECIATION TO STRENGTHEN BONDS

You have achieved consistency. You know the gratitude journal is working its quiet magic, lowering your stress, improving your sleep, and training your attention to find the good. That internal work is essential. It is the steady income of emotional resilience.

But here is the truth about human connection: we are not built to thrive in isolation. We are deeply social creatures. The highest form of gratitude, the practice that generates the most durable, life-altering change, is not solitary. It is **relational**.

When your appreciation shifts from a simple list in a journal to a structured piece of written appreciation addressed to another human being, the impact multiplies. This focused practice, often called a gratitude letter, is a high-leverage emotional action. It targets and strengthens the specific social bonds that support your life. Research confirms this targeted practice generates more intense benefits and longer-lasting effects than journaling alone. You are not just being kind. You are actively repairing and reinforcing the very social fabric that sustains your emotional health.

Why is writing a letter more powerful than a journal entry? It is about activation.

Your daily journal helps you manage the negativity bias inside your head. The letter forces you to process the good experience through the lens of *another person's agency* and *effort*. This is a massive cognitive leap. It activates stronger **social cognition processes** in your brain.

The emotional reward is intensified because you are engaging in the full reward circuit related to connection and prosocial behavior.

1. **Activating Social Pathways:** When you write a letter detailing how someone's effort helped you, you engage the neural pathways responsible for complex social behavior, including the areas linked to empathy and "theory of mind" (mPFC and dlPFC, as discussed in Book 3). You are actively thinking about their intentions, their effort, and the cost they incurred to help you.

2. **Durable Neuroplastic Change:** This targeted relational focus creates more robust and durable neural changes. It reinforces the brain's social pathways and the reward circuits associated with prosocial behavior, making the feeling of connection itself more valuable and lasting. The benefits, including sustained improvements in mood and life satisfaction, are often reported weeks and months after the letter is written and delivered.

3. **Overcoming Emotional Debt:** The negativity bias often creates emotional debt in relationships. We quickly absorb criticism or perceived slights (the cost) but fail to register or vocalize appreciation (the reward). This creates an unbalanced emotional ledger. The gratitude letter is a specific, powerful action that clears that debt, transforming a relationship from one of potential deficit to one of clear abundance.

The letter is not just a nice gesture. It is a strategically deployed tool designed to generate and solidify emotional resilience through confirmed social connection.

A letter only achieves these powerful benefits if it moves beyond vague compliments. It must convey genuine, specific appreciation. The goal is to make the recipient feel seen, valued, and understood at a deep, relational level.

The writing protocol involves three essential components that directly link the action back to the principles of NVC (Book 3) and the HEAL Method (Book 1).

1. Identify the Specific Contribution (The Observation)

You must start with verifiable facts, just like in NVC's **Observation** step. Identify a specific action, event, date, or quality of the person that profoundly impacted you. You must move past generic praise (e.g., "You are a kind person") to the specific, tangible evidence of their kindness.

- **Focus:** Be precise about the "when" and "what." Detail the moment so the recipient cannot doubt that you were paying attention.
- *Ineffective*: "Thank you for all your support over the years."
- *Effective*: "I am writing specifically about the Tuesday two months ago when I was completely swamped with the Smith account. You saw me panic, and without being asked, you took the lead on the client call, taking all the pressure off me."

This specificity is critical. It proves you were not just passively benefiting from their kindness. You were actively noticing their effort, which is a major reward in any relationship (Social Exchange Theory).

2. Describe the Emotional and Practical Impact (The Feeling and Need)

This is the emotional core of the letter. You must articulate the internal emotional impact their specific action had on you, linking it to a core, universal need that was met. This requires honest vulnerability.

- **Action Focus:** Describe the "before and after." What negative feeling did they help alleviate (e.g., fear, loneliness, panic), and what positive feeling did they create (e.g., safety, competence, peace)? This engages the listener's empathy.
- *Ineffective*: "That was a big help."
- *Effective*: "Before you stepped in on that call, I was feeling totally overwhelmed and panicked, which was violating my deep need for **professional competence** and **safety** in my job. Your action immediately met those needs. It gave me a sense of calm and competence back, which allowed me to think clearly and finish the project correctly."

This deep articulation moves the appreciation from a surface level to a profound human connection. The recipient understands their effort had a quantifiable, positive effect on your well-being, which is intrinsically rewarding (reward circuits, Book 3, Chapter 5).

3. Express Profound Thanks and Future Intent (The Commitment)

Conclude the letter by summarizing the lasting value of their action and, if appropriate, state your commitment to maintaining the bond.

- **Action Focus:** Reiterate the long-term emotional or practical resource their kindness created.
- *Effective:* "Thank you. That moment of support was not just a one-time favor; it built my confidence to handle the next crisis. Knowing I can rely on your partnership is something I deeply value. I commit to being there for you with the same calm and focus whenever you need it."

The Durable Benefits of Relational Gratitude

The sustained effects of gratitude letters validate their power as a superior tool for emotional strengthening.

- **Sustained Emotional Boost:** The positive emotions generated are not fleeting. Participants report measurable improvements in overall mood, life satisfaction, and interpersonal relationships for **weeks and months** after completing gratitude letter exercises. This durability proves that the practice creates lasting neural changes, building genuine emotional resilience, rather than merely temporary emotional states.
- **Reduced Toxic Comparison:** By intentionally focusing on the benevolence and positive intentions of others, the practice of writing appreciation letters actively counters toxic emotions like envy and resentment. You train your mind to look for connection and good intent, rather than focusing on the deficits that comparison (envy) creates.
- **Health and Coping Outcomes:** This relational gratitude supports the physiological benefits noted in Chapter 3: continued reduction in stress hormones (cortisol) and increased resilience against emotional setbacks, which is linked to better cardiac function. You use the power of connection to chemically regulate your body.

The Reciprocal Loop: Find-Remind-Bind Theory

The delivery of your written appreciation does more than just make the recipient feel good. It activates a powerful **reciprocal loop** that strengthens your entire social network. This loop is explained by the **Find-Remind-Bind Theory** of gratitude.

1. **Find:** Gratitude helps the giver *find* and recognize others who are valuable and worthy of sustained social connection (i.e., people who consistently provide support and kindness).

2. **Remind:** The explicit expression of gratitude *reminds* the recipient of their own prosocial behavior. This act is intrinsically rewarding and motivates them to continue acting kindly toward the grateful person ("I want to do this again").

3. **Bind:** The reciprocal cycle *binds* the two individuals together, deepening the social bonds and motivating both parties to seek continued connection.

This cycle means the inner strength you gain from gratitude directly increases your prosocial motivation, your desire to help and share with others, which is a key component of emotional health and social acceptance. By reinforcing the goodness received, you are cognitively and chemically motivated to contribute goodness back to the social exchange.

Action Plan: Moving from Journaling to Letters

Your task is to choose at least one person this week who has made a specific, positive impact and write them a structured letter of appreciation.

Step 1: Select the Target: Choose someone whose effort you have not fully acknowledged.

Step 2: Draft the Three-Part Script: Use the protocol outlined above to ensure your letter is specific, emotionally vulnerable, and committed to future connection.

Step 3: Deliver and Observe the Reward: The final step is delivering the letter, preferably in person, if possible. After the delivery, pause and reflect on the resulting feeling. This moment, the visible confirmation that your effort strengthened a valued bond, is the most potent reward. It is this relational feedback that cements the positive neuroplastic change more powerfully than a solitary journal entry.

By integrating written appreciation into your habits, you are using high-leverage emotional action to rewire your social brain. You are transforming passive observation into an active engine for connection, ensuring that your inner strength is constantly reinforced by the quality of your relationships.

CHAPTER 4

EXPAND YOUR FOCUS:

GRATITUDE FOR RESILIENCE AND HARD TIMES

You have successfully used gratitude to deepen your internal quiet. You are training your attention daily through journaling, and you have experienced the profound bonding power of written appreciation (Chapter 4). You know gratitude works when things are simply okay.

But life is not always okay.

Inevitably, genuine stress returns. You face a major financial reversal, a sudden conflict, or a serious professional setback. When these crises hit, the negativity bias screams loudest, threatening to hijack all the calm and clarity you have achieved. Your mind reverts to focusing on loss, risk, and lack.

The purpose of this chapter is to prepare you for that moment. We must ensure that your commitment to gratitude is not merely a fair-weather habit but a core psychological muscle that fires fastest under pressure. Gratitude, applied intentionally during genuine adversity, is your most powerful tool for building **resilience**, the ability to adapt and recover quickly from hardship. It prevents your mind from collapsing into toxic comparison and sustained despair.

Resilience is not about being tough or ignoring pain. It is about the efficiency and speed with which you can restore your body and mind to equilibrium after a shock. Without gratitude, the mind defaults to two deeply corrosive behaviors during a crisis:

1. The Collapse into Envy and Comparison

When suffering a setback, a job loss, a divorce, an illness, the mind has a dangerous knack for immediately comparing your life to a perceived ideal or to the apparent success of others. This comparison activates the toxic emotions of envy, jealousy, and resentment.

- **The Mechanism of Envy:** Envy is focusing on what is *missing* in your life relative to someone else's perceived abundance. If you are struggling financially, your mind finds every person enjoying ease. If you are facing relational trouble, your mind fixes on couples who seem happy. This comparison creates a sense of profound injustice and inadequacy, which is entirely self-defeating.

- **The Cost:** Envy consumes vast mental bandwidth, trapping you in a cycle of dissatisfaction and robbing you of the energy needed for practical problem-solving. It ensures that the emotional focus is entirely on *deficits* and *lack*, which reinforces the negativity bias.

2. The Mental Filter of Loss

During genuine hard times, the cognitive distortion known as the **Mental Filter** (Book 1) becomes intensely destructive. Your mind becomes hyper-focused on the specific loss, the health problem, the failed investment, the hurtful remark, while actively filtering out all the resources, support systems, and good things that remain present in your life.

This failure to see the full, balanced picture is what causes feelings of hopelessness. The world appears entirely dark because your mental filter is temporarily blocking out the light.

Gratitude is the direct, intentional counter-measure to both of these states. It forces the mind to shift its gaze from the *gap* (what is lost) to the *ground* (what remains, what is sufficient, and what is currently supporting you).

The practice of gratitude builds genuine internal fortitude by changing how you process difficult information. It does not deny the pain of the setback; it places the pain within a broader context of resources and support.

Studies show a strong correlation between feeling grateful and experiencing greater resilience and emotional strength. This happens because gratitude actively trains the mind to cope with difficult circumstances by adopting a **broader perception** and increased awareness of surrounding factors.

1. Focusing on the "What Remains"

When facing loss, your immediate instinct is to list what is gone. Gratitude forces you to list what is *still present* and functional.

- *Scenario*: You lose a significant project or client (financial loss).

- *Default Negative Focus*: "I lost the client. I am a failure. My finances are ruined." (Catastrophizing, Mental Filter).

- *Gratitude Resilience Focus*: "The loss is painful, but what remains? I still have my core professional competence. I still have a positive relationship with my past clients. I still have my health and my network. I still have two months of savings. I appreciate the financial security I built that allows me to withstand this setback."

This conscious reframing shifts your attention from the destructive thought of "ruin" to the constructive action of "resources." It affirms that the integrity of your life is defined by the whole picture, not one missing piece.

2. Maintaining Stress Tolerance

During a crisis, the body's natural response is to flood the system with cortisol and adrenaline. This keeps you in a debilitating state of high arousal. Resilience is measured by how effectively you can regulate this flood, preventing it from spiraling into anxiety or aggressive reaction (Book 2).

- **The Chemical Buffer:** Gratitude acts as a continuous emotional buffer. By maintaining a grateful state, even for small things, you continue to activate the parasympathetic nervous system, which helps lower the baseline levels of cortisol. This physiological dampening ensures that when the crisis hits, your stress system is not starting from an already hyper-aroused state.

- **The Proof:** Research has specifically shown that participants who experienced a reduction in stress hormones (cortisol) and exhibited better cardiac function were also more resilient to emotional setbacks and negative experiences. This underscores that gratitude is not just mental wishful thinking. It provides a real, chemical shield against the damaging effects of external stress.

By practicing gratitude in hard times, you are actively choosing to protect your body's stress tolerance threshold, ensuring that you can think clearly enough to engage your problem-solving skills (Book 2, Chapter 5) rather than collapsing into emotional paralysis.

Applying Gratitude in Crisis: The Reframing Lens

To maximize gratitude's impact during adversity, you need specific, high-leverage practices that directly challenge the "Mental Filter" and the "All-or-Nothing Thinking" (Book 1, Chapter 2) that thrive in crisis.

Action Tool 1: The "This is Tolerable" Practice

When the pressure is overwhelming, the mind often defaults to the catastrophic belief that the current suffering is unbearable. The "This is Tolerable" Practice forces an acceptance of the present reality while acknowledging the small things that prevent total collapse.

1. **Acknowledge the Pain (Fact):** State the difficulty directly without minimizing it. *Example: "I am feeling deep anxiety about my finances."*

2. **Identify the Tolerable Present:** Immediately shift attention to the small, objective facts that are *currently* making the situation non-terminal.

   - *Example Focus:* "I am breathing easily right now. I have a roof over my head tonight. I have food in the refrigerator. My physical body is not in immediate danger. The current moment is **tolerable**."

3. **Find Gratitude in the Unseen Support:** Express appreciation for the often-unseen infrastructure that keeps the crisis from becoming a total catastrophe. *Example: "I appreciate the consistent effort of my partner who is working hard, and I am grateful for the structural security of our home."*

This practice grounds you firmly in the present moment, which is a known benefit of expressing gratitude. It pulls your focus away from the speculative, catastrophic future and into the factual, manageable present, enabling you to conserve your energy for real problem-solving.

Action Tool 2: Gratitude for the "Dark Teacher"

This advanced application involves finding appreciation not just *despite* the adversity, but sometimes *for* the adversity itself, viewing it as a "Dark Teacher" or a catalyst for growth. This is the ultimate expression of resilience.

- **The Focus:** You are not grateful *for* the suffering, but grateful *for the clarity or competence* the suffering forced you to develop.

- *Scenario:* A relational conflict that was painful but necessary (Book 3).

- *Gratitude Focus:* "I am grateful that the conflict forced us to finally use the DESC Script and define our boundaries (Chapter 3). Before the fight, we never had the courage to set these limits. I appreciate the **clarity** and **strength** that the pain delivered."

This form of gratitude helps you transform the energy of failure or loss into the energy of learning and growth. It is a powerful form of cognitive restructuring, actively replacing the sense of helplessness with a sense of growth and agency. The consistent practice of this perspective is what allows people to cope with difficult circumstances with a broader, more resourceful mindset.

The Role of Relational Gratitude in Crisis

When under acute stress, the tendency is to isolate, withdrawing from others to manage shame or fear. This isolation is dangerous because it removes the very social support systems that buffer stress and promote prosocial behavior.

This is where the relational practices from Chapter 4 become vital.

- **Reinforcing the Bond:** When you are struggling, expressing gratitude to those who are helping you, even for small efforts, reinforces the **reciprocal loop** (Find-Remind-Bind Theory). You remind the helper that their effort is seen and valued, which motivates them to continue providing support. This is critical for stabilizing the social exchange during a high-cost period.

- **The Strength of Connection:** Expressing gratitude, even when you feel depleted, encourages prosocial behavior and increases the desire to spend time with others, countering the isolation driven by anxiety. Social support is crucial for mitigating the negative emotional effects of stress, anxiety, and loneliness.

The consistent practice of relational gratitude, even if it is just a text message appreciating a friend's patience, ensures that your lifeline remains intact during the storm.

The Unwavering Inner Strength

The practices in this chapter, focusing on what remains, auditing for tolerance, and reframing adversity, ensure that gratitude moves from a simple feeling to an **unwavering inner strength**.

This strength is quantifiable: you are chemically regulating your stress response, emotionally counteracting toxic comparison, and cognitively maintaining a broad, solution-oriented perspective, even when the pressure is immense.

By committing to gratitude, you are seizing control of your emotional destiny by ensuring your focus is on abundance, not lack. This final, integrated practice is the most powerful tool for maintaining your resilient outlook, preparing you for the final book, where we will translate this inner strength into the external integrity of self-respect and clear boundaries.

CHAPTER 5

GIVE IT BACK: GRATITUDE AND INCREASING PROSOCIAL BEHAVIOR

You have done the deep work. You have trained your mind to find the good, to appreciate the specific efforts of others, and to use that focus to calm your body and lower your stress hormones. You have built a serious, durable internal reserve of emotional resilience.

But what is inner strength for, if not to be spent?

If you keep that abundance bottled up, it stagnates. The greatest function of gratitude is relational: it serves as the most reliable indicator that you are ready to engage in **prosocial behavior**, the actions intended to help, share, and cooperate with others. When you feel genuinely grateful, you are chemically and cognitively motivated to contribute kindness back into the social world, completing a powerful, positive feedback loop that stabilizes your relationships and reinforces your own peace.

This commitment to external generosity is the final step in this book. It ensures that your kind speech (Book 3) is consistently backed by generous action. We are translating inner appreciation into external momentum.

Why Kindness is Not Optional: The Prosocial Mandate

Prosocial behaviors are simply actions intended to help other people, driven by a fundamental concern for their feelings and welfare. Holding a door open, sharing a resource, offering comfort, or cooperating are all part of this. They are the behavioral opposite of the hurtful and hostile habits you are discarding.

Why must you make this a priority? Because kind action is necessary for the health of your social life and your own mental state:

1. **The Social Glue:** Prosocial actions forge connections and hold the fabric of social life together. They help you establish social support, which is critical for coping with personal hardships. When you are kind, you build the safety net you will inevitably need.

2. **The Mood-Boosting Effect:** Kindness is its own reward system. Research has consistently shown that people who frequently engage in prosocial behaviors are more likely to experience better moods. It gets better: people who help others tend to experience negative moods *less frequently*. Helping is an active way to keep the negativity bias at bay (Book 1).

3. **Stress Management:** Need a reliable way to reduce the impact of stress? Help someone else. Research found that engaging in prosocial behaviors helps mitigate the negative emotional effects of stress on the helper. When you focus outward to assist another person, you constructively redirect cognitive energy away from your internal worries, giving your mind a functional, positive task.

You are not being asked to be a martyr. You are being asked to engage in an action that is scientifically proven to improve your own mood, reduce your stress, and solidify your social safety net.

The Reciprocal Engine: Find-Remind-Bind Theory

How exactly does feeling grateful (an internal state) lead to a powerful motivation to act (an external state)? The **Find-Remind-Bind Theory** provides the scientific roadmap for this reciprocal cycle. This theory confirms that expressing thanks is not the conclusion of the process; it is the catalyst for the next round of connection.

1. **Find:** Gratitude first helps the individual *find* and recognize others who are valuable and worthy of sustained social connection, those who reliably provide support and kindness. You sharpen your social intelligence by prioritizing healthy, supportive relationships.

2. **Remind:** The expression of gratitude, whether through a quick text or a detailed letter (Chapter 4), *reminds* the recipient of their own prosocial behavior. This act is intrinsically rewarding to the helper and motivates them to continue acting kindly toward the grateful person. Your thanks acts as positive reinforcement for their generosity.

3. **Bind:** The resulting reciprocal cycle *binds* the two individuals together, strengthening the social bond. This deepens the relationship and motivates both parties to seek continued connection, stabilizing the social exchange.

This entire mechanism confirms that gratitude is a powerful, direct predictor of prosocial motivation. By acknowledging the support you receive, you are chemically and cognitively motivated to repay that kindness, creating a durable, positive loop in your social exchanges. Your inner strength is literally multiplied by the strength of your connections.

Action Tool 1: The Daily Kindness Commitment

To actively engage this reciprocal cycle, you must integrate small, low-cost acts of kindness into your daily routine. This turns your internal appreciation into external momentum. This principle is supported by research showing that prompting individuals to engage in kind acts yields benefits beyond personal happiness, promoting better social acceptance and overall well-being.

Action Focus: Proactive, Measurable Kindness

The act must be low-cost and easily achievable. This leverages the **SMART goal** principles you mastered in Book 1 (Chapter 5), guaranteeing a successful win that reinforces your motivation (dopamine release).

1. **Verbal Validation:** Commit to giving one sincere, specific compliment or verbal validation today. The focus must be on **effort or competence**, not just appearance. Don't be vague. *Example: Instead of saying, "Your presentation was fine," say, "I really appreciated the specific effort you put into structuring that opening section; the way you handled the data made the entire*

complex argument immediately clear." This uses your Kind Speech skills (Book 3) to deliver a clear, high-reward message that reinforces their competence.

2. **Removing a Burden:** Look for a small burden you can quietly remove from someone else's path, especially in a shared environment. *Example: Without being asked, take out a communal recycling bin, or silently wipe down the shared kitchen counter at work.* This small, unsolicited act of support reinforces the social bond by demonstrating attention and care, fulfilling the other person's need for **ease** and **support** (NVC, Book 3).

3. **Offer Presence:** Intentionally set aside your phone and offer a few minutes of **undivided attention** to someone who is speaking to you. *Example: Fully listen to a colleague or partner recount a stressful event without interrupting, distracting yourself, or formulating your own response.* This fulfills the basic human need for presence, validation, and being truly heard, which is a powerful prosocial act that mitigates their stress.

These actions are deliberate attempts to inject positive rewards into your social environment, ensuring your relationships are defined by mutual support and abundance.

Action Tool 2: Gratitude as a Strategy Against Envy

Prosocial behavior is not just about doing favors. It is a powerful psychological strategy for managing complex internal emotional dynamics, specifically those related to toxic comparison and material scarcity (Book 4, Chapter 5).

When you feel that sharp twinge of envy regarding another person's success, a big promotion, a new piece of property, or effortless ease, your mind is locked on focusing on *lack* and *injustice*. This internal state often leads to passive-aggressive behavior or hostility toward the person you envy, damaging the relationship. Gratitude provides a functional alternative.

Action Focus: Appreciating the Process, Not the Outcome

1. **Acknowledge the Pain (Fact):** State the feeling without judgment: "I feel a sharp twinge of envy when I see my colleague's new leadership title."

2. **Shift to Process Gratitude:** Immediately shift your focus to appreciating the *process, effort,* or *competence* that person likely invested to achieve that goal. You must engage your Empathy

Circuits (Book 3) to see their struggle. *Example: "I appreciate the consistent dedication and early mornings my colleague clearly exerted over the last year to master those skills. I am grateful for their visible example of competence and hard work; it shows what is possible."*

3. **Translate to Self-Action:** Convert that appreciation into a positive, low-cost action for yourself. This turns envy into motivation. *Example: "I will immediately send them a congratulatory note (prosocial behavior), and then I will use the next hour to work on my own SMART goal for professional skill development (Book 1, Chapter 5)."*

By appreciating their process, you transform the toxic energy of envy into the functional energy of motivation and prosocial action. This prevents the corrosive effects of envy from damaging your relationships, fulfilling your personal value of *integrity* by aligning your actions with your best self.

Integrating External Action with Internal Strength

The practices in this chapter ensure that your external actions reinforce the deep internal strength you have built across all four books.

- **Fuels Kind Speech (Book 3):** Your mastery of assertive communication is strongest when it comes from a place of gratitude and generosity, not demand. Gratitude for a reliable partner makes it easier to use the DESC script with care and acceptance when addressing a conflict, rather than reverting to criticism and aggression. The emotional reserve provided by gratitude (low cortisol, high positive affect) acts as a buffer, ensuring your assertive requests are delivered with the respect that makes them effective.

- **Reinforces Integrity (Book 5):** Living a life of integrity requires aligning your actions with your core values (Book 5, Chapter 6). If your values include "kindness," "community," or "support," then the consistent practice of prosocial behavior ensures that your external actions align with your internal principles. This alignment is the highest form of self-respect.

- **Combats Hostility (Book 2):** Prosocial commitment provides a healthy, positive outlet for emotional energy, preventing the accumulation of resentment and stress that often fuels aggressive outbursts. Helping others mitigates the negative emotional effects of your own stress.

The inner strength you have built through gratitude is now your engine for kindness. By moving from internal appreciation to external, measurable action, you are contributing to a positive, resilient social exchange that supports your well-being and strengthens your connections. This commitment to prosocial action is the final step before we focus on the external integrity of self-respect and boundaries.

CONCLUSION

THE GRATITUDE HABIT: MAINTAINING YOUR NEW OUTLOOK AND HEALTH

You have arrived at a significant turning point. This book was your training camp for emotional self-sufficiency. You took the idea of being thankful and turned it into a structured, daily habit. You now know that genuine gratitude is not just a nice feeling you wait for. It is a powerful, active tool you generate and control.

We must conclude with a clear understanding: the emotional quiet you feel now is not luck. It is the direct, measurable result of consistent effort. You have ensured that the strength you built is reliable, verifiable, and self-sustaining. This is how you make an outlook based on abundance, not scarcity, your new, permanent way of life.

The Science of Proof: You Are Resilient

The greatest reward for mastering gratitude is the objective proof that your internal systems are repairing. You are seeing a quantifiable decrease in the negative chemistry that defined your past habits.

1. Measurable Relief from Worry and Despair

The emotional toll of constant negativity and hostility is immense. You tackled this burden head-on. The systematic work you did, forcing your mind to track positive data daily through journaling, has provided clinical relief you can trust.

- **Anxiety Reduction:** It is not a small thing. Studies confirm that people who consistently used gratitude interventions experienced a significant reduction in anxiety symptoms. This shows up as a **7.76% lower score on the Generalized Anxiety Disorder (GAD-7) assessment** compared to control groups. That drop in anxiety is your freedom. It proves that your mind is now less consumed by the pervasive "what-if" scenarios that previously paralyzed you.

- **Depression Relief:** Similarly, the same analysis found that gratitude interventions led to a significant reduction in depressive symptoms, achieving a **6.89% lower score on the Patient Health Questionnaire-9 (PHQ-9)**. This proves that the daily, deliberate focus on what is present and functional actively counteracts the sense of hopelessness and deficit that fuels depression. Gratitude forces your mind to find evidence of sufficiency, which is the direct cognitive antidote to despair.

This objective evidence means your mind is quieter and less prone to worry and negative rumination. It is a functional success.

2. Physiological Regulation and Resilience

Your gratitude practice has become a powerful, continuous maintenance program for your physical health and the calm you mastered in Book 2.

- **Cortisol Detox:** Chronic stress, the foundation of negative habits, is chemically maintained by the stress hormone, **cortisol**. By consistently dwelling on feelings of safety and contentment through journaling and savoring, you activated the parasympathetic nervous system (the brake). This behavioral choice leads to a measurable **reduction in cortisol levels**. This reduction is vital because lowered cortisol supports immune function and actively counteracts the negative neuroplasticity that impairs emotional regulation in the PFC (Book 1).

- **Improved Cardiac Function and Resilience:** Studies indicate that the sustained emotional state promoted by gratitude is linked to **better cardiac function** and measurable resilience against emotional setbacks. When your body is regulated by gratitude, it is quicker to adapt and recover from stress.

- **Sleep Quality:** The intentional shift in attention before bedtime allows you to successfully interrupt the psychological arousal that causes insomnia and rumination (Book 2). Studies consistently confirm that people who practice gratitude journaling report **better quality sleep**. This improved sleep, in turn, strengthens the regulatory power of your Prefrontal Cortex (PFC), enhancing your emotional control and memory capacity the following day.

You are now physically, chemically, and neurologically more resilient to the pressures of the external world because your internal focus is on sufficiency and safety.

The Sustained Mechanism: Making the Good Stick

The durability of these changes relies on your mastery of neuroplastic principles: sensitization and savoring. You have successfully taught your brain to prioritize the positive.

1. **Creating "Velcro for the Good":** Your brain operates on sensitization: repeated activation makes neural circuits more responsive. You spent this book using your **Gratitude Journal** and the **HEAL Method** (Book 1) to force your mind to focus intently on the good for extended periods (savoring). This sustained focus is what facilitates neuroplastic change, ensuring that your brain becomes faster and more efficient at registering and holding onto positive input (the "Velcro for the good").

2. **Relational Reinforcement:** The practice of **Written Appreciation** (Chapter 4) further cemented this change by reinforcing your **social cognition** circuits. By consistently acknowledging the efforts of others, you tapped into the highly rewarding reciprocal loop (**Find-Remind-Bind Theory**, Chapter 6). When you express gratitude, the recipient is motivated to continue their prosocial behavior, and you are motivated to sustain the grateful habit because you receive the reward of reinforced connection. This social reinforcement makes the habit of gratitude intrinsically self-sustaining.

3. **Countering Toxic Emotions:** This consistent, active focus on abundance ensures that you move beyond the toxic cycle of **envy and comparison** that destroys self-worth (Chapter 5). By

consciously focusing on the *assets* and *competence* you possess and the *resources* that surround you, you build a powerful cognitive shield against the internal pressure of perceived lack.

The inner strength you have built is now the non-negotiable emotional resource that stabilizes and fuels the entire five-book system.

- **Fuels Kind Speech and Assertiveness (Book 3):** Your mastery of assertive communication is now delivered from a place of emotional sufficiency, not neediness. Gratitude provides the generous emotional reserve that allows you to be clear and firm (assertive) without becoming demanding or aggressive. You can approach conflict (DESC Script) from a position of "I have plenty, but this is my need," rather than "I need you to fill my empty tank."

- **Supports Agency (Book 1):** Gratitude directly counteracts the feeling of **learned helplessness** (Book 1, Chapter 5). When you face a large problem, your gratitude practice ensures your mind automatically focuses on the **assets** you possess (your health, your network, your skills) rather than the perceived deficit. This shift from focusing on *loss* to focusing on *resources* enables you to launch a strong, solution-oriented action plan.

- **Increases Integrity (Book 5):** When you consistently engage in prosocial behavior (Chapter 6), driven by your gratitude, your external actions align with your internal values of generosity and kindness. This integrity is the highest form of self-respect, and it is the key to setting clear, confident boundaries. The individual who feels abundant is the one who can confidently say "no" when necessary.

The consistency of your daily gratitude practice is now the primary factor in maintaining your positive outlook and health. It is the engine that generates the necessary emotional momentum to keep the entire system running smoothly, ensuring that your emotional state is resilient, reliable, and fundamentally optimistic.

You have secured the internal foundation for a life of emotional clarity. Now, we translate this profound inner strength into the external competence of defining your worth and setting healthy limits.

REFLECTION QUESTIONS

Prosocial behaviour

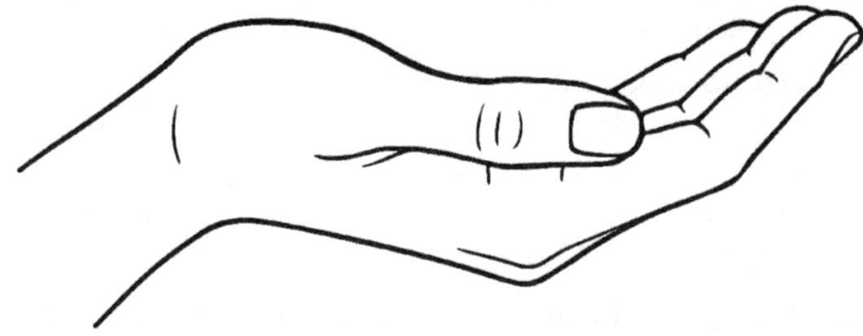

1. Think about your sleep this past week. Did you fall asleep faster or feel more rested? Describe one specific, measurable physical health metric (e.g., time to fall asleep, a subjective score of morning stress) that has improved since starting your evidence-based gratitude journal. How do you quantify this change?

2. Tell me about a time this week where you felt that familiar impulse toward **envy or toxic comparison.** How did you deliberately apply the resilience technique of focusing on "what remains" (Chapter 5) to shift your perspective and conserve energy?

3. Recall one successful **Accountable Apology** or assertive request you made this week (Book 3). How did the emotional reserve and acceptance you cultivated through gratitude make that difficult conversation easier to start and maintain?

4. What was one act of low-cost, proactive **prosocial behavior** (Chapter 6) you engaged in this week? How did the resulting feeling of connection or competence compare to a purely internal journal entry?

5. Look at your journal. Describe a recent entry that went beyond a simple list of objects. Describe the specific, detailed focus you used (What, Why, and How) to successfully *Enrich* and *Absorb* that positive experience. What durable feeling did it leave you with?

BOOK FIVE

DEFINE YOUR SPACE:
PRACTICAL ACTIONS TO SPREAD RESPECT

INTRODUCTION
RESPECT IS RECIPROCITY:
THE FOUNDATION OF HEALTHY RELATIONSHIPS

Congratulations. You made it to the final stage. You achieved profound internal change: you silenced the inner critic (Book 1), you mastered physical and emotional control (Book 2), you learned to speak with clear kindness (Book 3), and you fortified your inner strength with sustained gratitude (Book 4).

But here is where the work gets real. All that hard-won internal peace, that calm, that self-worth, is fragile if you do not protect it. If you fail to define your space, if you do not set and enforce clear personal limits, every resource you built will be systematically drained by others. Your patience will be exhausted by people who chronically disrespect your time, and your energy will be depleted by demands you feel too weak to refuse.

The essential truth of sustaining a positive life is that internal strength must translate into external integrity. The skill that makes this possible is **respect**. We must understand respect not as a soft, abstract ideal, but as a practical, predictable principle that governs all human interaction. We define respect as **reciprocity**, the balanced, mutual regard that ensures every relationship provides equitable value. This book provides the direct, actionable frameworks to establish that balance permanently.

The Problem Defined: The High Cost of the Unbalanced Exchange

Chronic rudeness, hostility, and disrespect are not random character flaws; they are the primary indicators that a relationship system is broken. The science that explains this failure is **Social Exchange Theory (SET)**.

SET is a psychological and sociological framework that posits that all social behavior, from a quick work email to a decades-long marriage, results from a continuous, if often subconscious, calculation. Individuals engage in interaction by weighing the potential **rewards** they receive against the **costs** they incur in that relationship. We choose and maintain relationships that maximize personal benefits and minimize personal disadvantages.

In this framework, respect is the ultimate reward.

- **Rewards** include validation, clear communication, emotional security, shared time, and support (all skills you mastered in Book 3 and 4).

- **Costs** include stress, time wastage, emotional dumping, energy depletion, and, critically, consistent **disrespect** or **rudeness**.

When you consistently engage with hostile habits, negativity, aggression, or a refusal to honor time, you impose a high cost on the other person. SET suggests that people will typically diminish or end a relationship if the **costs consistently outweigh the rewards**, especially if their efforts are not returned.

The Failure of Inequity: Why Relationships Break

Hostile and negative habits destroy relationships by creating **inequity**. Inequity occurs when one person perceives that their effort, time, and emotional investment are not being reciprocated, making the exchange feel unbalanced. This imbalance is where resentment takes root.

The failure to define your space, the collapse into passive compliance or the explosive reaction of aggression, is always a failure to manage this balance.

1. **The Passive Cost Accumulation:** If you default to passive behavior (Book 3, Chapter 3), you allow others to routinely impose costs on you: taking too much of your time, demanding emotional labor, or ignoring your stated needs. When you fail to state your needs, you are teaching the other person that they can safely ignore your wants. This lack of self-respect accumulates internally as resentment, which is repressed anger. This drives up your personal cost until the relationship is no longer tolerable.

2. **The Aggressive Cost Imposition:** Conversely, if you react aggressively, you impose extreme emotional costs on the other person (fear, humiliation, defensiveness). While aggression may achieve short-term compliance, the long-term relational cost is devastating, destroying mutual trust and ensuring the person will eventually withdraw or retaliate.

The path to spreading respect begins with an honest audit of your own relational ledger. You must identify where you are allowing costs to accumulate unchecked and where you are inadvertently imposing unfair costs on others. The functional solution is to establish yourself as a high-value partner in social exchange, one who gives respect generously, but who requires it to be reciprocated predictably.

The Foundation of Boundaries: Protecting Your Mental Health

The practical action for defining your value and ensuring reciprocity is **boundary setting**.

A boundary is simply a limit you identify for yourself and apply through clear communication or deliberate action. Boundaries are not tools for controlling others; they are declarations of self-care necessary to maintain security and health in all relationships, at work and at home.

Setting healthy boundaries is not optional; it is a critical component of maintaining the emotional stability you built in Books 1 and 2.

- **Preventing Burnout and Depletion:** Establishing clear boundaries, especially between your work life and personal life (workplace boundaries), is a proven self-care practice that actively reduces the risk of **workplace burnout**. Warning signs that your boundaries are weak include chronic energy depletion, feelings of negativism related to work, and increased mental distance from your job.

- **Protecting Emotional Integrity:** Boundaries protect your emotional well-being from undue stress, projection, or emotional labor imposed by others. They ensure that you do not take on the responsibility for other people's emotional states or poor choices, which is a major source of internal stress.

- **Defining Your Value:** When you set clear limits, you demonstrate that your time, energy, and needs are important. This action reinforces your internal self-respect and confirms to others that your needs must be considered in the social exchange, which, paradoxically, earns their respect.

Boundaries fall into several key categories: emotional (protecting your well-being), physical (defining your space), material (protecting belongings), time (protecting your schedule), and workplace (protecting work-life balance). Mastering the communication of these boundaries is the central focus of this book.

The Final Step: Integrity as the Highest Respect

The ability to set and maintain boundaries is ultimately rooted in **self-respect** and **integrity**.

Integrity means that your external behavior aligns with your core internal values, the principles that truly guide your decisions and actions. When you are forced to violate your boundaries, such as saying "yes" when you desperately want to say "no", you experience misalignment. This misalignment leads to stress, resentment, and a collapse in self-respect because your actions betrayed your inner sense of what is right.

The path forward requires deep self-reflection to clarify those guiding values: What aspects of your personality are you most proud of? When do you feel most in control of your life? This emotional self-reflection is itself supported by meta-analytic evidence for addressing negative emotional states like anxiety and depression.

By aligning your actions with your values, you establish consistency. An individual who is consistent, assertive, and respectful of their own needs is an individual who is predictable and trustworthy. This integrity is the highest form of respect you can offer yourself and others.

This final book synthesizes all the skills you have learned, calm, assertiveness, and self-worth, into a concrete, five-part plan for external integrity.

1. **Define the Limits (Chapter 2):** You will move from vague discomfort to establishing clear, structured boundaries across emotional, time, and workplace categories, treating them as non-negotiable requirements for mental health maintenance.

2. **Communicate with Conviction (Chapter 3):** You will use the assertive communication skills (DESC Script) and needs-based language (NVC) to voice your boundaries clearly, ensuring they are understood as declarations of self-care, not impositions of control.

3. **Audit the Exchange (Chapter 4):** You will learn how to systematically audit your key relationships using SET principles, ensuring fairness and reciprocity are maintained, and identifying where you need to assertively re-balance the rewards and costs.

4. **Validate Others (Chapter 5):** Spreading respect requires a move beyond self-focus. You will learn to give credit where due, actively validating the contributions and efforts of others, which reinforces prosocial motivation (Book 4) and counters hostile self-centeredness.

5. **Achieve Alignment (Chapter 6):** You will engage in deep self-reflection to clarify your core values and assess the current misalignment in your life. The goal is to make small, consistent behavioral choices that reflect your true self, cementing the highest form of self-respect.

The journey ends here, but the work of maintenance begins. You have the internal capacity. Now, you will learn the external skills to define your worth and maintain your peace forever.

CHAPTER 1

SET CLEAR LIMITS: ESTABLISHING BOUNDARIES FOR MENTAL HEALTH

You have internalized the necessity of respect as reciprocity. You know that if your relationships are to thrive, the rewards must balance the costs, and you must establish yourself as a high-value partner in that exchange.

The transition from intellectual understanding to practical execution begins here. This chapter is your instruction manual for the single, most necessary action required to maintain that balance: **setting boundaries**.

Many people view boundaries as inherently hostile, rigid demands that restrict freedom. This is entirely wrong. Boundaries are not tools for controlling other people. They are essential acts of self-care and declarations of self-respect. They are the limits you identify for yourself and apply through clear communication to maintain your security, health, and emotional stability in all relationships, at work and at home. If you fail to set limits, you guarantee that all the emotional and physiological resources you built in Books 1, 2, and 4 will be systematically drained until you are depleted and resentful.

Setting healthy boundaries is not a luxury. It is a critical component of maintaining your mental and emotional health. If you are struggling with chronic exhaustion, perpetual resentment, or a feeling that your life is not your own, it is a clear signal that your boundaries are weak or nonexistent.

The benefits of setting and maintaining clear boundaries are measurable and directly counteract the negative habits you are working to eliminate:

1. **Protecting Against Burnout:** Establishing clear boundaries, especially in professional environments (workplace boundaries), is a proven form of self-care that actively reduces the risk of **workplace burnout**. Burnout is a serious condition defined by chronic energy depletion, increased mental distance from one's job, and feelings of negativism related to work. When you fail to draw lines around your time and effort, you invite this depletion.

2. **Reinforcing Self-Respect:** When you set clear limits, you send an undeniable message to yourself and to the world: "My time, energy, and needs are important and worthy of protection." This action reinforces your internal sense of self-respect and integrity (Book 5, Chapter 6).

3. **Preventing Resentment:** Passive behavior, saying "yes" when you desperately mean "no", does not eliminate conflict. It merely delays it, turning it inward where it ferments as **resentment**. Resentment is repressed anger, which fuels irritability and eventual aggressive outbursts (reactive aggression, Book 2). Boundaries are the healthy emotional release valve that prevents this toxic buildup.

By defining your space, you are actively choosing to protect the emotional stability (low HRV, high gratitude) you built over the previous four books.

Identifying Your Boundary Categories

Boundaries are often complex because they apply to many different aspects of your life. Moving from vague discomfort to clear action requires identifying the specific category where your limits are being violated most frequently.

Boundaries fall into several key categories:

Boundary Type	Definition and Function	Example of a Clear Limit
Emotional Boundaries	Protecting your well-being from undue stress, projection, or emotional labor imposed by others. You are not responsible for managing another person's feelings.	"I can listen for five minutes, but I cannot be your crisis counselor; I need you to find professional help for that."
Time Boundaries	Protecting the use and misuse of your time, ensuring your schedule is respected and that commitments are honored.	"I do not check or respond to work emails after 5:30 PM, regardless of urgency."
Workplace Boundaries	Protecting your professional balance. This defines when and how you engage with professional duties outside of your designated time / role.	"I will communicate my working hours clearly in my email signature."
Physical Boundaries	Defining your physical space and comfort levels, including personal touch and proximity.	"I am not comfortable hugging people I have just met."
Material Boundaries	Protecting your personal belongings, money, or resources from being misused or taken without consent.	"Please ask before borrowing my tools, and please return them by the end of the day."

The first actionable step is auditing your life to find the category where you are experiencing the most frequent pain, stress, or resentment. That is the area that requires immediate attention and the implementation of a firm, well-communicated limit.

Action Tool 1: The Discomfort Audit

Most people recognize a boundary violation only *after* the fact, when they are already feeling anger or resentment. To set effective boundaries, you must learn to recognize the **early physical and emotional signals** that a limit is being crossed. This uses the self-reflection skills you mastered in Book 2 (recognizing early warning signs of anger/stress).

Action Focus: Connecting Signal to Source

Commit to auditing your emotional and physical responses over the next three days, looking for the physical manifestation of discomfort.

Signal (Internal Feeling / Sensation)	Source (External Action / Person)	Underlying Need Violated
Tightness in chest, anxiety surge (Book 2)	When my relative asks for financial help again.	**Autonomy, Financial Safety**
Immediate mental exhaustion, energy depletion (Burnout sign)	When my coworker dumps her weekend crisis on me every Monday morning.	**Emotional Boundary, Ease, Time**
Ruminating resentment (Chapter 3, Book 2)	When my spouse consistently leaves their work items on the shared kitchen table.	**Order, Respect for Shared Space**
Impulse to avoid or lie (Passive behavior)	When my manager asks me to take on a project outside of my scope after hours.	**Time Boundary, Professional Integrity**

By identifying the specific action that triggers the physical and emotional discomfort, you transition from saying "I feel bad" to stating the problem factually: "My time boundary is being crossed by requests after 5:30 PM." This clarity is essential, as it allows you to move to the next stage: establishing the limit.

Action Tool 2: Establishing Clarity—The "When/I will" Rule

A boundary is only effective if it is clear, specific, and backed by a predictable action on your part. Vague limits are easily crossed and quickly lead back to resentment.

The most effective boundaries follow the **"When X happens, I will do Y"** structure. This removes emotional volatility and frames the boundary as a statement of your personal action, not a demand for the other person's obedience.

1. Define the Limit Factually:

The limit must target a specific, observable behavior (Observation, NVC).

- *Ineffective Limit:* "Don't be so negative around me." (Too vague, easily denied.)
- *Factual Limit:* "When you start complaining about work for more than three minutes, or use judgmental language about our team."

2. Define Your Predictable Action:

The action must be something *you* control. This maintains your agency and integrity.

- *Ineffective Action:* "You need to change the subject." (Demands they change.)
- *Predictable Action:* "I will change the subject, or I will end the conversation and leave the room."

Example Boundary Scripts (Internal):

- **Time Boundary:** "When a meeting runs 10 minutes past the scheduled end time, **I will politely stand up and say I have a hard stop.**"
- **Emotional Boundary:** "When a friend starts calling me to exclusively complain about their partner for the third time this week, **I will interrupt and suggest they seek professional counseling.**"
- **Work Boundary:** "When a colleague emails me with a non-urgent request on Saturday, **I will not open the email and I will reply on Monday morning during scheduled hours.**"

This structured approach transforms the boundary from a subjective feeling into an objective rule, making it easier to enforce and harder for others to violate. You are utilizing the assertive communication skills (DESC script, Book 3) to deliver a clear, specific request (S: Specify) followed by a predictable consequence (C: Consequences), all framed around your core need for health and integrity.

Protecting Against Boundary Violation (The Backlash)

When you first begin setting boundaries, you will likely face resistance, resentment, or even anger from those accustomed to your passive compliance. This backlash is not proof that the boundary is wrong. It is proof that the old, inequitable system (SET) is being successfully disrupted.

To navigate this resistance, you must be prepared to protect the boundary with the emotional regulation you have mastered:

1. **Maintain Calm (Book 2):** When the other person becomes angry or aggressive, immediately revert to your physiological tools (4-7-8 breathing) to keep your PFC online. Their anger is a predictable cost of the relational exchange; do not let it trigger your reactive aggression.

2. **Repeat, Do Not Debate:** Avoid arguing, justifying, or over-explaining. You are not asking for permission; you are stating a fact about yourself. Repeat the boundary statement clearly and calmly. *Example: "I understand you are frustrated, but I still need to leave at 5:30 PM."*

3. **Follow Through:** This is the most crucial step. A boundary is not a verbal agreement; it is an action. If you state the limit, you must follow through with the consequence (e.g., leaving the room, not replying to the email) to prove to yourself and the other person that you mean it.

This consistent, predictable follow-through is what cements your self-respect and earns the respect of others. By moving away from vague discomfort to clear, consistent limits, you define your value and protect the internal peace you worked so hard to build.

CHAPTER 2

USE THE BOUNDARY SCRIPT:

COMMUNICATING NEEDS WITH CONVICTION

You have completed the essential pre-work. You know that a boundary is a necessary act of self-care (Chapter 2), and you have successfully identified the specific areas where your time, energy, or emotional space are being violated. You have named the threat.

Now comes the hard part: the external execution.

A boundary is just a thought until it is voiced. The moment you move from internal decision to external communication, you face the fear of confrontation, rejection, or causing offense. This fear often leads people to deliver boundaries passively, with a whisper, a joke, or an apology, or aggressively, with a hostile demand that triggers immediate resistance. Both approaches destroy the boundary before it can take root.

The integrity of your internal peace depends on your ability to voice your limits with **conviction and care**. You need a precise, structural framework that guarantees your message is delivered clearly, reduces the listener's defensiveness, and aligns your external actions with your internal self-respect. This chapter gives you that framework by adapting your assertive communication skills (Book 3) to the high-stakes task of boundary setting.

The Anatomy of Conviction: Assertiveness as Integrity

A boundary is an assertive declaration. **Assertiveness** is the core skill that allows you to express your thoughts, feelings, and beliefs directly and honestly while strictly respecting the rights of others. When it comes to boundaries, assertiveness is not optional; it is the delivery system for mutual respect.

Why is assertive delivery necessary for a boundary to work?

1. **Passive Delivery Fails Integrity:** If you deliver a boundary passively, for example, saying, "I guess I really shouldn't work late again, maybe?", you send the message that the limit is negotiable. You signal that your needs are less important than the other person's potential discomfort. This fuels resentment in you (repressed anger) and teaches the other person that they can safely ignore your limit, driving the relational ledger back into inequity (Social Exchange Theory, Chapter 1).

2. **Aggressive Delivery Fails Connection:** If you deliver the boundary aggressively, for example, yelling, "Stop calling me after 6 PM! You are so selfish!", you trigger the listener's defense mechanisms. Their amygdala lights up, the PFC shuts down, and they stop hearing your need. The boundary gets lost in the static of their emotional reaction. Aggression may force temporary compliance through fear, but it destroys mutual trust, which is the long-term cost you are trying to avoid.

Assertive communication, when defining a boundary, is the middle path. It uses clear, direct language that avoids hostility, ensuring the message is about the *limit* and *your need*, not a judgment of the *other person's character*. This is why you built the internal calm in Book 2: to keep your physiology regulated while you execute this high-stakes script.

The Core Tool: The Boundary Script (DESC Adaptation)

You will use the **DESC Script** (Describe, Express, Specify, Consequences) as your primary tool for asserting boundaries. This structure forces clarity, prevents emotional tangents, and ensures you state both the limit and the non-hostile outcome.

When adapting the DESC script for a boundary, the focus shifts to defining your personal action rule.

D: Describe the Factual Violation

Start by describing the factual behavior that is violating your limit. This must be an objective **Observation** (NVC principle) that is verifiable and devoid of judgment or emotional language.

- **Action Rule:** Use neutral language to state the *specific*, recurring behavior that is the problem.
- *Ineffective:* "You are always dumping your problems on me."
- *Effective:* "I have noticed that for the last three weekends, you have called me on Sunday morning to discuss your work stress for over forty-five minutes."

E: Express the Impact on Your Needs

Next, you must connect the factual violation to the internal cost it is creating. This is where you use the vulnerability of "I" statements to express the resulting feeling and, crucially, the underlying **Need** (NVC principle) that is being violated.

- **Action Rule:** Connect the behavior to a genuine human need (e.g., rest, autonomy, safety, energy).
- *Ineffective:* "I feel like you don't respect me." (This is a blame word/judgment.)
- *Effective:* "I feel completely drained and overwhelmed by these lengthy calls. My deep need for **rest** and **emotional autonomy** on my one day off is not being met."

By defining the boundary in terms of your need for *rest*, you elevate the discussion from a petty demand to a necessary requirement for self-care.

S: Specify the New Action Rule (The Boundary)

This is the non-negotiable step. You must specify the clear, actionable rule you are setting moving forward. The limit must be clear, specific, and easily understood by the other person. This is your declaration of self-respect.

- **Action Rule:** State the limit directly, using a phrase that signals personal control.
- *Ineffective:* "I need you to stop being so dependent on me." (Vague, demands they change.)
- *Effective:* "I need to establish a time boundary: From now on, I can listen for a maximum of **fifteen minutes** on Sunday, and I need to hear you actively transition to a different topic."

C: Consequences (Specify Your Predictable Action)

The final step is to specify the consequence. Critically, this consequence must focus on the **predictable action that *you* will take** to enforce the boundary, not on punishing the other person. This maintains your agency and integrity.

- **Action Rule:** State the consequence calmly. It is a factual statement of what happens next if the limit is breached.
- *Ineffective*: "If you call me again, I will hang up, and I won't talk to you for a week." (Punishment/Aggression.)
- *Effective*: "If the call goes over fifteen minutes, I will calmly remind you of my time boundary and then **end the call**. I will not be able to answer your call again until Monday morning."

Case Study: Asserting a Workplace Boundary

The DESC script is particularly potent in the workplace, where boundaries often blur between professional hours and personal time (Workplace Boundaries, Chapter 2).

Scenario: Your manager frequently sends non-urgent tasks via text message after 8:00 PM, violating your time boundary and causing you anxiety.

DESC Step	Assertive Boundary Script	Purpose / Alignment
D: Describe	"I've noticed that I often receive task requests via text message from you after 8:00 PM and on weekends."	Factual **Observation** (Chapter 2, Book 3). Neutralizes defensiveness.
E: Express	"Receiving these messages late causes me to feel anxious and interrupt my family time, violating my need for **rest** and a clear **work-life balance**."	Links action to core **Need** (NVC) and internal cost (stress, burnout).
S: Specify	"I need us to establish that all non-emergency communications will be sent via email during standard business hours (9 AM–5 PM)."	Clear, **Specific** rule. Actionable requirement.

DESC Step	Assertive Boundary Script	Purpose / Alignment
C: Consequences	"If a non-emergency text is sent after hours, I will not open it or see it until the next morning at 9:00 AM. This way, I can ensure my focus and energy are maintained for peak productivity during the day."	States **My Action** (I will not open it) and frames the outcome as a **Positive Consequence** for the shared goal (productivity).

This script transforms the situation from a complaint about rudeness to a proposal for functional efficiency, which is a key reward in the workplace social exchange (SET).

The Neurocognitive Power of Assertion

Executing a boundary script successfully is a high-leverage action that reinforces every positive neural pathway you have built.

1. **Restoring Agency (Countering Helplessness):** Successfully asserting a boundary provides a massive, immediate psychological reward. You took purposeful action (Chapter 5, Book 1) and that action produced a result (the boundary was stated, your needs were defended). This measurable success triggers dopamine release, affirming your belief in personal agency and directly counteracting the neurochemical deficits of learned helplessness.

2. **Strengthening Self-Esteem and Coping:** Assertiveness itself is a core coping skill. By directly and respectfully standing up for your interests, you eliminate the toxic buildup of resentment (repressed anger). Research confirms that assertive communication helps control stress and anger, improves coping skills, boosts self-esteem, and earns the respect of others. The consistent practice of this skill reinforces your internal worth.

3. **Measurable Efficacy:** This is not anecdotal. Assertiveness training produces measurable behavioral change. Studies show that participants who undergo assertiveness training experience significant improvement in their assertiveness levels. For example, in clinical settings, 23.5% of participants improved their assertiveness category after structured training, compared to only 4% who regressed. Your structured script is the methodology for this measurable growth.

A boundary is not a verbal agreement; it is an action. The conviction behind the boundary rests entirely on your willingness to execute the stated consequence calmly and predictably.

When you first assert a boundary, you will inevitably face **backlash**. The other person is invested in the old, inequitable system where your compliance was the predictable reward. Their resistance, anger, guilt-tripping, or dismissal, is not proof that your boundary is wrong; it is proof that the old system is being successfully disrupted.

Navigating the Backlash:

1. **Emotional Regulation is Primary (Book 2):** Their anger will likely trigger your emotional warning signs. Immediately revert to your physiological tools (4-7-8 breathing) to keep your PFC online. Do not let their hostility trigger your reactive aggression.

2. **Repeat, Do Not Debate:** Do not fall into the trap of arguing or justifying the boundary. Your boundary is a statement of fact about your self-care, not an argument to be won. Calmly repeat the core limit: "I understand you are frustrated, but I still need to end the call now."

3. **Execute the Consequence:** If the limit is crossed, you must follow through with your stated action (C: Consequences). If you said you would end the call, you must end the call. This is the moment your integrity is tested. Consistent follow-through is what moves the boundary from a suggestion to a rule, cementing your self-respect and earning predictable respect from others.

By committing to the conviction of your script and the integrity of your follow-through, you define your value and protect the internal peace you worked so hard to build. This establishes the necessary stability to ensure fairness and reciprocity in all your most important relationships.

CHAPTER 3

HONOR THE EXCHANGE:
ENSURING FAIRNESS IN SOCIAL RELATIONSHIPS

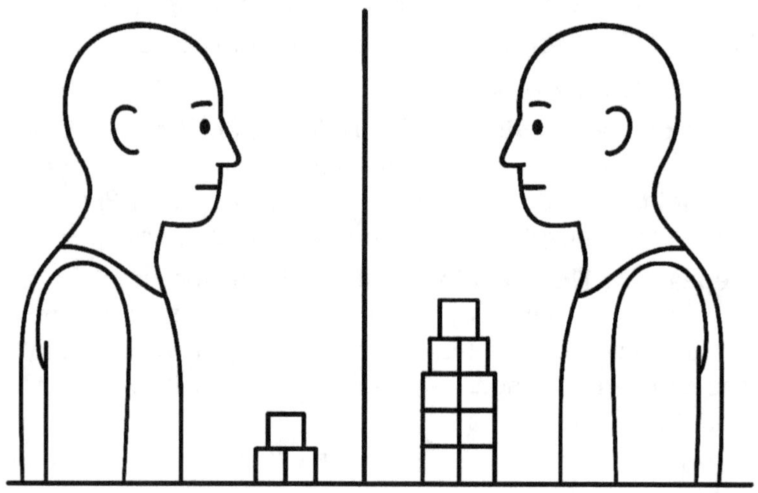

You have achieved the capacity for self-respect. You know how to set clear limits and communicate your boundaries assertively, using your calm voice to define your space (Chapter 3). This mastery is crucial because it ensures that your internal resources are protected from passive depletion.

But boundaries are only half of the equation. To truly **spread respect**, you must actively audit the health of your most important relationships. Respect is not a feeling; it is a calculation of fairness, and it is governed by the principles of **reciprocity**.

This chapter provides the tools for that audit. We will use the framework of **Social Exchange Theory (SET)** to identify where your relationships are imbalanced, where you are allowing costs to accumulate, and where you need to assertively negotiate a more equitable contribution. Healthy relationships are built on balanced exchanges, not martyrdom or constant, unreciprocated effort.

Social Exchange Theory (SET) is the foundational concept for understanding how respect functions in relationships. As established in the introduction, SET states that social behavior results from weighing the **rewards** received against the **costs** incurred.

The stability of all social relationships, from professional partnerships to family dynamics, depends heavily on the **norm of reciprocity**. This social contract suggests two things:

1. **Return Benefits:** People should return the benefits or rewards they receive from others.

2. **Avoid Unreciprocated Obligation:** People try to avoid creating or sustaining relationships where they are consistently giving more than they receive, or vice versa.

In the relational ledger, emotional energy, time, support, and financial resources are all viewed as *costs* or *investments*. Kindness, respect, and validation are *rewards*. A relationship is deemed successful and stable when the rewards and costs for both parties are perceived as roughly balanced, or **equitable**.

If you consistently give more emotional energy, time, or support than you receive, if your costs always outweigh your rewards, the exchange will be viewed as inequitable, and the relationship will eventually become unstable, often leading to resentment and breakdown.

The Problem of Inequity: Comparison Levels

The feeling that a relationship is unfair is not just based on the absolute rewards you receive. It is based on a psychological benchmark called the **comparison level (CL)**.

Your comparison level is your personal standard. It is what you believe you deserve to receive in a specific type of relationship, based on past experience and social context.

- **Relationship A (CL Violation):** If you are consistently listening to a friend's problems for two hours a week, but they cancel every time you need support, you are violating your comparison level for a *reciprocal friendship*. Your costs are high; your rewards are low.

- **The Internal Cost:** This violation damages your self-respect and fuels the toxic buildup of resentment (repressed anger, Book 2, Chapter 3). You feel exploited, undervalued, and angry, even if you never express it.

Identifying inequity is crucial for both self-respect and relational longevity. You must stop allowing inequitable exchanges to deplete your resources and violate your standard of worth.

Action Tool 1: The Relational Ledger Audit

You must transition from vague feelings of being "used" to objective identification of inequity. The Relational Ledger Audit forces you to quantify the exchange in your key relationships using the SET framework.

Action Focus: Auditing Investments and Returns

Choose three key relationships (one professional, one personal, one family) where you feel chronic stress or resentment. Audit the exchange over the last month by focusing only on observable actions.

Relationship Partner	My Investment (Costs / Effort)	Their Contribution (Rewards / Return)	Equity Status (Balanced / Deficit)
Colleague (Jerry)	Spent 3 hours fixing Jerry's error; offered validation after his review.	Jerry gave one five-minute compliment; failed to attend my presentation.	**Deficit.** My emotional and time cost significantly outweighs the return.
Friend (Sarah)	Listened to her job stress for 4 phone calls; initiated all plans.	Sarah sent a thoughtful birthday card; listened intently to my one problem.	**Slight Deficit.** Rewards are high quality, but I carry all the labor of initiation.

The Principle: If you consistently identify a **Deficit** in the relationship, you have discovered a boundary problem that needs assertive communication. The current exchange is violating your comparison level, and it is a drain on your emotional resources (your inner strength). This relationship is a liability to your sustained peace.

Action Tool 2: Negotiating Reciprocity with Assertiveness

Once you identify an inequity, you cannot wait for the other person to change magically. You must assertively communicate the need for a more equitable contribution. This is the moment where your Kind Speech skills (Book 3) become the tools for self-defense.

Action Focus: Using DESC to Rebalance the Ledger

You must use the **DESC Script** (Describe, Express, Specify, Consequences) to initiate the conversation, focusing on the need for fairness (equity).

Scenario: You audited your relationship with your colleague, Jerry, and identified a consistent deficit of effort and support.

DESC Step	Script for Asserting Reciprocity	Principle
D: Describe	"Jerry, I noticed that I spent about three hours fixing that bug in your code last week, and I spent an hour listening to your concerns about your review, but you missed my presentation yesterday."	Neutral **Observation** (Facts).
E: Express	"I felt depleted and unsupported by that exchange. I need our working relationship to meet my need for **equity** and **mutual support**."	Links feeling to core **Need** (NVC).
S: Specify	"I need us to agree on a better balance. For our relationship to continue working well, I need you to be present and engaged during my major professional events."	**Specific** request for observable behavior (Attendance / Engagement).
C: Consequences	"If we both commit to being present and engaged for each other's key moments, we both benefit from higher visibility and confidence. If I cannot rely on this, I will need to limit my assistance to only urgent, immediate tasks."	States the **Positive Consequence** (mutual benefit) and your predictable **Action** (re-setting the boundary / limit) if the inequity persists.

This assertive action reinforces mutual respect and prevents you from feeling exploited or depleted. You are not fighting; you are simply maintaining the health of the social contract.

The Role of Integrity in the Exchange

The ability to successfully negotiate reciprocity is deeply linked to your internal integrity (Book 5, Chapter 6).

If you value **kindness** (Book 4), you must be willing to give support. But if you also value **self-respect** and **autonomy**, you must be willing to defend your limits. When you assertively demand equity, you are aligning your actions with your values: you respect the other person enough to be honest (kindness), and you respect yourself enough to be firm (autonomy).

When you follow through on the consequence (C: Consequences), you prove that your boundary is not arbitrary, it is rooted in a non-negotiable value. This consistent follow-through is what moves the boundary from a mere suggestion to a reliable relational fact, which in turn earns the respect and trust of others.

Respect as a Living Agreement

Respect is not a given; it is a living agreement that requires continuous auditing and negotiation. By using the principles of Social Exchange Theory, you gain the objective, rational framework needed to identify and correct inequity.

You now possess the tools to ensure that your relationships are balanced, fair, and mutually rewarding. You have moved from passively enduring unbalanced relationships to actively and competently creating healthy, reciprocal exchanges. This foundation of fairness ensures that your inner strength is protected and that the integrity of your actions is always aligned with your highest self-respect.

CHAPTER 4

GIVE CREDIT WHERE DUE: RESPECTING OTHERS' CONTRIBUTIONS AND AGENCY

You've come this far because you stood up for yourself. You've learned to set firm boundaries, express your true needs, and check whether your relationships are fair and balanced (Chapter 4). This strong focus on valuing yourself is important. It helps protect your emotional energy.

But respect isn't something you can just keep to yourself like a treasure. It's more like a flowing exchange where both sides give and take. If you only pay attention to what you deserve, you might slip into a different kind of self-focus. You might start noticing only your own hard work and forget to appreciate what others bring to the table.

Here's the simple truth: One big problem with old, unhealthy habits is not recognizing the effort, sacrifices, and worth of the people you depend on. Ignoring this, failing to give credit where it's due, makes your new kindness seem hollow. It can look like you care only about your side of things.

This chapter talks about the last key step in respect: really recognizing others' efforts and choices. This skill makes sure your clear words come with true appreciation behind them. Giving credit isn't just polite, it's a crucial way to build strong social bonds, boost your own happiness, and push back against the selfishness and hostility of old habits.

The Cost of Staying Quiet: Minimizing Others' Work

If you think back to times you were rude or dismissive, it's often because you lost perspective. You were stuck on your own pain and effort, and couldn't see what the other person was doing or intending.

This failure to recognize others often comes from harmful mental patterns:

- Minimizing and Mislabeling: This is when you downplay someone else's effort or intentions. For example, when a coworker finishes a task, your mind might say, "That was easy for them," or "They were just doing their job." This stops you from seeing their work as a real contribution in your relationship. When you don't give back, it quickly leads to imbalance and resentment. Studies show that hostile behavior can often be linked to these types of mental errors where people undervalue others to feel better about themselves.

- The Blame Habit: Just like anger can lead to blaming others, rude behavior often comes with refusing to own up to shared problems while pointing fingers at others. Focusing only on someone's flaws stops you from noticing their good work. This lack of credit harms relationships. It denies people the basic need to be seen and appreciated and weakens the motivation to keep investing effort. When people's efforts are always ignored, staying involved feels too costly.

Why Recognition Matters: A Helpful Action

Giving credit and recognizing others is a strong, intentional way to be helpful, it shows you care about their feelings and rights. This kindness is the outward sign of the gratitude you've built inside (Book 4).

Benefits of Giving Recognition:

- Lifts Your Mood: When you genuinely recognize someone else, you get a mood boost in return. It's the brain's reward for being kind. Studies show people who regularly help others feel happier and experience fewer bad moods. Being generous in this way helps keep your own emotional balance strong.

- Reduces Stress: Helping others by recognizing their effort shifts your focus away from your own worries, lowering your stress levels. This mental shift works well with the calming strategies you learned earlier (Book 2).

- Strengthens Give and Take: Giving credit is a simple, low-effort way to add value to your relationships. When you acknowledge a coworker's role, they feel appreciated and are encouraged to keep cooperating. This makes your connections steadier and more positive (Find-Remind-Bind Theory, Book 4).

So, giving recognition isn't just about making others feel good, it's also key to your own mental health and to building strong, lasting relationships.

Action Tool 1: Recognize Effort and Intent

The main goal here is to make sure the other person feels truly "seen" for the work they put in, not just for the final result. Be clear and specific about what you notice, focusing on how they did it more than just what they achieved.

Action Steps:

- Try to give three specific compliments today, pointing out effort and the process.

- Focus on effort, not just results. Instead of saying, "Your presentation was great," say, "I noticed how much you practiced for that presentation; your preparation really showed."

- Focus on intent, not just outcome. Instead of "The house looks clean," try, "I appreciate how you cleaned the kitchen to give me a break; that really means a lot."

- Recognize effort even when things don't turn out perfectly. For example, "That solution didn't work, but I really value the initiative you took to research it. We'll use what you learned next time."

Doing this kind of focused recognition makes your praise feel real and valuable, encouraging others to keep being helpful toward you.

Action Tool 2: The Power of Public Credit

In groups, whether at work, with friends, or family, giving credit publicly is a great way to spread respect and build positivity. When others see recognition being shared openly, it sends a strong message of generosity.

Action Steps:

- When you get praise for a team's success, quickly give credit to others who helped. For example, say, "Thanks, but this success really comes down to Sarah's careful data work and David's patience with the client."
- Even in simple talks, recognize someone's role in supporting a point. For example, "That's a good point, and I appreciate you speaking up to make it clear for everyone."

This shows you have enough confidence in yourself not to hoard credit. Sharing recognition like this builds trust and marks you as a supportive leader and teammate.

Respect Flows Both Ways

By mastering how to show respect outwardly, you complete a big transformation. You've set your limits to protect your peace. You've checked for fairness in your dealings. Now you add the step of giving credit and recognition to others.

Doing this consistently makes your relationships healthier and more balanced. When you show appreciation, it encourages others to keep giving their best, stabilizing your social circle (Find-Remind-Bind Theory).

You've shifted from hostile habits to generous actions. You give respect and expect it back. This flow keeps your inner strength safe and your outer life honest. The final chapter will help you tie this all together by living out your core values.

CHAPTER 5

LIVE YOUR VALUES:

ALIGNING BEHAVIOR WITH SELF-RESPECT

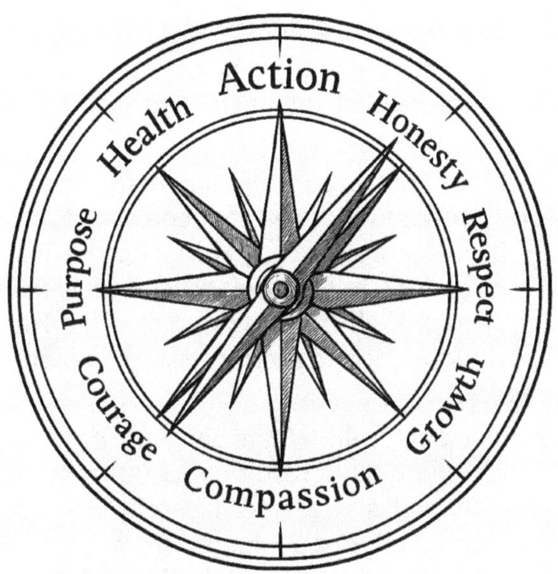

You have reached the final layer of self-respect. You have built the external defense system: clear boundaries, assertive scripts, and a commitment to reciprocal fairness (Chapters 2–5). This structural work ensures that your relationships are balanced and protected from exploitation.

But all these external actions are fragile if they are not rooted in an internal anchor. If you stand up for your time (a time boundary) but deep down you don't believe your work is meaningful, the boundary will eventually collapse. If you apologize for hostile speech (relational repair) but your actions immediately fall back into old, selfish patterns, your words lack authenticity.

The ultimate measure of respect, and the final action required for permanent change, is **integrity**. Integrity means that your external behavior aligns perfectly with your core internal values, the principles that truly guide your decisions and actions. When your actions betray your values, you experience immediate, measurable distress. This chapter teaches you how to identify those core values and systematically align your daily choices with them, cementing the highest form of self-respect.

The Problem of Misalignment: When Actions Betray Beliefs

Everyone holds a set of core values, deep-seated beliefs about what is good, right, and worthwhile (e.g., honesty, freedom, connection, competence, health). These values are the blueprint for your ideal self.

However, the destructive habits of negativity and hostility create a profound state of **misalignment** between that ideal blueprint and your daily reality.

- **The Cost of Betrayal:** Misalignment occurs when you consistently choose an action that contradicts a core value. For example, if your core value is **Honesty**, but you routinely tell small lies or omit facts to avoid difficult conversations, you are betraying yourself. If your core value is **Health**, but you chronically overwork and sacrifice sleep, you are violating your own integrity.

- **The Psychological Toll:** When behavior deviates substantially from clear values, the result is chronic stress, feelings of inauthenticity, and a severe collapse in self-respect. You feel out of control and disconnected from your true self. This emotional distress is a powerful trigger for reverting to old negative patterns, like passive-aggressive behavior or rumination (Book 2).

The commitment in this chapter is to close the gap between who you say you are and what you actually do. This consistency, this integrity, is what makes your asserted boundaries feel unshakable.

Action Tool 1: The Core Value Clarification Audit

You cannot align your life with values you cannot clearly name. The first step is deep, intentional self-reflection to clarify your true guiding principles. This self-reflection is supported by meta-analytic evidence as an effective tool for addressing negative emotional states like anxiety and depression.

Action Focus: Defining Your Personal Constitution

Ask yourself these four foundational questions. Write down one to three words that represent the core value that guides your answer.

1. **Identity:** What aspects of your personality are you most proud of, even when they are challenged? (This reveals values like **Courage** or **Kindness**.)

2. **Fulfillment:** When do you feel most fulfilled, capable, and authentically yourself? (This reveals values like **Competence** or **Connection**.)

3. **Control:** When do you feel most in control of your life, and what conditions created that feeling? (This reveals values like **Autonomy** or **Order**.)

4. **Aspiration:** If you knew you could not fail, what would your life look like? (This reveals values like **Impact** or **Contribution**.)

Your Result: Compile a list of your 5 to 7 highest-ranking values (e.g., Health, Honesty, Connection, Autonomy, Competence). This list becomes your personal constitution, the objective standard against which all future decisions are measured.

Action Tool 2: The Alignment Assessment

Once your values are clear, you must ruthlessly assess the current level of misalignment in your daily life. This is the moment where you apply the clear, factual observation skills of NVC (Book 3) to your own behavior.

Action Focus: Identifying the Integrity Gaps

Choose your top three core values. For each value, identify one specific habit or boundary failure that is actively undermining it.

Core Value	Specific Misaligned Habit	Cost of Misalignment
Health	Routinely accepting late-night calls, leading to less than 6 hours of sleep.	Violates the basic need for rest; weakens PFC and emotional regulation (Book 2).
Honesty	Telling "white lies" to a partner to avoid difficult conflict about finances.	Erodes trust (relational cost) and causes internal anxiety / shame (personal cost).
Autonomy	Saying "yes" to colleagues' last-minute requests when my schedule is already full.	Leads to resentment and violates the time boundary (Chapter 2); reinforces passive behavior.

The identification of these gaps is the most powerful step. It moves the feeling of being "stuck" from a vague emotional problem to a concrete, solvable behavioral problem. You realize: "My anxiety is not random; it is the natural consequence of betraying my value of Health through poor sleep."

Action Tool 3: Behavioral Alignment Through Small Wins

Closing the integrity gap requires committing to small, measurable behavioral choices that directly honor your values. This uses the principle of **Action to Create Hope** (Book 1, Chapter 5), affirming that your efforts produce results and rebuilding your sense of agency.

Action Focus: SMART Alignment Goals

For each misalignment identified, create a small, manageable, **SMART** goal that aligns your behavior with the value immediately.

Value and Gap	Actionable Alignment Goal (SMART)	Reinforcing Principle
Health (Less than 6 hours sleep)	**Goal:** Tonight, I will turn off all screens and be in bed by 10:30 PM, regardless of task completion.	Honors the **Time Boundary** (Chapter 2) and reinforces the value of Health.
Honesty (White lies about money)	**Goal:** This week, I will draft the DESC Script (Book 3) to initiate an honest, factual conversation about our spending limit on Thursday evening.	Uses **Assertive Communication** to align with Honesty; replaces avoidance with competence.
Autonomy (Saying yes when busy)	**Goal:** The next time a colleague makes a last-minute request, I will pause, check my calendar, and assertively say, "Thank you for asking; I will need to check my capacity and get back to you in an hour."	Uses **Behavioral Inhibition** (Book 2) to pause the passive impulse and honor the boundary.

This process ensures that every word you speak and every action you take is a deliberate choice that reflects your true self and your vision of success. This internal consistency is not only emotionally rewarding, it generates the highest form of self-respect.

The ability to live your values with consistency is the ultimate outcome of mastering respect. You have moved from a place where negative habits defined your character to a place where deliberate, value-driven actions define your integrity.

This integrity is the most powerful resource for maintaining the entire system:

- **Boundary Enforcement:** When you know a boundary is tied to your non-negotiable value of **Health** or **Autonomy**, it becomes infinitely easier to enforce it calmly and predictably (Chapter 3). You are not being mean; you are simply upholding your personal constitution.

- **Trust and Reciprocity:** People trust an individual whose actions are predictable and whose values are clear. This consistency is a high reward in the social exchange (SET, Chapter 4), stabilizing your relationships and earning you predictable respect.

You have defined your space. You have asserted your value. Now, you live the change. The final chapter summarizes the maintenance required to ensure a life of sustained integrity and mutual respect.

CONCLUSION

A LIFE OF INTEGRITY: SUSTAINING MUTUALLY RESPECTFUL INTERACTIONS

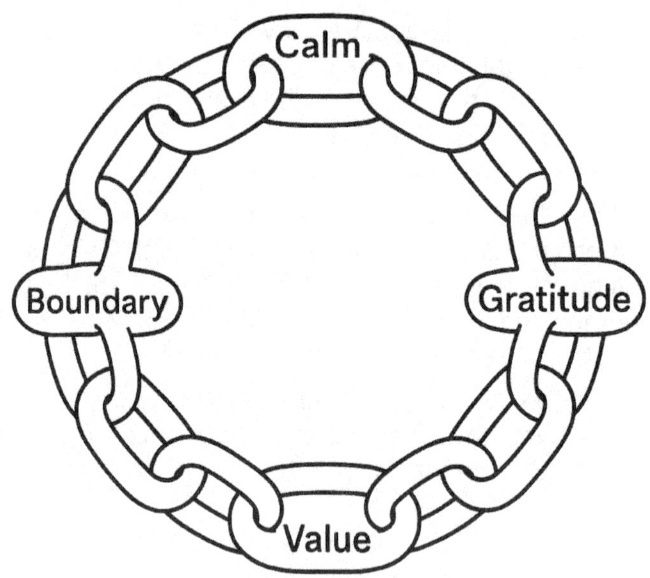

You have completed the entire process. This book was the final test. It moved you from internal self-worth to external action, ensuring that your life is defined by consistency, boundaries, and mutual respect.

The transformation across these five books is total. You replaced the chaotic cycles of negativity, rudeness, and hostility with a self-sustaining system of calm, clarity, and integrity. You did not just learn how to *feel* better; you learned how to *be* better, a predictable, reliable, and respectful agent in all your relationships.

This final chapter serves as a summation of the whole system, confirming how the external integrity you mastered here is the key to maintaining every single positive change you made. The life you want, one of deep connection and unwavering self-respect, depends on your commitment to this continuous maintenance.

The durable success of this program rests on the fact that every skill is interconnected. The skills you learned in the first four books are the resources you spend here in Book 5 to define and defend your value.

1. The Anchor: Integrity and Values

The ultimate foundation for sustained respect is **integrity**, the perfect alignment between your words, your actions, and your core values (Chapter 6).

- **The Action:** You identified your highest values (e.g., Health, Honesty, Autonomy) and audited your life for **misalignment** (Action Tool 2, Chapter 6). You committed to small, measurable **SMART** goals that directly honored those values (e.g., going to bed on time to honor Health).

- **The Result:** This consistency generates the highest form of self-respect. When you uphold your values, your boundaries (Chapter 2) become non-negotiable. You are not being mean when you say "no" to a late request; you are simply upholding your personal constitution. This conviction is what earns respect from others, stabilizing the relational exchange.

2. The Defense System: Boundaries and Assertiveness

Integrity makes your defense system predictable and effective, preventing the slow drain of resentment and burnout.

- **The Action:** You learned to set firm, specific **boundaries** (Chapter 2) and communicate them with conviction using the **DESC Script** (Chapter 3). This forces you to assert your needs clearly and respectfully, rather than falling into passive compliance or aggressive demands (Book 3).

- **The Result:** Assertive action directly reduces stress and prevents the toxic buildup of resentment (repressed anger, Book 2) that fuels future hostile outbursts. By taking control of your time, emotional energy, and professional space, you protect the emotional reserves you built through gratitude (Book 4). This protects against burnout, which is a major symptom of weak boundaries.

3. The Exchange: Reciprocity and Prosocial Flow

Your external interactions are now defined by fairness and generosity, replacing the old habits of minimization and self-centeredness.

- **The Action:** You mastered the **Relational Ledger Audit** (Chapter 4) to identify and assertively correct inequitable exchanges (SET). Simultaneously, you committed to actively **giving credit where due** (Chapter 5), acknowledging the effort and agency of others.

- **The Result:** This commitment to **reciprocity** ensures that your relationships are mutually beneficial, not exploitative. By reinforcing the goodness received (through validation), you motivate others to contribute goodness back, stabilizing the entire social system (Find-Remind-Bind Theory, Book 4). You are moving from a hostile, scarcity-based mindset to one of generous, sustainable abundance.

Maintenance: The Action Plan for Sustained Integrity

The transformation is complete, but the maintenance is continuous. Your daily practice must now integrate all five systems to ensure that the entire mechanism of control, clarity, and competence remains functional.

When a crisis occurs, when you feel the heat of anger, the urge to be rude, or the collapse of self-respect, you must use this integrated action sequence:

1. **Immediate Physiological Check (Book 2):** When you feel the first sign of stress or anger (the "burn"), immediately engage the **4-7-8 breathing protocol** to prevent cognitive shutdown. Calm the body first.

2. **Cognitive Audit (Book 1):** With your PFC back online, quickly check your interpretation: Are you using the **Hostile Attribution Bias** (Book 2) or **Catastrophizing** (Book 1)? Is the thought aligned with your core value of **Honesty** or **Fairness** (Book 5, Chapter 6)?

3. **Assertive Response (Book 3 & 5):** If a boundary has been crossed, or a need is unmet, do not ruminate (Book 2). Instead, immediately prepare and deliver the **DESC Boundary Script** (Chapter 3) or the **Accountable Apology** (Book 3, Chapter 6).

4. **Problem-Solving (Book 2):** Once calm and asserted, move immediately to the **5-Step Problem-Solving Model** to address the root cause of the conflict, ensuring a constructive solution replaces the impulsive reaction.

5. **Re-Focus and Recharge (Book 4):** Use the **Gratitude Journal** and the **HEAL Method** (Book 1) to restore your positive affect. By focusing on what remains and savoring a small moment of peace, you lower cortisol and replenish the emotional reserves spent during the conflict.

This integrated system ensures that you respond to any threat not with the old default of negativity and hostility, but with deliberate, competent, and respectful action.

The Call to a Life of Integrity

You now possess the complete toolkit for defining your destiny. You have proven that every word, thought, and action is a choice you can control. You have moved from a place where you felt like a passive victim of your emotions to a place where you are the assertive, responsible agent of your life.

The ultimate reward is not just reduced stress, but genuine **integrity**, the unshakable self-respect that comes from knowing your external life perfectly reflects your highest internal values. This integrity is the foundation of a life where mutual respect is predictable, conflict is constructive, and kindness is effortless.

Live the change.

REFLECTION QUESTIONS

1. Identify one core personal value (e.g., Health, Honesty, Autonomy) that you violated this past week. Describe the specific misaligned habit and state the small, measurable **SMART goal** you will implement immediately to realign your behavior.

2. Describe one boundary you successfully asserted (or failed to assert) using the **DESC Script** this week. If you succeeded, what part of the script was most powerful? If you failed, what specific consequence did you fail to execute?

3. Audit one key relationship using the **Relational Ledger Audit** (Chapter 4). What specific, quantifiable investment (cost) are you putting in that is not being reciprocated, and what assertive request will you make to re-balance that exchange?

4. Describe one successful instance where you gave **Public Credit** or specific validation to someone (Chapter 5). How did this act of generosity reinforce your own sense of abundance (Book 4), and what was the immediate positive response from the recipient?

5. Reflecting on the entire five-book series: Identify one skill from Book 2 (Calm Anger) and one skill from Book 5 (Spread Respect) that you used together this week to achieve integrity. (e.g., Used 4-7-8 breathing to calmly enforce a Time Boundary).

OVERALL CONCLUSION

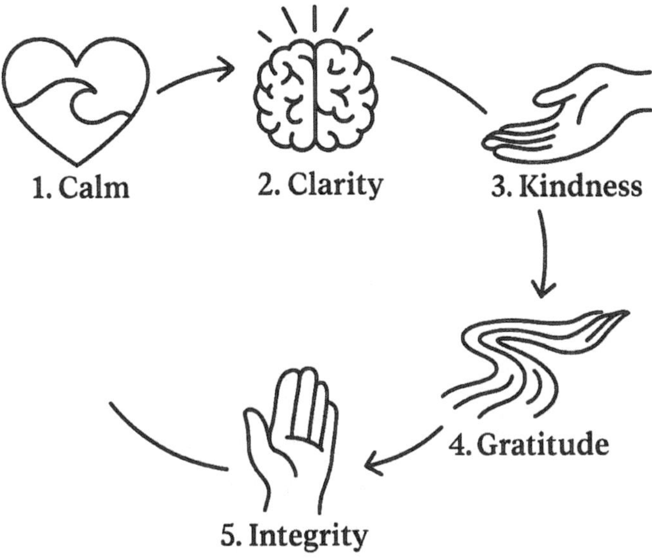

From Negative to Effective: Synthesizing the Five Skills

You have reached the end of the structural phase of this program. You replaced chronic, damaging habits with a complete, integrated system for living with integrity. You did not just learn coping tricks; you leveraged neuroplasticity to physically change the pathways in your brain that once dictated negativity, rudeness, and hostility.

The final strength of this transformation lies in the fact that your five books are not separate courses. They form a closed, self-sustaining system where each skill is the necessary prerequisite and resource for the next. This sequence ensures that your change is durable.

1. The Physiological Prerequisite: Calm Enables Clarity

The journey began by securing the body's state, recognizing that you cannot reason your way out of a physiological alarm.

- **Book 2 (Calm Anger)** provides the essential physical regulation: the **4-7-8 breathing protocol** and the control over your vagus nerve. This immediate intervention stops the adrenaline surge, lowers your heart rate, and prevents the emotional brain (amygdala) from hijacking your actions.

- **The Connection to Book 1 (Positivity):** This physical calm is the non-negotiable step that restores resources to your **Prefrontal Cortex (PFC)**. Without a regulated PFC, you cannot successfully execute the cognitive work of Book 1: identifying the **Triple Column Technique (TCT)** distortions or challenging your **Catastrophizing**. The calm body *enables* the rational mind.

2. The Internal Engine: Agency Fuels Generosity

Once the mind is calm and clear, you built the internal engine for action, ensuring motivation does not collapse when things get difficult.

- **Book 1 (Positivity)** and **Book 4 (Gratitude)** solved the problem of inertia. By committing to small, successful **SMART goals** (Book 1, Chapter 5), you directly counteracted **learned helplessness**, affirming agency and restoring the flow of dopamine necessary for motivation and hope.

- **The Connection to Resilience:** This internal engine is continuously maintained by **Gratitude (Book 4)**. Daily journaling and savoring lower your stress hormone, **cortisol**. This chemical stability acts as an emotional buffer, ensuring that when setbacks occur, you approach them from a position of abundance and resource (resilience), rather than deficit and panic.

3. The External System: Integrity Commands Respect

The stable, resourceful, and calm internal self must then define its space in the world.

- **Book 3 (Kind Speech)** provides the communication framework: the **Nonviolent Communication (NVC)** model and the **DESC Script**. These tools ensure that you articulate your needs and feelings clearly and respectfully, replacing the old, destructive language of blame and demands.

- **The Connection to Book 5 (Respect):** This assertive communication is the essential tool for **Book 5 (Respect)**. You use the DESC script to establish clear, non-negotiable **boundaries** (Chapter 3, Book 5). This action prevents the accumulation of costs (time, energy, resentment) that otherwise destroy the relational balance (Social Exchange Theory, Chapter 4, Book 5). When you speak assertively and honor your values, you stabilize your relationships and earn predictable respect.

The system is a loop: Calm body (Book 2) enables clear thought (Book 1), which fuels generous action (Book 4), which is then used to define and defend your space (Book 5), protecting the resources needed to remain calm (Book 2). Your commitment to integrity ensures this loop runs without interruption.

Action Maintenance: How to Troubleshoot Setbacks

The shift you have achieved is permanent, but maintenance is required. A resilient life is not one without problems. It is one where you have a predictable, structured sequence to follow when problems occur.

When you inevitably face an internal regression, a moment of rage, a slip into passive avoidance, or a wave of self-criticism, you must immediately treat the event not as a personal failure, but as a **system failure** that requires troubleshooting.

The 5-Phase Troubleshooting Sequence:

Phase 1: The Physiological Reset (Stop the Surge)

- **The Signal:** You feel the physical "burn": rapid heart rate, jaw clenching, shallow breath. You are experiencing sympathetic overdrive.

- **The Intervention:** Stop all external action. Immediately revert to the **4-7-8 breathing protocol**. Execute four full cycles (4-second inhale, 7-second hold, 8-second exhale). Your only job is to restore physiological calm.

- **The Test:** Re-check your heart rate or subjective tension. Did the physical symptoms measurably decrease? If not, repeat the breathing or use a physical redirect (walking, stretching) until calm is regained.

Phase 2: The Cognitive Diagnostic (Check the Story)

- **The Signal:** A torrent of angry, judgmental, or helpless thoughts floods your mind, often fueled by rumination.

- **The Intervention:** Engage the **Triple Column Technique (TCT)** (Book 1, Chapter 2). Identify the specific **Cognitive Distortion** (**Catastrophizing, Blaming Others, Labeling**). Ask the core question: **What is the objective, factual evidence for this thought?**

- **The Test:** Does the thought align with your core values (Book 5, Chapter 6)? If the thought contradicts **Honesty** or **Fairness**, dismiss it as an irrational pattern and immediately focus on a constructive thought replacement.

Phase 3: The Relational Correction (Reassert Integrity)

- **The Signal:** You realize you said "yes" when you meant "no," or you allowed a boundary to be violated, leading to resentment (SET inequity).

- **The Intervention:** Formulate and deliver a correction using the **DESC Assertive Script** (Book 3, Chapter 3 and Book 5, Chapter 3). You are not apologizing for the boundary; you are asserting your limit. Your delivery must be calm (due to Phase 1) and firm.

- **The Test:** Did you follow through on the consequence? If you fail to execute the consequence, the boundary collapses. Immediately schedule a specific time to re-assert the limit and execute the necessary consequence (e.g., cutting the meeting short, turning off the phone).

Phase 4: The Agency Restoration (Action to Overcome Inertia)

- **The Signal:** You feel overwhelmed, immobilized, or hopeless, the signature of **learned helplessness**.

- **The Intervention:** Choose the **smallest possible SMART goal** that honors a core value (Book 1, Chapter 5 and Book 5, Chapter 6). This is a guaranteed, low-cost win (e.g., spending 15 minutes organizing one drawer, sending one difficult email).

- **The Test:** Did you complete the specific action? Completion instantly triggers the dopamine reward, affirming your agency and breaking the cycle of inertia.

Phase 5: The Resilience Recharge (Refill the Well)

- **The Signal:** You feel emotionally depleted, experiencing low mood or increased irritability.

- **The Intervention:** Use the **HEAL Method** (Book 1) or engage in structured **Gratitude Journaling** (Book 4). Savor a small moment of competence or safety for 15 to 30 seconds, focusing on the physical sensation of contentment.

- **The Test:** Did you choose to focus on what **remains** (resources) rather than what is **lost** (deficits)? This continuous positive sensitization lowers stress chemistry and replenishes your emotional well-being.

You now possess the complete, scientific blueprint for a life defined by respect and clarity. This is no longer a self-help book; it is a reference manual for your new operating system.

The only remaining action is maintenance.

1. **Commit to Daily Check-ins:** Continue your daily Gratitude Journaling (Book 4) and your morning LKM/Mindfulness practice (Book 1). These habits are the low-cost investments that maintain high emotional returns (low stress, high resilience).

2. **Treat Boundaries as Sacred:** Your boundaries are the physical expression of your self-respect. Never violate them for the comfort of others. The moment you compromise your integrity, you invite hostility and negativity back into your life.

3. **Lead with Kindness and Accountability:** Use your skills to actively contribute to the social contract. Be assertive, not aggressive. Give credit where due. And when you inevitably fail, use the **Accountable Apology** (Book 3, Chapter 6) and the **Problem-Solving Model** (Book 2, Chapter 5) to repair the rift and strengthen the bond.

The transformation is yours. Go live a life of integrity, clarity, and unwavering self-respect.

CHECKLIST

YOUR PRINT AND GO SHEET TO KEEP AND REVISIT

This sheet is your summary of the **Action Maintenance System**. It moves you from internal regulation to external integrity. Use this list daily and especially when you feel the first signs of stress, anger, or inertia.

System	Daily Action Plan: Maintenance & Prevention	Crisis Intervention: Stop the Surge
Book 4: Inner Strength (Recharge)	**Gratitude Savoring:** Write down 3 specific things you are grateful for. Focus on the *why* and *how*, savoring the feeling for 15 seconds.	**Resilience Check (Chapter 5):** When facing loss or anxiety, identify what **remains** (resources, health, network) rather than focusing on the deficit.
Book 1: Positivity (Cognitive Reset)	**HEAL Method:** Actively enrich and absorb one small positive moment for 15 seconds.	**TCT Audit (Chapter 2):** Immediately identify and label the core thought error (**Catastrophizing, Blaming Others, Labeling**).

Book 5: Respect (Integrity)	**Value Alignment:** Review your top 3 core values (Health, Honesty, etc.). Commit to one small **SMART action** today that honors one of these values.	**Relational Ledger Audit (Chapter 4):** Check the exchange. If resentment is present, define the specific **inequity** that needs asserting.
Book 5: Respect (Giving Credit)	**Prosocial Action:** Give one piece of specific, high-value validation today (Acknowledge **effort** or **intent**, not just the result).	**Empathy Check (Chapter 5):** When reacting to a colleague, quickly ask: "What non-hostile **Contextual Stressor** might be driving their behavior?"

The Crisis Sequence: When Conflict Hits

Use this structured sequence to move from an emotional outburst (hostility) to a constructive solution (integrity).

Phase	Action Tool	Goal
1. Stop the Burn (Book 2)	**4-7-8 Breathing Protocol:** Inhale 4, Hold 7, Exhale 8 (repeat 4 times).	**Restore PFC Function.** Stop the physiological surge and calm the amygdala.
2. Check the Story (Book 2 / 1)	**Reality Testing:** Isolate the factual observation from the **Hostile Attribution Bias** Generate 3 non-hostile alternative explanations for the behavior.	**Prevent Rumination.** Force the mind out of the toxic replay loop and into objective data.
3. Assert the Limit (Book 3 / 5)	**DESC Boundary Script:** Define the limit clearly and assertively. D (Describe fact) → E (Express need) → S (Specify rule) → C (Consequence: *Your* action).	**Uphold Integrity.** Defend your boundary with conviction.

4. Problem-Solve (Book 2)	**5-Step Model:** Use the controlled calm to initiate structured problem-solving (Step 1: Define the factual problem).	**Find a Solution.** Address the root cause of the conflict, replacing helplessness with competence.
5. Repair the Rift (Book 3 / 5)	**Accountable Apology:** If you contributed to the damage, apologize by naming the specific behavior and the **violated need** (e.g., need for respect), followed by a clear commitment to future action.	**Rebuild Trust.** Close the accountability gap and reinforce the relational bond.

HERE'S ANOTHER BOOK BY VIVIAN WHITMORE THAT YOU MIGHT LIKE

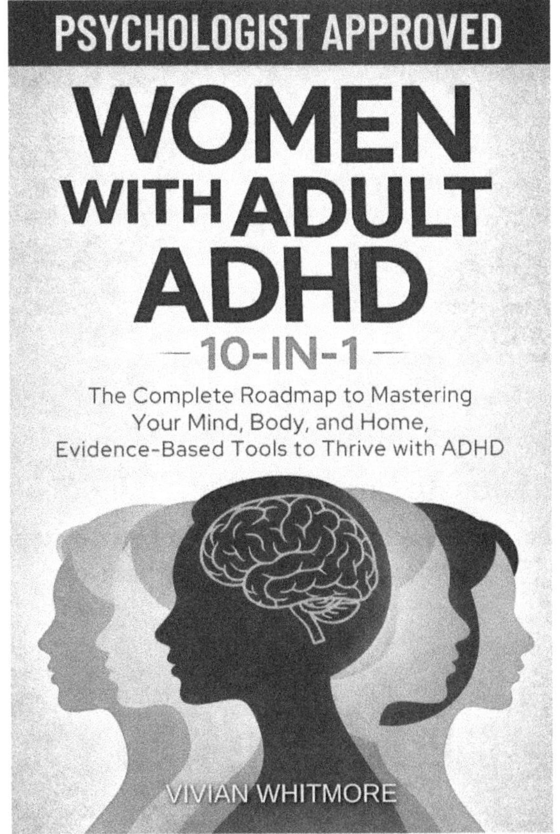

Claim Your Free Bonus

As a thank you for reading, I've put together a powerful digital bonus pack to help you apply what you've learned — even if you only have a few minutes a day.

 **Inside you'll find:**

✔ Quick-access emotional reset tools

✔ A printable clarity map for focus and purpose

✔ 30 powerful journaling prompts

✔ Daily progress & reflection trackers

✔ A mini affirmation deck for calm and confidence

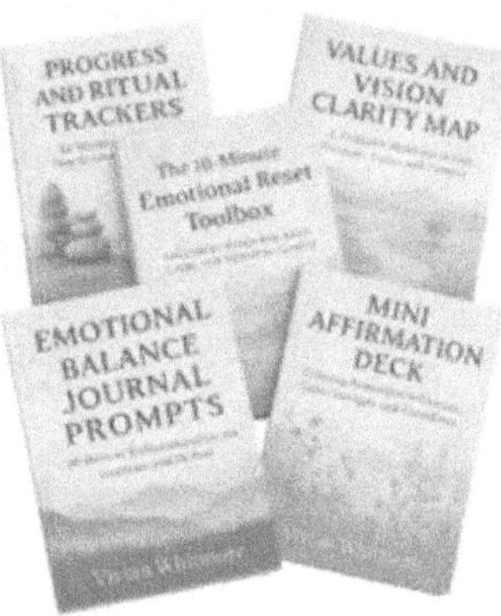

Access below to download your full bonus pack:

https://livetolearn.lpages.co/vivian-withmore-how-to-stop-ruining-your-relationships-10-in-1-paperback/

Or, scan the QR code

RESOURCES

**Part 1: How to Stop Being Toxic 5-in-1
Introduction**

- Anger Management for Substance Use Disorder and Mental Health Clients: A Cognitive–Behavioral Therapy Manual (Substance Abuse and Mental Health Services Administration).

- Emotional Intelligence: Why It Can Matter More Than IQ – Daniel Goleman.

- The Body Keeps the Score – Bessel van der Kolk (Focus on trauma and emotional regulation).

- Nonviolent Communication: A Language of Life – Marshall B. Rosenberg.

- The Healing Power of Empathy – Marshall B. Rosenberg.

- The Seven Principles for Making Marriage Work – John M. Gottman (Focus on validation and communication patterns).

- Your Perfect Right: Assertiveness and Equality in Your Life and Relationships – Robert E. Alberti and Michael L. Emmons.

- The Assertiveness Workbook: How to Express Your Ideas and Stand Up for Yourself – Randy J. Paterson.

- Set Boundaries, Find Peace: A Guide to Reclaiming Yourself – Nedra Glover Tawwab.

- Boundaries: Where You End and I Begin – Anne Katherine.

- Codependent No More: How to Stop Controlling Others and Start Caring for Yourself – Melody Beattie.

- Codependency for Dummies – Darlene Lancer.

- The State of Affairs: Rethinking Infidelity – Esther Perel.

- After the Affair: Healing the Pain and Rebuilding Trust When a Partner Has Been Unfaithful – Janis A. Spring.

Book 1: Control Anger - Action Steps to Master Your Reactions

- Substance Abuse and Mental Health Services Administration (SAMHSA). Anger Management for Substance Use Disorder and Mental Health Clients: A Cognitive-Behavioral Therapy Manual.

URL: https://library.samhsa.gov/sites/default/files/angermanagement manual508compliant.pdf

- Hofmann, S. G., et al. The efficacy of incorporating mental imagery in cognitive restructuring techniques on reducing hostility.
URL: https://www.researchgate.net/publication/353362096_The_efficacy_of_incorporating_mental_imagery_in_cognitive_restructuring_techniques_on_reducing_hostility_A_randomized_controlled_trial

- Segal, J., Smith, M. Anger Management Tips and Techniques. HelpGuide.org
URL: https://www.helpguide.org/relationships/communication-anger-management.htm

- Verywell Mind. Anger Management Strategies.
URL: https://www.verywellmind.com/anger-management-strategies-4178870

- Verywell Mind. Learn Assertive Communication in Five Simple Steps.
URL: https://www.verywellmind.com/learn-assertive-communication-in-five-simple-steps-3144969

- A Cognitive Connection. 5 CBT Techniques for Anger.
URL:
- https://acognitiveconnection.com/cognitive-behavioral-therapy-techniques-for-anger-management

- Mayo Clinic. Anger Management: 10 Tips to Tame Your Temper.
URL: https://www.mayoclinic.org/healthy-lifestyle/adult-health/in-depth/anger-management/art-20045434

- Overcome With Us. 9 Helpful CBT Skills for Anger Management.
URL: https://www.overcomewithus.com/blog/9-helpful-cbt-skills-for-anger-management

- Goleman, D. Emotional Intelligence: Why It Can Matter More Than IQ.

- First Session. How to Use I Statements.
URL: __https://www.firstsession.com/resources/how-to-use-i-statements

Book 2: Build Empathy - Understand and Connect Emotionally

- Greater Good Science Center. How to Develop Empathy Skills. URL: https://greatergood.berkeley.edu/topic/empathy/definition
- Psychology Today. Cultivating Empathy. URL: https://www.psychologytoday.com/us/basics/empathy
- Harvard Health Publishing. The Science of Empathy. URL: https://www.health.harvard.edu/blog/empathy-can-be-taught-2021041422333
- ResearchGate. Emotional Intelligence and Empathy in Relationships. URL: https://www.researchgate.net/publication/327065137_The_role_of_emotional_intelligence_and_empathy_in_relationships
- TED Talks on Empathy (Search TED platform for various talks)

Book 3: Talk with Respect - Effective Communication Techniques

- Patterson, K., et al. Crucial Conversations: Tools for Talking When Stakes Are High.
- Verywell Mind. Effective Communication Skills. URL: https://www.verywellmind.com/effective-communication-skills-5183787
- MindTools. Assertive Communication Techniques. URL: https://www.mindtools.com/pages/article/newCS_98.htm
- ResearchGate. Psychological Safety in Team Communication. URL: https://www.researchgate.net/publication/379315835_The_Role_of_Psychological_Safety_in_Team_Communication_Implications_for_Human_Resource_Practices

PsychCentral. Communication Barriers and Remedies.

- URL: https://psychcentral.com/lib/the-art-of-effective-communication/
- Conflict Resolution Resources from Counseling and Psychology Experts (general theme)

Book 4: Set Boundaries - Define Your Limits and Protect Your Space

- PsychCentral. Understanding the Cycle of Guilt.
  URL: https://psychcentral.com/blog/understanding-the-cycle-of-guilt/

- Verywell Mind. Learn Assertive Communication in Five Simple Steps.
  URL: https://www.verywellmind.com/learn-assertive-communication-in-five-simple-steps-3144969

- Melody Beattie. Codependent No More: How to Stop Controlling Others and Start Caring for Yourself.

URL: https://www.melodybeattie.com/codependent-no-more/

- Self-Compassion.org. About Dr. Kristin Neff.
  URL: https://self-compassion.org/

- Positive Psychology. How to Set Healthy Boundaries.
  URL: https://positivepsychology.com/great-self-care-setting-healthy-boundaries/

- ResearchGate. Personal Boundaries and Mental Health.
  URL:
  https://www.researchgate.net/publication/379852826_Personal_boundaries_definition_role_and_impact_on_mental_health

- Annapolis TRICARE. Create Healthy Boundaries.
  URL:
  https://annapolis.tricare.mil/Portals/109/Documents/Behavioral%20Health/Create%20Healthy%20Boundaries.pdf

- The Knowledge Academy. When I Say No, I Feel Guilty.
  URL: https://www.theknowledgeacademy.com/blog/books-on-assertiveness/

Book 5: Fix Broken Trust - Rebuild Security Through Consistency

- Psychology Today. How to Rebuild Trust in 7 Steps.
  URL: https://www.psychologytoday.com/us/blog/compassion-matters/201901/how-rebuild-trust-in-7-steps

- Mindfully Minding Me. Couples Therapists Tips for Rebuilding Trust.
  URL: https://mindfullymindingme.com/how-to-rebuild-trust/

- APA. Acceptance and Commitment Therapy Overview.

URL: https://www.apa.org/ptsd-guideline/patients-and-families/act

- The Knowledge Academy. Daring Greatly and Vulnerability. URL: https://www.theknowledgeacademy.com/blog/vulnerability-and-leadership/

- ResearchGate. Psychological Safety in Team Communication. URL: https://www.researchgate.net/publication/379315835_The_Role_of_Psychological_Safety_in_Team_Communication_Implications_for_Human_Resource_Practices

- Maxwell School. Reflective Listening Techniques.

- Positive Psychology. Empathic Listening. URL: https://positivepsychology.com/empathic-listening/

- Overcome With Us. 9 Helpful CBT Skills for Anger Management. URL: https://www.overcomewithus.com/blog/9-helpful-cbt-skills-for-anger-management

- Counselling Tutor. The Meaning of Attending.

- The Body Keeps the Score — Bessel van der Kolk (book)

- Bay Area CBT Center. Top 10 Manipulation Tactics.

- Emerald. Employee Trust Repair Practices Scale Development.

- Crucial Learning Blog. Crucial Conversations Principles.

Resources for Overall Conclusion:

- **Positive Psychology**. Build Trust in a Relationship: 12 Ways to Build Trust. URL: https://positivepsychology.com/build-trust/

- **Mindfully Minding Me**. Couples Therapists' Tips for How to Rebuild Trust After It Has Been Broken. URL: https://www.mindfullymindingme.com/blog/couples-therapists-tips-for-how-to-rebuild-trust-after-it-has-been-broken

- **APA**. Acceptance and Commitment Therapy. URL: https://www.apa.org/education/ce/acceptance-commitment.pdf

- **The Knowledge Academy**. Daring Greatly: How the Courage to be Vulnerable Transforms the Way We Live, Love, Parent, and Lead. (Referencing Brené Brown's work on vulnerability). URL:

https://www.theknowledgeacademy.com/blog/books-on-assertiveness/

- **Investopedia**. Prospect Theory. (Referencing the psychological weight of losses over gains). URL: https://www.investopedia.com/terms/p/prospecttheory.asp

- **Psychology Today**. How to Rebuild Trust in 7 Steps. URL: https://www.psychologytoday.com/us/blog/toxic-relationships/202109/how-to-rebuild-trust-in-7-steps

- **PsychCentral**. Understanding the Cycle of Guilt. URL: https://psychcentral.com/blog/understanding-the-cycle-of-guilt

- **Cornell Health**. Assertive Communication Skills. URL: https://health.cornell.edu/sites/health/files/pdf-library/assertive-communication-skills.pdf

- **SAMHSA**. Anger Management for Substance Use Disorder and Mental Health Clients: A Cognitive–Behavioral Therapy Manual. URL: https://library.samhsa.gov/sites/default/files/anger_management_manual_508_compliant.pdf

- **Verywell Mind**. Anger Management Strategies. URL: https://www.verywellmind.com/anger-management-strategies-4178870

- **ResearchGate**. The efficacy of incorporating mental imagery in cognitive restructuring techniques on reducing hostility. URL:(https://www.researchgate.net/publication/353362096_The_efficacy_of_incorporating_mental_imagery_in_cognitive_restructuring_techniques_on_reducing_hostility_A_randomized_controlled_trial)

- **HelpGuide.org**. Setting Healthy Boundaries in Relationships. URL: https://www.helpguide.org/relationships/social-connection/setting-healthy-boundaries-in-relationships

- **Annapolis TRICARE**. Create Healthy Boundaries. URL:(https://annapolis.tricare.mil/Portals/109/Documents/Behavioral%20Health/Create%20Healthy%20Boundaries.pdf?ver=2020-09-14-081212-590)

- **Wikipedia**. Extinction (psychology). URL: https://en.wikipedia.org/wiki/Extinction_(psychology)

- **ResearchGate**. Personal boundaries: definition, role, and impact on mental health. URL:

https://www.researchgate.net/publication/379852826_Persona l_boundaries_definition_role_and_impact_on_mental_healthOsob istisni_kordoni_viznacenna_rol_ta_vpliv_na_psihicne_zdorov'a

- **Mayo Clinic**. Anger Management: 10 Tips to Tame Your Temper. URL: https://www.mayoclinic.org/healthy-lifestyle/adult-health/in-depth/anger-management/art-20045434

- **Verywell Mind**. The Extinction Burst in Psychology. URL: https://www.verywellmind.com/what-is-an-extinction-burst-2795855

- **ResearchGate**. Mindfulness-Based Relationship Enhancement. URL:(https://www.researchgate.net/publication/222830032_Mi ndfulness-Based_Relationship_Enhancement)

- **ResearchGate**. The Role of Psychological Safety in Team Communication. URL:(https://www.researchgate.net/publication/379315835_Th e_Role_of_Psychological_Safety_in_Team_Communication_Impli cations_for_Human_Resource_Practices)

- **Maxwell School of Citizenship and Public Affairs**. Reflective Listening. URL: https://www.maxwell.syr.edu/docs/default-source/ektron-files/reflective-listening-neil-katz-and-kevin-mcnulty.pdf?sfvrsn=f1fa6672_7

- **Positive Psychology**. Empathic Listening. URL: https://positivepsychology.com/empathic-listening/

- **Overcome With Us**. 9 Helpful CBT Skills for Anger Management. URL: https://www.overcomewithus.com/blog/9-helpful-cbt-skills-for-anger-management

- **Counselling Tutor**. The Meaning of Attending. URL: https://counsellingtutor.com/basic-counselling-skills/the-meaning-of-attending/

- **Goleman, D.** Emotional Intelligence: Why It Can Matter More Than IQ. (Discussing emotional management and the amygdala's role in hijacking rational thought).

- **The Body Keeps the Score** – Bessel van der Kolk (Focus on trauma and emotional regulation).

- **The Knowledge Academy**. When I Say No, I Feel Guilty. URL: https://www.theknowledgeacademy.com/blog/books-on-assertiveness/

Book 1: Rewire Your Brain: Action Steps to Boost Positivity

<u>Introduction</u>

- https://pmc.ncbi.nlm.nih.gov/articles/PMC3652533/
- https://pmc.ncbi.nlm.nih.gov/articles/PMC7047599/

<u>Chapter 1</u>

- https://fortmyerstherapist.com/cbt-technique-using-triple-column-technique-change-thoughts-change-life/

<u>Chapter 2</u>

- https://pmc.ncbi.nlm.nih.gov/articles/PMC8475916/
- https://pmc.ncbi.nlm.nih.gov/articles/PMC10440210/

<u>Chapter 3</u>

- https://rickhanson.com/online-courses/positive-neuroplasticity-training/
- https://rickhanson.com/topics-for-personal-growth/the-negativity-bias/

<u>Chapter 4</u>

- https://medium.com/@msjag416/dopamine-and-learned-helplessness-why-motivation-disappears-and-how-it-comes-back-39853a4f49a7
- https://www.chapterstreatment.com/post/taking-action-a-guide-to-action-oriented-therapy

<u>Chapter 5</u>

- https://www.kevinwgrant.com/blog/item/breaking-free-from-self-judgment

<u>Conclusion</u>

- https://digitalcommons.pcom.edu/cgi/viewcontent.cgi?article=1024&context=capstone_projects

Book 2: Take Back Control: Techniques to Calm Anger Now

<u>Introduction</u>

- https://www.centerwatch.com/clinical-trials/listings/NCT06697587/enhanced-cognitive-reappraisal-and-emotion-awareness-training-ecreat-for-maladaptive-anger-inhibition-a-pilot-study

- https://pmc.ncbi.nlm.nih.gov/articles/PMC3490066/

Chapter 1

- https://www.psychologytoday.com/us/blog/the-athletes-way/201905/longer-exhalations-are-an-easy-way-to-hack-your-vagus-nerve
- https://www.healthline.com/health/4-7-8-breathing

Chapter 2

- https://pmc.ncbi.nlm.nih.gov/articles/PMC4849278/
- https://pmc.ncbi.nlm.nih.gov/articles/PMC12452349/

Chapter 3

- https://pmc.ncbi.nlm.nih.gov/articles/PMC3490066/
- https://cogbtherapy.com/cbt-blog/2014/5/4/hhy104os08dekc537dlw7nvopzyi44

Chapter 4

- https://pmc.ncbi.nlm.nih.gov/articles/PMC10243415/
- https://pmc.ncbi.nlm.nih.gov/articles/PMC4176893/
- Chapter 5
- https://pubmed.ncbi.nlm.nih.gov/26592092/
- https://www.neuroregulation.org/article/view/23500

Conclusion

- https://mindful.health/anger-management-techniques/

Book 3: Connect Clearly: Actionable Models for Kind Speech

Introduction

- https://www.verywellmind.com/being-direct-vs-being-rude-8739387
- https://www.verywellmind.com/what-is-prosocial-behavior-2795479

Chapter 1

- https://www.theoaktreepractice.com/resources/relationships/how-nonviolent-communication-can-transform-your-relationship/
- https://www.hatching-dragons.com/blog/nonviolent-communication-principles-practice-benefits

<u>Chapter 2</u>

- https://www.mayoclinic.org/healthy-lifestyle/stress-management/in-depth/assertive/art-20044644
- https://www.mdpi.com/2071-1050/13/20/11504

<u>Chapter 3</u>

- https://pmc.ncbi.nlm.nih.gov/articles/PMC2717040/
- https://pmc.ncbi.nlm.nih.gov/articles/PMC3021497/

<u>Chapter 4</u>

- https://pubmed.ncbi.nlm.nih.gov/34963634/
- https://www.kevinwgrant.com/blog/item/breaking-free-from-self-judgment

<u>Chapter 5</u>

- https://www.natibeltran.com/the-complete-guide-to-nonviolent-communication-for-purpose-driven-leaders/
- https://www.hatching-dragons.com/blog/nonviolent-communication-principles-practice-benefits

Book 4: Build Inner Strength: Daily Habits for Practicing Gratitude

<u>Introduction</u>

- https://www.scielo.br/j/eins/a/m8kqK5vgZ9wb4DxRtD877bd

<u>Chapter 1</u>

- https://www.piedmont.org/living-real-change/the-life-changing-effects-of-gratitude

<u>Chapter 2</u>

- https://positivepsychology.com/neuroscience-of-gratitude/

<u>Chapter 3</u>

- https://www.cannelevate.com.au/article/gratitude-letters-research-written-appreciation-wellbeing/

<u>Chapter 4</u>

- https://positivepsychology.com/neuroscience-of-gratitude/

<u>Chapter 5</u>

- https://www.mindful.org/the-science-of-gratitude/

<u>Conclusion</u>

- https://www.scielo.br/j/eins/a/m8kqK5vgZ9wb4DxRtD877bd

Book 5: Define Your Space: Practical Actions to Spread Respect

<u>Introduction</u>

- https://www.ebsco.com/research-starters/social-sciences-and-humanities/social-exchange-theory

<u>Chapter 1</u>

- https://health.ucdavis.edu/blog/cultivating-health/how-to-set-boundaries-and-why-it-matters-for-your-mental-health/2024/03

<u>Chapter 2</u>

- https://www.mayoclinic.org/healthy-lifestyle/stress-management/in-depth/assertive/art-20044644

- https://www.ahrq.gov/teamstepps-program/curriculum/mutual/tools/desc.html

<u>Chapter 3</u>

- https://en.wikipedia.org/wiki/Social_exchange_theory

<u>Chapter 4</u>

- https://www.verywellmind.com/what-is-prosocial-behavior-2795479

- https://pmc.ncbi.nlm.nih.gov/articles/PMC3490066/

<u>Chapter 5</u>

- https://www.therapyroute.com/article/100-therapy-questions-for-self-awareness-healing-and-growth-by-therapyroute

<u>Conclusion</u>

- https://cogbtherapy.com/cbt-blog/2014/5/4/hhy104os08dekc537dlw7nvopzyi44

- https://www.mayoclinic.org/healthy-lifestyle/stress-management/in-depth/assertive/art-20044644